A TREASURY OF
ALBERT SCHWEITZER

A Treasury of
Albert Schweitzer

edited by
Thomas Kiernan

GRAMERCY BOOKS
New York • Avenel

This 1994 edition is published by Gramercy Books,
distributed by Random House Value Publishing, Inc.,
40 Engelhard Avenue, Avenel, New Jersey 07001.
By arrangement with Philosophical Library.

Random House
New York • Toronto • London • Sydney • Auckland

Printed and bound in the United States of America

Library of Congress Cataloging-in-Publication Data
Schweitzer, Albert, 1875-1965.
    A treasury of Albert Schweitzer.
        p. cm.
    Originally published: New York: distributed by
the Citadel Press by arrangement with Philosophical Library, 1965.
    Includes bibliographical references.
    ISBN 0-517-11957-9
    1. Philosophy. 2. Life. 3. Religion. 4. Man
5. Schweitzer, Albert, 1875-1965.
B2430.S372T73 1994
193—dc20   94-11809
                                                      CIP

8 7 6 5 4 3 2 1

REVERENCE FOR LIFE
Selections made by Thomas Kiernan.

THE LIGHT WITHIN US
Selections made by Richard Kik. The original German edition
Vom Licht in Uns was published by Verlag, J. F. Steinkopf,
Stuttgart.

PILGRIMAGE TO HUMANITY
Translated by Walter E. Stuermann. Material edited by
Dr. Rudolf Frabs; originally published by Reclam Verlag, Stuttgart,
under the title *Weg zur Humanitat*.

PHILOSOPHY OF RELIGION
Selected and translated by Kurt F. Leidecker. This study
based on Kantian metaphysics from *The Critique of Pure Reason*
to *Religion Within the Limits of Reason Alone*.

HAND LETTERING BY LINDA KOSARIN

CONTENTS

BOOK TWO

The Light Within us

97

BOOK THREE

Pilgrimage to Humanity

Development

Editor's Preface

It is more than fifty years since Albert Schweitzer went to Lambaréné, in what is now Gabon, to practice medicine and found a hospital. In that time he has become a universal symbol of altruism, self-sacrifice and dedication.

Within the more recent past, however, there has developed a highly vocal coterie of critics of Dr. Schweitzer, both in and outside Africa. With the emergence of the new Africa, where self-determination is an at least partially realized fact and colonial rule is fast disintegrating, the mission of Schweitzer has been brought under question. While Schweitzer's medical methods and philosophy were considered suitable for colonial Africa, they are now adjudged hopelessly anachronistic.

However valid much of the criticism may be, it cannot be forgotten that when Schweitzer first arrived in Lambaréné in 1913 he ran real risks, endured real hardships, and made a real contribution to the health and welfare of those among whom he chose to live. It must be remembered that Schweitzer, through his continuing devotion to the principles he set out to follow, became one of the greatest humanitarians of our time, and that, although criticisms concerning his medical methods may, from a medical point of view, be valid, his reputation as a humanitarian cannot be tarnished.

Because of Schweitzer's fame as a medical missionary, other, equally important aspects of his life are not so well known. Schweitzer was, among other things, an accomplished musician, an authority on the Bible (his early investigations of the New Testament set the pace for later, more esoteric, Biblical studies), an expert on animals and plant life, and a thinker whose concern with the problems of the human spirit and whose methods of expressing this concern raised him to the stature of one of our foremost philosophers.

As this book went to press, the sad news came of the death of Albert Schweitzer. The mortal man has passed from us but his ideas and vision are immortal.

THOMAS KIERNAN
1965

A TREASURY OF
ALBERT SCHWEITZER

Book One

Reverence for Life

Feeling for Animal Life

A S FAR BACK as I can remember I was saddened by the amount of misery I saw in the world around me. Youth's unqualified *joie de vivre*, I never really knew, and I believe that to be the case with many children, even though they appear outwardly merry and quite free from care.

One thing that specially saddened me was that the unfortunate animals had to suffer so much pain and misery. The sight of an old limping horse, tugged forward by one man while another kept beating it with a stick to get it to the knacker's yard at Colmar, haunted me for weeks.

It was quite incomprehensible to me—this was before I began going to school—why in my evening prayers I should pray for human beings only. So when my mother had prayed with me and had kissed me good night, I used to add silently a prayer that I had composed myself for all living creatures. It ran thus: "O, heavenly Father, protect and bless all things that have breath; guard them from all evil, and let them sleep in peace."   [1]

⊒ A deep impression was made on me by something which happened during my seventh or eighth year. A friend and I had with strips of India rubber made ourselves catapults, with which we could shoot small stones. It was spring and the end of Lent, when one morning my friend said to me, "Come along, let's go on to the Rebberg and shoot some birds." This was to me a terrible proposal, but I did not venture to refuse for fear he should laugh at me. We got close to a tree which was still without any leaves, and on which the birds were singing beautifully to greet the morning, without showing the least fear of us. Then stooping like a Red Indian hunter, my companion put a bullet in the leather of his catapult and took aim. In obedience to his nod of command, I did the same, though with terrible twinges of conscience, vowing to myself that I would shoot directly he did. At that very moment the church bells began to ring, mingling their music with the songs of the birds and the sunshine. It was the Warning-bell, which began half an hour before the regular peal-ringing, and for me it was a voice from heaven. I shooed the birds away, so that they flew where they were safe from my companion's catapult, and then I fled home. And ever since then, when the Passiontide bells ring out to the leafless trees and the sunshine, I reflect with a rush of grateful emotion how on that day their music drove deep into my heart the commandment: "Thou shalt not kill."

From that day onward I took courage to emancipate myself from the fear of men, and whenever my inner convictions were at stake I let other people's opinions weigh less with me than they had done previously. I tried also to unlearn my former dread of being laughed at by my school fellows. This early influence upon me of the commandment not to kill or to torture other creatures is the great experience of my childhood and youth. By the side of that all others are insignificant. [1]

⊒ While I was still going to the village school we had a dog with a light brown coat, named Phylax. Like many others of his kind, he could not endure a uniform, and always went for the postman. I was, therefore, commissioned to keep him in order whenever the postman came, for he was inclined to bite, and had already been guilty of the crime of attacking a policeman. I therefore used to take a switch and drive him into a corner of the yard, and keep him there till the postman had gone. What a feeling of pride it gave me to stand, like a wild beast tamer, before him while he barked and showed his teeth, and to control him with blows of the switch whenever he tried to break out of the corner! But this feeling of pride did not last. When, later in the day, we sat side by side as friends, I blamed myself for having struck him; I knew that I could keep him back from the postman if I held him by his collar and stroked him. But when the fatal hour came round again I yielded once more to the pleasurable intoxication of being a wild beast tamer! [1]

⊒ During the holidays I was allowed to act as driver for our next door neighbor. His chestnut horse was old and asthmatic, and was not allowed to trot much, but in my pride of drivership I let myself again and again be seduced into whipping him into a trot, even though I knew and felt that he was tired. The pride of sitting behind a trotting horse infatuated me, and the man let me go on in order not to spoil my pleasure. But what was the end of the pleasure? When we got home and I noticed during the unharnessing what I had not looked at in the same way when I was in the cart, viz., how the poor animal's flanks were working, what good was it to me to look into his tired eyes and silently ask him to forgive me?

On another occasion—it was while I was at the Gymnasium, and at home for the Christmas holidays—I was driving a sledge when a neighbor dog, which was known to be vicious, ran yelping out of the house and sprang at the horse's head. I thought I was fully justified in trying to sting him up well with the whip, although it was evident that he only ran at the sledge in play. But my aim was too good; the lash caught him in the eye, and he rolled howling in the snow. His cries of pain haunted me; I could not get them out of my ears for weeks. [1]

⊒ I have twice gone fishing with rod and line just because other boys asked me to, but this sport was soon made impossible for me by the treatment of the worms that were put on the hook for bait, and the wrenching of the mouths of the fishes that were caught. I gave it up, and even found courage enough to dissuade other boys from going. [1]

Respect for Life

▣ From experiences like these, which moved my heart and often made me feel ashamed, there slowly grew up in me an unshakeable conviction that we have no right to inflict suffering and death on another living creature unless there is some unavoidable necessity for it, and that we ought all of us to feel what a horrible thing it is to cause suffering and death out of mere thoughtlessness. And this conviction has influenced me only more and more strongly with time. I have grown more and more certain that at the bottom of our heart we all think this, and that we fail to acknowledge it and to carry our belief into practice chiefly because we are afraid of being laughed at by other people as sentimentalists, though partly also because we allow our best feelings to get blunted. But I vowed that I would never let my feelings get blunted, and that I would never be afraid of the reproach of sentimentalism.

I never go to a menagerie because I cannot endure the sight of the misery of the captive animals. The exhibiting

of trained animals I abhor. What an amount of suffering
and cruel punishment the poor creatures have to endure in
order to give a few moments' pleasure to men devoid of all
thought and feeling for them!   [1]

Mutual Knowledge

◨ After all, is there not much more mystery in the relations of man to man than we generally recognize? None of us can truly assert that he really knows someone else, even if he has lived with him for years. Of that which constitutes our inner life we can impart even to those most intimate with us only fragments; the whole of it we cannot give, nor would they be able to comprehend it. We wander through life together in a semi-darkness in which none of us can distinguish exactly the features of his neighbor; only from time to time, through some experience that we have of our companion, or through some remark that he passes, he stands for a moment close to us, as though illumined by a flash of lightning. Then we see him as he really is. After that we again walk on together in the darkness, perhaps for a long time, and try in vain to make out our fellow traveller's features.

To this fact, that we are each a secret to the other, we have to reconcile ourselves. To know one another cannot mean to know everything about each other; it means to feel mutual affection and confidence, and to believe in one another. A man must not try to force his way into the personality of another. To analyze others—unless it be to help back to a sound mind someone who is in spiritual or intellectual confusion—is a rude commencement, for there is a modesty of the soul which we must recognize, just as we do that of the body. The soul, too, has its clothing of which we must not deprive it, and no one has a right to say to another: "Because we belong to each other as we do, I have a right to know all your thoughts." Not even a mother may treat her child in that way. All demands of that sort are foolish and unwholesome. In this matter giving is the only valuable process; it is only giving that stimulates. Impart as much as you can of your spiritual being to those who are on the road with you, and accept as something precious what comes back to you from them.   [1]

Riddles of Existence

◪ Science teaching had something peculiarly stimulating for me. I could not get rid of the feeling that it was never made clear to us how little we really understand of the processes of Nature. For the scientific school books I felt a positive hatred. Their confident explanations—carefully shaped and trimmed with a view to being learnt by heart, and, as I soon observed, already somewhat out of date—satisfied me in no respect. It seemed to me laughable that the wind, the rain, the snow, the hail, the formation of clouds, the spontaneous combustion of hay, the tradewinds, the Gulf Stream, thunder and lightning, should all have found their proper explanation. The formation of drops of rain, of snow flakes, and of hailstones had always been a special puzzle to me. It hurt me to think that we never acknowledge the absolutely mysterious character of Nature, but always speak so confidently of explaining her, whereas all that we have really done is to go into fuller and more complicated descriptions, which only make the mysterious more mysterious than ever. Even at that age, it became clear to me that what we label Force or "Life" remains in its own essential nature forever inexplicable.

Thus I fell gradually into a new habit of dreaming about the thousand and one miracles that surround us, though fortunately the new habit did not, like my earlier thoughtless daydreams, prevent me from working properly. The habit, however, is with me still, and gets stronger. If during a meal I catch sight of the light broken up in a glass jug of water into the colors of the spectrum, I can at once become oblivious of everything around me, and unable to withdraw my gaze from the spectacle.

Thus did love for history and love for science go hand in hand, and I gradually recognized that the historical process too is full of riddles, and that we must abandon forever the hope of really understanding the past. [1]

The Meaning of Philosophy

◪ The purpose of all philosophy is to make us aware as thinking beings of the intelligent and intimate relationship with the universe in which we have to stand, and of the way in which we must behave in the presence of the stimuli that come from it.

One kind of philosophy is able to bring man and the universe together only by doing violence to nature and the world and by forcing the world into harmony with man's thought.

The other, the insignificant nature philosophy, leaves the world and nature as they are, and compels man to find himself and assert himself in them as a spiritually and creatively triumphant being. The first philosophy is ingenious, the second elementary. The first proceeds from one mighty manifestation of thought to another, as they appear in the great speculative systems of German philosophy, and we are carried away with admiration for them. This philosophy has its day and disappears. The second,

· 25 ·

the plain and simple nature philosophy, remains. An elementary philosophy, which first of all tried to find intelligent expression in the Stoics and then perished with them because it failed to achieve an affirmative view of the world and of life, strives always to come into its own. This nature philosophy has come down to us in an imperfect form. It tried once again in Spinoza and in the eighteenth-century rationalism to think through to the affirmation of the world and life. When it was unable to do so, violence took the place of effort. The great speculative philosophy brought forth its systems of compulsion. At that time, when everyone was blinded by a world prostrate before thought, there was one man who was not blinded, who remained loyal to the elementary and humble nature philosophy, aware that it had not been able to think its way through to an affirmative conclusion in that eighteenth century in which he lived, but certain that it would have to do so; and he worked toward that end in the simple way which was his inner nature.

When I myself became aware of this and turned back to this nature philosophy—recognizing that it is our appointed task to bring it to an affirmative position in relation to the world and life, in so simple a fashion that all thoughtful people throughout the world would have to share in this thinking, and therein find peace with the infinite and incentive for creative activity—then I realized that Goethe was the man who had held out at the abandoned post where we were once more mounting guard and beginning to work again. [II]

Goethe

◲ Once again I met Goethe when my laborious student years had ended and I went out into the world of medicine. It was as if I conversed with him in the primeval forest. I had always supposed that I should go there as a doctor. In the early years, whenever there was building or similar material work to be done, I took pains to pass it on to others who seemed to me fitted for it or hired for that sort of work. Soon I had to admit that this would not do. Either they did not appear, or they were not qualified to forward the work. So I accustomed myself to work which was very different from my medical duties. But the worst came later. In the closing months of 1925, a great famine endangered my hospital, and I was forced to lay out a plantation for the hospital so that in any future period of famine we might be able to keep our heads in some measure above water. I had to superintend the clearing of the jungle myself. The motley array of voluntary workers assembled from among those who attended the patients would recognize no authority but that of the "Old Doctor," as I was called there. So for weeks and months I stood in the jungle trying to wrest fruitful land from it, and tormented by unruly workers. Whenever I was in complete despair, I thought of Goethe, who had imagined his Faust, in the end, busily regaining land from the sea where men might live and find nourishment. So Goethe stood beside me in the gloomy forest as the great smiling comforter who understood me.

If I needs must mention something else that I owe to Goethe, it is this—that a deep concern for justice goes with him everywhere. When, at the turn of the century, theories began to prevail that whatever had to be done should be done without regard to the right, without regard to the fate of those affected by the change, and since I myself did not know how these theories which influenced us all were to be met, it was a real experience for me to find everywhere in Goethe a longing to avoid the sacrifice of the right in doing what had to be done. Ever and again with deep emotion, I turn over the final pages of *Faust*, which—whether in Europe or in Africa—I always read at Eastertide. There Goethe tells of the final experience of Faust, his last guilty action, when he determines to get rid of the hut which stands in his way by a slight and well-intentioned act of violence, because, as he says, he is tired of justice. But this well-intentioned act of violence becomes in its execution a frightful deed of violence, in which people lose their lives, and the hut goes up in flames. That Goethe should add this episode at the conclusion of his *Faust*, although it retards the action, gives us a deep insight into the way in which his concern for justice and his longing to achieve without hurting worked within him.

My final and lasting experience with Goethe arose from the extremely vital way in which Goethe shared in the whole life of his time, its thought and its activity. The currents of the age surged through him. That is the thing that impresses one, not only in the young Goethe and the mature Goethe, but also in the old Goethe. While the mail coach was still crawling along the highway, and it seemed that the industrial age was only faintly foreshadowed, for him the industrial age was already there. He was busy with the problem that it presented, the replacement of the worker by the machine. If he is no longer master of his material in *Wilhelm Meister's Travels*, it is not simply because the old man no longer has the creative power which was formerly at his command, but because the material has grown into something immeasurable and intractable, because this old man is putting into this material his whole experience and his whole concern for the future age, because this old man is endeavoring to become, among the men of his time, one who understands the new age and has grown to be a part of it. This is what deeply impresses one in the aging Goethe.

These were the contacts with Goethe through which I came close to him. He does not inspire one. He brings forth no theories that provoke enthusiasm. What he offers us is always what he himself has experienced in thought and deed, what he has molded into higher forms of reality. We come nearer to him only in experience. Because of an experience that corresponds with his, he ceases to be a stranger and becomes a confidant with whom we feel ourselves united in admiring friendship.

My own fate has been such that I have vitally experienced in the very fiber of my being the fortunes of our age and concern about our humanity. That I may experience these things as a free man, in a time when so many whom we need as free personalities are confined in some narrow calling, that I, like Goethe, may serve as a free man because of a fortunate combination of circumstances—this seems to me a grace that lightens my laborious life. Everything that I can accomplish in my work seems to me only a thankful acknowledgment to fortune for this great favor.

Goethe before us lived through this labor and this anxiety for his time. Circumstances have become more chaotic than even he, with his clear vision, could foresee. Mightier than circumstances must our strength be if we are to become, in the midst of them, men who understand our age, men who are an integral part of it.

Goethe's spirit places a threefold obligation upon us: We must wrestle with circumstances, so that those who are imprisoned by them in their exhausting jobs may nevertheless be able to preserve their spiritual lives. We must wrestle with men, so that, distracted as they constantly are by the external things so prominent in our time, they may find the road to inwardness and remain on it. We must wrestle with ourselves and with everyone else, so that, in an age of confusion and inhumanity, we may remain loyal to the great humane ideals of the eighteenth century, translating them into the thought of our age and attempting to realize them.

This is our task, each in his own life, each in his own calling, in the spirit of the great child of Frankfort, whose birthday we celebrate in his birthplace today. This child of Frankfort does not, I think, move away from us with the passing of the years—but draws closer to us. The more progress we make, the more clearly we recognize Goethe as the man who, in the midst of a profound and comprehensive experience, was concerned for his age and labored for it, as we must do; the man who wished to understand his time and to become a part of it.

All this he accomplished with the abounding gifts that had been laid in his cradle here by fortune. It is for us to act as men who have received only one small pound, but who still want to be found faithful in our stewardship. So may it be!   [II]

⊐⌐ What is Goethe's word to us, to us human beings plunged as we are in terrible need? Has he a special message for us?

Yes, he has.

All that thought in which a man embraces, not simply the people of a single age, but humanity itself composed of individual human beings—and this is true of Goethe's thought as it is true of hardly any other—has something superior to every age in it. Society is something temporal and ephemeral; man, however, is always man.

So Goethe's message to the men of today is the same as to the men of his time and to the men of all times: "Strive for true humanity! Become yourself a man who is true to his inner nature, a man whose deed is in tune with his character."

But, the question rises, can we still achieve such human personality in the midst of the frightful circumstances of our day? Is the least sign of material and spiritual independence, which the individual must possess if he is to realize this end, to be found among us? The circumstances of our time are indeed such that material independence is hardly known any more by the men of our day, and even their spiritual independence is sorely threatened. All kinds of unnatural conditions are developing daily among us, in such a way that man ceases to feel any longer that he is in every respect a being that belongs to nature and to himself, and becomes more and more a creature submissive to society.

So the question is raised which would have been considered impossible only a few decades ago: Do we still desire to remain faithful to the ideal of human personality even in the midst of hostile circumstances, or are we now on the contrary loyal to a new ideal for humanity which ordains that man shall achieve a differently ordered fulfillment of his nature in the restless merging of his being in organized society?

What, however, can this mean except that we, like Faust, have erred terribly in detaching ourselves from nature and in surrendering ourselves to the unnatural?

After all, what is now taking place in this terrible epoch of ours except a gigantic repetition of the drama of Faust upon the stage of the world? The cottage of Philemon and Baucis burns with a thousand tongues of flame! In deeds of violence and murders a thousandfold, a brutalized humanity plays its cruel game! Mephistopheles leers at us with a thousand grimaces! In a thousand different ways mankind has been persuaded to give up its natural relations with reality, and to seek its welfare in the magic formula of some kind of economic and social witchcraft, by which the possibility of freeing itself from economic and social misery is only still further removed!

And the tragic meaning of these magic formulas, to whatever kind of economic and social witchcraft they may belong, is always just this, that the individual must give up his own material and spiritual personality and must live only as one of the spiritually restless and materialistic multitude which claims control over him.

That economic relations would some day eventuate in such a destruction of the independence of the individual, Goethe could not foresee. But with that capacity for mysterious foreboding in which he becomes aware of the danger of machinery, the early introduction of which he witnesses, he foresees that the spiritual independence of mankind will be threatened by the appearance of mob rule. This premonition is the basis for his unconquerable aversion to all revolutionaries. The revolutionary is for him the will of the masses bent on overthrowing the will of the individual. Himself a witness of the earliest manifestations of mob rule in the French Revolution and in the wars for freedom, he is profoundly conscious that therewith something appears on the scene the consequences of which will be immeasurable. Hence his hesitant attitude toward the wars for freedom, which was the occasion of so many misunderstandings. He wants freedom for his people, of course, but the manifestation of the mass mind bent on it makes him feel very uneasy, as we learn from a conversation in 1813 with the history professor Luden of Jena, in the course of which he reveals thoughts filled with profound emotion which at other times he keeps shut up within him.

Goethe is the first who feels something like a concern for man. At a time when others are still unconcerned, it dawns upon him that the great problem in the coming evolution of things will be this: how the individual can assert himself in the face of the multitude.

In this anxious foreboding, which he cherishes within him, and which lies behind many a stormy word which brought upon him the reproach that he was a reactionary and did not understand the signs of the time, there is also concern for his nation. He knows that no other nation so offends against its nature, in the renunciation by its own people of their spiritual independence, as his own nation, this people that he loves with such proud reserve. Yet he knows well that the deep communion with nature, the spirituality, and the need for spiritual independence, which constitute his own being, are manifestations of the soul of his people in him.

And now, a hundred years after his death, it has come to pass, through a calamitous development determined by events and through the influence of that development upon the economic, the social and the spiritual everywhere, that the material and the spiritual independence of the individual, so far as it is not already destroyed, is most seriously threatened. We remember the death of Goethe in this most portentous and fateful hour which has ever struck for mankind. He is summoned as no other poet or thinker to speak to us in this hour. He looks into our time as one most out of place in it, for he has absolutely nothing in common with the spirit in which it lives. But he comes with the most timely counsel, for he has something to say to our time which it is essential that it should hear.

What does he say to it?

He says to it that the frightful drama that is being enacted in it can come to an end only when it sets aside the economic and social magic in which it has trusted, when it forgets the magic formulas with which it deludes itself, when it is resolved to return at any cost to a natural relationship with reality.

To the individual he says: Do not abandon the ideal of personality, even when it runs counter to developing circumstances. Do not give it up for lost, even when it seems no longer tenable in the presence of opportunistic theories which would make the spiritual conform only to the material. Remain men in possession of your own souls! Do not become human things which have offered hospitality to souls which conform to the will of the masses and beat in time with it.

Not everything in history is ordained to be overthrown in the process of constant change, as it seems to superficial observers; on the contrary, ideals that carry within themselves enduring worth will adjust themselves to changing circumstances and grow stronger and deeper in the midst of them. Such an ideal is that of human personality. If it is given up, then the human spirit will be destroyed, which will mean the end of civilization, and even of humanity.

Therefore, it is significant that in this time our eyes should rest on Goethe, the messenger to true and noble humanity, and that his thoughts should spread in every possible way among the people. May his "be yourself" that resounds from them, and contains in this fateful hour for humanity the significance of a historical watchword for the world, make us brave to withstand the spirit of the time and even in the most difficult circumstances to preserve for ourselves and for others as much opportunity as possible for true humanity. And may it be true—for this is the critical thing!—that we, each of us in the measure of his given capacity, may also bring to pass the simple humanity of "let man be noble, kindly, and good," and that this ideal may be among us not simply as thought, but also as power.

[II]

The Sanctuary of Thought

GLORIOUS ACTIVITY

🔲 Again and again we unite with gratitude to the God who has directed us to such a glorious sphere of activity, gratitude to the kind people who make it possible for us through the gifts they send for the work.   [III]

GRACE FOR WORK

🔲 Our real strength for the work we find every day anew is the realization of the grace which comes to us in that we are allowed to be active in the service of the mercy of Jesus among the poorest of the poor. It is this consciousness which unites us. In this we feel ourselves lifted above the not always small difficulties which work among primitives who cannot be accustomed to any discipline brings with it.
          [III]

THOUGHT DEMANDS ACQUIESCENCE

🔲 Only when thinking becomes quite humble can it set its feet upon the way that leads to knowledge. The more profound a religion is, the more it realizes this fact—that what it knows through belief is little compared with what it does not know. The first active deed of thinking is resignation—acquiescence in what happens. Becoming free, inwardly, from what happens, we pass through the gate of resignation on the way to ethics. [IV]

DISSONANCE AND HARMONY

The spirit of the age dislikes what is simple. It no longer believes the simple can be profound. It loves the complicated, and regards it as profound. It loves the violent. That is why the spirit of the age can love Karl Barth and Nietzsche at the same time. The spirit of the age loves dissonance, in tones, in lines and in thought. That shows how far from thinking it is, for thinking is a harmony within us. [IV]

REALISTIC THINKING

Thinking which keeps contact with reality must look up to the heavens, it must look over the earth, and dare to direct its gaze to the barred windows of a lunatic asylum. Look to the stars and understand how small our earth is in the universe. Look upon earth and know how minute man is upon it. The earth existed long before man came upon it. In the history of the universe, man is on earth for but a second. Who knows but that the earth will circle round the sun once more without man upon it? Therefore we must not place man in the center of the universe. And our gaze must be fixed on the barred windows of a lunatic asylum, in order that we may remember the terrible fact that the mental and spiritual are also liable to destruction. [IV]

THE RIDDLE OF THE UNIVERSE

⊐ All thinking must renounce the attempt to explain the universe. We cannot understand what happens in the universe. What is glorious in it is united with what is full of horror. What is full of meaning is united to what is senseless. The spirit of the universe is at once creative and destructive—it creates while it destroys and destroys while it creates, and therefore it remains to us a riddle. And we must inevitably resign ourselves to this.   [IV]

THE RELIGION OF THE AGE

⊐ If one reviews the development of religion since the middle of the nineteenth century, one understands the tragic fact that although really living religion is to be found among us, it is not the leaven that leavens the thinking of our age.   [IV]

CONTEMPT FOR THINKING

⊐ Karl Barth, who is the most modern theologian, because he lives most in the spirit of our age, more than any other has that contempt for thinking which is characteristic of our age. He dares to say that religion has nothing to do with thinking. He wants to give religion nothing to do with anything but God and man, the great antithesis. He says a religious person does not concern himself with what happens to the world. The idea of the Kingdom of God plays no part with him. He mocks at what he calls "civilized Protestantism." The church must leave the world to itself. All that concerns the church is the preaching of revealed truth. Religion is turned aside from the world.   [IV]

THE IDEALS WE NEED

⧉ Humanity has always needed ethical ideals to enable it to find the right path, that man may make the right use of the power he possesses. Today his power is increased a thousandfold. A thousandfold greater is now the˙ need for man to possess ethical ideals to point the way. Yet at the very moment when this happens, thinking fails. In this period of deepest need thinking is not giving to humanity the ideals it needs so that it may not be overwhelmed. Is that our destiny? I hope not. I believe not. I think that in our age we are all carrying within us a new form of thought which will give us ethical ideals.   [IV]

THINKING DROPS THE TILLER

⧉ In modern thinking the same thing happens as in religion. Thinking drops the tiller from its hand in the middle of the storm. It renounces the idea of giving to human beings ideals by the help of which they can get on with reality. It leaves them to themselves, and that in a most terrible moment. For the present moment *is* terrible. Man has won power over the forces of nature and by that has become superman—and at the same time most miserable man! For this power over the forces of nature is not being used beneficially, but destructively.   [IV]

THE PHILOSOPHY OF VALUES

⧉ The philosophy of values resorts to a type of thinking which becomes dualistic. It asserts that there are spiritual truths alongside theoretical truths, and that all valuable conviction has truth in itself—a dangerous assertion. The real father of this doctrine of double truth is Hume. To escape skepticism, Hume says, we need convictions which will help us to live, and in regard to which we ask, not, Are they true? but, Are they necessary for our life? [IV]

PRAGMATISM

⊐〕 What is pragmatism compared with this philosophy of values? [The philosophy of Hume.] It is a philosophy of values which has given up the criterion of ethics. Pragmatism says: Every idea that helps me to live is truth. Europeans got this pragmatism sent, all ready for use, from America, in William James. So modern thinking arrives at the doctrine of double truth. The theory of double truth is a spiritual danger. If there is a double truth, there is no truth. The sense of sincerity is blunted and the last thing that thinking can give humanity is a feeling for truth—for sincerity is fundamental in all spiritual life and when this fundamental is shaken, there is no spiritual life remaining. In pragmatism, not only sincerity and truth, but ethics is in danger. For ethics is no longer the criterion of what is valuable. Pragmatism is filled with the spirit of realism. It permits men to take their ideals from reality.   [IV]

BY WORKS OF LOVE

⊐〕 It constituted a great difficulty for the non-dogmatic religion when theological science at the end of the nineteenth century was forced to admit that the ethical religion of Jesus shared the supernatural ideas of late-Jewish belief in the Messianic kingdom, and indeed that it also shared with it its expectation of the approaching end of the world.

Here it becomes clear that there is no purely historical foundation for religion. We must take the ethical religion of Jesus out of the setting of His world-view and put it in our own. Whereas He expected the Kingdom of God to come at the end of the world, we must endeavor, under the influence of the spirit of His ethical religion, to make the Kingdom of God a reality in this world by works of love.   [IV]

THE ETHICS OF MATERIALISM

▤ The ethics of materialism is unnecessary. Society has no need that the individual should serve it. Society does not need his morality; it can force upon him the sociology which it holds to be best. Herbert Spencer was not only a great thinker but a great prophet. He expressed anxiety lest the state should by violence force the individual to submit to it. He was right. The ethics of materialism has not triumphed, for in our days we have experienced the state destroying the individual in order to make the individual its servant. Therefore, the ethics of materialism is no religion.   [IV]

THE MACHINE AND SOCIAL PROBLEMS

▤ Because he has power over the forces of nature, man built machines which took work away from man, and this makes social problems of such magnitude that no one would have dreamed of them forty years ago. In some cities now air raid practices are held, with sirens shrieking and all lights out. People shove something over their heads which makes them look like beasts, and rush into cellars, while flying through the air appears the superman, possessing endless power for destruction. [IV]

DOES EVERYTHING SERVE PROGRESS?

Hegel dares to say that everything serves progress. The passions of rulers and of peoples—all are the servants of progress. One can only say that Hegel did not know the passions of people as we know them, or he would not have dared to write that! [IV]

Religion Is Not a Force

▣ "Is religion a force in the spiritual life of our age?" I answer in your name and mine, "No!" There is still religion in the world; there is much religion in the church; there are many pious people among us. Christianity can still point to works of love and to social works of which it can be proud. There is a longing for religion among many who no longer belong to the churches. I rejoice to concede this. And yet we must hold fast to the fact that religion is not a force. The proof? The war! [IV]

DOGMATIC RELIGION

▣ Dogmatic religion is based on the creeds, the early church and the reformation. It has no relations with thinking, but emphasizes the difference between thinking and believing. This religion further is more dominated by the thought of redemption than by that of the Kingdom of God. It has no wish to influence the world. That is characteristic

· 44 ·

of all the ancient creeds—that the idea of the Kingdom of God finds no expression in them. [IV]

RELIGION AND CIVILIZATION

▱ Why did the idea of the Kingdom of God have no significance in the early church? It was closely connected with the expectation of the end of the world. And when hope of the coming of the end of the world had faded, the idea of the Kingdom of God lost its force as well. So it came about that the creeds were not at the same time preoccupied with the idea of redemption. Only after the reformation did the idea gradually arise that we men and women in our own age must so understand the religion of Jesus that we endeavor to make the Kingdom of God a reality in this world. It is only through the idea of the Kingdom of God that religion enters into relationship with civilization. [IV]

RELIGION TURNS ITS BACK

▱ In recent times a tendency has appeared in dogmatic religion which completely turns its back on thinking and at the same time declares that religion has nothing to do with the world and civilization. It is not its business to realize the Kingdom of God on earth. This extreme tendency is mainly represented by Karl Barth. [IV]

WHEN OUR AGE BEGAN

▱ In the nineteenth century the spirit of realism rose against the spirit of idealism. The first personality in which it was realized was Napoleon I. The first thinker in whom it announced itself was the German philosopher Hegel. Men have not, Hegel maintained, to transform reality in order to bring it into accord with ideals devised by thinking. Progress takes place automatically in the natural course of events. The passions of ruling personalities and of peoples in some way or other are in the service of progress—even war is. The view that ethical idealism is a form of sentimentality of which no use can be made in the world of reality began with Hegel. He was first to formulate the theory of rationalism. He wrote: "What is reasonable is real, and what is real is reasonable." On the night of June 25, 1820, when that sentence was written, our age began, the age which moved on to the World War—and which perhaps someday will end civilization!   [iv]

When Thinking Was Religious

⊒ The religion of our age gives the same impression as an African river in the dry season—a great river bed, sand banks, and between, a small stream which seeks its way. One tries to imagine that a river once filled that bed; that there were no sand banks but that the river flowed majestically on its way; and that it will someday be like that again. Is it possible, you say, that once a river filled this bed? Was there a time when ethical religion was a force in the spiritual life of the time? Yes, in the eighteenth century. Then ethical religion and thinking formed one unity. Thinking was religious, and religion was a thinking religion. Because it was conditioned by ethical religious ideas, the thinking of that period undertook to represent reality to itself as it should be. It possessed ethical ideals in accordance with which it transformed reality.   [IV]

EIGHTEENTH CENTURY RELIGION

⊒ The religion of the eighteenth century undertook a great work of reform. It waged war against superstition and ignorance. It obtained recognition for humanity in the eyes of the law. Torture was abolished, first in Prussia in the year 1740 through a cabinet order of Frederick the Great. It was demanded of the individual that he should place himself at the service of the community. English emigrants formulated in America for the first time the rights of man. The idea of humanity began to gain in significance. People dared to grasp the thought that lasting peace must reign on earth. Kant wrote a book on *Everlasting Peace* (1795), and in it represented the thought that even politics must submit to the principles of ethics. Finally, an achievement which the spirit of the eighteenth century brought about in the nineteenth century, came the abolition of slavery.

The religious-ethical spirit of the eighteenth century desired then to make the Kingdom of God a reality on earth. [IV]

TWO CURRENTS IN RELIGION

In religion there are two different currents: one free from dogma and one that is dogmatic. That which is free from dogma bases itself on the preaching of Jesus; the dogmatic bases itself on the creeds of the early church and the reformation. The religion free from dogma is to some extent the heir of rationalistic religion. It is ethical, limits itself to the fundamental ethical verities, and endeavors, so far as is in its power, to remain on good terms with thinking. It wants to realize something of the Kingdom of God in the world. It believes itself identical with the religion of Jesus. All the efforts of historical-theological science in the nineteenth century are aimed at proving that Christian dogma began with St. Paul and that the religion of Jesus is non-dogmatic, so that it can be adopted in any age. [IV]

A RELIGION THAT UTTERS NO COMMANDS

⊐ The ethical religion of the philosophers of the second half of the nineteenth century is not firmly grounded. Its idea of God is quite incomplete. What is ethical in such teaching has no force. It lacks compulsive power and enthusiasm, and so this fine philosophical religion has had no significance for the thinking of the world in general. It is something which cannot be placed in the center of things; it is too delicate, too cautious, it utters no commands. [IV]

THE DEFEAT OF RELIGION

⊐ Religion was powerless to resist the spirit through which we entered the war. It was overcome by this spirit. It could bring no force against the ideals of inhumanity and unreasonableness which gave birth to the war, and when war had broken out, religion capitulated. It became mobilized. It had to join in helping to keep up the courage of the peoples. To give each people courage to go on fighting, one had to explain that they were fighting for their existence and for the spiritual treasures of humanity. Religion helped to give this conviction. It is easy to understand why it did this. It seemed a necessity. It remains true, however, that in the war religion lost its purity and lost its authority. It joined forces with the spirit of the world.

The one victim of defeat was religion. And that religion *was* defeated is apparent in our time. For it lifts up its voice, but only to protest. It cannot command. The spirit of the age does not listen. It goes its own way.   [IV]

What Do I Think?

How did it come about that ethical ideas could not oppose the inhuman ideals of the war? It was due to the spirit of practical realism. I place at opposite extremes the spirit of idealism and the spirit of realism. The spirit of idealism means that men and women of the period arrive at ethical ideals through thinking, and that these ideals are so powerful that men say: We will use them to control reality. We will transform reality in accordance with these ideals. The spirit of idealism desires to have power over the spirit of realism. The spirit of practical realism, however, holds it false to apply ideals to what is happening. The spirit of realism has no power over reality. If a generation lives with these ideas, it is subject to reality. This is the tragedy which is being enacted in our age. For what is characteristic of our age is that we no longer really believe in social or spiritual progress, but face reality powerless.

[IV]

THE RELATIONSHIP OF LOVE

◿ Let me give you a definition of ethics: It is good to maintain life and further life; it is bad to damage and destroy life. However much it struggles against it, ethics arrives at the religion of Jesus. It must recognize that it can discover no other relationship to other beings as full of sense as the relationship of love. Ethics is the maintaining of life at the highest point of development—my own life and other life—by devoting myself to it in help and love, and both these things are connected. [IV]

THE PROGRESS OF ETHICS

◿ There is a development under way by which the circle of ethics always grows wider, and ethics becomes more profound. This development has been in progress from primitive times to the present. It is often halted, hindered by the absence of thought among men—I dare to say through that absence of thought which characterizes thought! But yet the development goes on to its end. The circle described by ethics is always widening. Primitive man has duties only toward his nearest relations. All other living beings are to him only things; he mistreats them and kills them, without compunction. Then the circle widens to the tribe, to the people, and grows ever wider until at last man realizes his ethical association with the whole of humanity. This represents an enormous act of thinking. [IV]

SHALL WE MAKE OR SUFFER HISTORY?

◿ One truth stands firm. All that happens in world history rests on something spiritual. If the spiritual is strong, it creates world history. If it is weak, it suffers world history. The question is, shall we make world history or only suffer it passively? Will our thinking again become ethical-religious? Shall we again win ideals that will have power over reality? This is the question before us today.   [IV]

THE MYSTERY OF THE UNIVERSE

Modern thinkers emancipated from Kant . . . want to get at religion by saying: All this knowledge of the world through science is only a description of the world, from which man derives nothing. What we must know is the essential nature of the universe. The thing we must be pre-occupied with is the mystery of our life. How we understand the mystery of our life is the mystery of the universe. They say: We know the universe by intuition, not by reason. Our life knows the life in the world, and through our life we become one with the life of the universe. This thinking therefore is mysticism.

But ethics plays no part in this form of thought. The great problem of what man is aiming at plays no part in it.

[IV]

ETHICS AND HUMANITY

Consider Plato and Aristotle. Their ethics is narrow-hearted. They were occupied only with their fellow citizens. Slaves and foreigners did not concern them. Then with stoicism the circle begins to widen. That was the greatest manifestation of Greek thought. (Forgive me this heresy!) Then in Seneca, Epictetus, Marcus Aurelius, the idea suddenly crops up that ethics is concerned with all humanity.

Thought arrives at that intuitive knowledge which you find
already in the prophets of Israel and which is explained by
Jesus. [IV]

INCOMPLETE ETHICS

Materialism proclaims war against metaphysics. It
wants only the positive—what one can really know—and
by that it declares its intention of living. The ethics of
materialism consists in saying: You must live for the good
of the community. Has this form of ethics really the significance of a religion? Can a man understand the purpose of
his life when he says: I live for the good of the community?
No! The ethics of materialism is incomplete. It hangs in the
air. [IV]

UNETHICAL RELIGION

Karl Barth—whom I personally value greatly—
came to the point when he had to concern himself with the
world, which in theory he did not want to do. He had to
defend the freedom of religion against the state. And he
did it with courage. But it shows that his theory is false! It
is something terrible to say that religion is not ethical. Karl
Barth is a truly religious personality, and in his sermons
there is much profound religion. But the terrible thing is
that he dares to preach that religion is turned aside from
the world and in so doing expresses what the spirit of the
age is feeling. [IV]

ALL LIFE IS VALUABLE

The deeper we look into nature, the more we recognize

that it is full of life, and the more profoundly we know that all life is a secret and that we are united with all life that is in nature. Man can no longer live his life for himself alone. We realize that all life is valuable and that we are united to all this life. From this knowledge comes our spiritual relationship to the universe.   [IV]

THE HIGHEST RATIONALITY

Today there is an absence of thinking which is characterized by a contempt for life. We waged war for questions which, through reason, might have been solved. No one won. The war killed millions of men, brought suffering to millions of men, and brought suffering and death to millions of innocent animals. Why? Because we did not possess the highest rationality of reverence for life. And because we do not yet possess this, every people is afraid of every other, and each causes fear to the others. We are mentally afflicted one for another because we are lacking in rationality. There is no other remedy than reverence for life, and at that we must arrive.   [IV]

ETHICS AND THE ANIMAL CREATION

Slowly in our European thought comes the notion that ethics has not only to do with mankind but with the animal creation as well. This begins with St. Francis of Assisi. The explanation which applies only to man must be given up. Thus we shall arrive at saying that ethics is reverence for *all* life.   [IV]

WE WANDER IN DARKNESS

We wander in darkness now, but one with another we all have the conviction that we are advancing to the light; that again a time will come when religion and ethical thinking will unite. This we believe, and hope and work for, maintaining the belief that if we make ethical ideals active in our own lives, then the time will come when peoples will do the same. Let us look out toward the light and comfort ourselves in reflecting on what thinking is preparing for us.   [IV]

WHAT DO I THINK?

Descartes built an artificial structure by presuming that man knows nothing, and doubts all, whether outside himself or within. And in order to end doubt he fell back on the fact of consciousness: *I think*. Surely, however, that is the stupidest primary assumption in all philosophy! Who can establish the fact that he thinks, except in relation to thinking *something?* And what that something is, is the important matter. When I seek the first fact of consciousness, it is not to know if I think, but to get hold of myself. Descartes would have a man think once, just long enough to establish the certainty of being, and then give over any further need of meditation. Yet meditation is the very thing I must not cease. I *must* ascertain whether my thoughts are in harmony with my will-to-live.   [V]

SPIRITUAL HARMONY

As we know life in ourselves, we want to understand life in the universe, in order to enter into harmony with it.

Physically we are always trying to do this. But that is not the primary matter; for the great issue is that we shall achieve a spiritual harmony. Just to recognize this fact is to have begun to see a part of life clearly.   [v]

REASON AND GOODNESS

⊒ Whatever is reasonable is good. . . . To be truly rational is to become ethical.   [v]

ABSOLUTE ETHICS

⊒ Every ethic has something of the absolute about it, just as soon as it ceases to be mere social law. It demands of one what is actually beyond his strength. Take the question of man's duty to his neighbor. The ethic cannot be fully carried out without involving the possibility of complete sacrifice of self. Yet philosophy has never bothered to take due notice of the distinction. It has simply tried to ignore absolute ethics, because such ethics cannot be fitted into tabulated rules and regulations. Indeed, the history of world teachings on the subject may be summarized in the motto: "Avoid absolute ethics, and thus keep within the realm of the possible."   [v]

INTEREST IN LIFE

⊒ There is in each of us the will-to-live, which is based on the mystery of what we call "taking an interest." We cannot live alone. Though man is an egoist, he is never completely so. He *must* always have some interest in life about him. If for no other reason, he must do so in order to make his own life more perfect. Thus it happens that we want to devote ourselves; we want to take our part in perfecting our ideal of progress; we want to give meaning to the life in the world. This is the basis of our striving for harmony with the spiritual element.   [v]

THE INSIGNIFICANCE OF MAN

When we consider the immensity of the universe, we must confess that man is insignificant. The world began, as it were, yesterday. It may end tomorrow. Life has existed in the universe but a brief second. And certainly man's life can hardly be considered the goal of the universe. Its margin of existence is always precarious. Study of the geologic periods shows that. So does the battle against disease. When one has seen whole populations annihilated by sleeping sickness, as I have, one ceases to imagine that human life is nature's goal. In fact, the Creative Force does not concern itself about preserving life. It simultaneously creates and destroys. Therefore, the will-to-live is not to be understood within the circle of Creative Force. Philosophy and religion have repeatedly sought the solution by this road; they have projected our will to perfection into nature at large, expecting to see its counterpart there. But in all honesty we must confess that to cling to such a belief is to delude ourselves.   [v]

WHAT KNOWLEDGE TELLS ME

I ask knowledge what it can tell me of life. Knowledge replies that what it can tell me is little, yet immense. Whence this universe came, or whither it is bound, or how it happens to be at all, knowledge cannot tell me. Only this:

that the will-to-live is everywhere present, even as in me. I do not need science to tell me this; but it cannot tell me anything more essential. Profound and marvelous as chemistry is, for example, it is like all science in the fact that it can lead me only to the mystery of life, which is essentially in me, however near or far away it may be observed.   [v]

IS MAN THE END OF NATURE?

The effort for harmony never succeeds. Events cannot be harmonized with our activities. Working purposefully toward certain ends, we assume that the Creative Force in the world is doing likewise. Yet, when we try to define its goal, we cannot do so. It tends toward developing a type of existence, but there is no coordinated, definite end to be observed, even though we think there should be. We like to imagine that Man is nature's goal; but facts do not support that belief.   [v]

SPIRITUAL EXALTATION

One realizes that he is but a speck of dust, a plaything of events outside his reach. Nevertheless, he may at the same time discover that he has a certain liberty, as long as he lives. Sometime or another all of us must have found that happy events have not been able to make us happy, nor unhappy events to make us unhappy. There is within each of us a modulation, an inner exaltation, which lifts us above the buffetings with which events assail us. Likewise, it lifts us above dependence upon the gifts of events for our joy. Hence, our dependence upon events is not absolute; it is qualified by our spiritual freedom. Therefore, when we speak of resignation it is not sadness to which we refer, but the triumph of our will-to-live over whatever happens to us. And to become ourselves, to be spiritually alive, we must have passed beyond this point of resignation.   [v]

SINCERITY

▣ Resignation is the very basis of ethics. Starting from this position, the will-to-live comes first to veracity as the primary ground of virtue. If I am faithful to my will-to-live, I cannot disguise that fact, even though such disguise or evasion might seem to my advantage. Reverence for my will-to-live leads me to the necessity of being sincere with myself. And out of this fidelity to my own nature grows all my faithfulness. Thus, sincerity is the first ethical quality which appears. However lacking one may be in other respects, sincerity is the one thing which he must possess. Nor is this point of view to be found only among people of complex social life. Primitive cultures show the fact to be equally true there. Resignation to the will-to-live leads directly to this first virtue: sincerity.   [v]

THE MYSTERY OF LIFE

▣ The essential thing to realize about ethics is that it is the very manifestation of our will-to-live. All of our thoughts are given in that will-to-live, and we but give them expression and form in words. To analyze reason fully would be to analyze the will-to-live. The philosophy that abandons the old Rationalism must begin by meditation on itself. Thus, if we ask, "What is the immediate fact of my consciousness? What do I self-consciously know of myself, making abstractions of all else, from childhood to old age? To what do I always return ?" we find the simple fact of consciousness in this, *I will to live*. Through every stage of life, this is the one thing I know about myself. I do not say, "I am life"; for life continues to be a mystery too great to understand. I only know that I cling to it. I fear its cessation—death. I dread its diminution—pain. I seek its enlargement—joy.   [v]

I CLING TO LIFE

When my will-to-live begins to think, it sees life as a mystery in which I remain by thought. I cling to life because of my reverence for life. For, when it begins to think, the will-to-live realizes that it is free. It is free to leave life. It is free to choose whether or not to live. This fact is of particular significance for us in this modern age, when there are abundant possibilities for abandoning life, painlessly and without agony.   [v]

LIFE IS A TRUST

The question which haunts men and women today is whether life is worth living. Perhaps each of us has had the experience of talking with a friend one day, finding that person bright, happy, apparently in the full joy of life; and then the next day we find that he has taken his own life! Stoicism has brought us to this point, by driving out the fear of death; for, by inference it suggests that we are free to choose whether to live or not. But if we entertain such a possibility, we do so by ignoring the melody of the will-to-live, which compels us to face the mystery, the value, the high trust committed to us in life. We may not understand it, but we begin to appreciate its great value. Therefore, when we find those who relinquish life, while we may not condemn them, we do pity them for having ceased to be in possession of themselves. Ultimately, the issue is not whether we do or do not fear death. The real issue is that of reverence for life. [v]

HINDERING OR HELPING

What shall be my attitude toward other life? It can only be of a piece with my attitude towards my own life. If I am a thinking being, I must regard other life than my own with equal reverence. For I shall know that it longs for fullness and development as deeply as I do myself. Therefore, I see that evil is what annihilates, hampers, or hinders life. And this holds good whether I regard it physically or spiritually. Goodness, by the same token, is the saving or helping of life, the enabling of whatever life I can influence to attain its highest development. [v]

REVERENCE AND RESIGNATION

The first spiritual act in man's experience is reverence for life. The consequence of it is that he comes to realize his dependence upon events quite beyond his control. Therefore he becomes resigned. And this is the second spiritual act: resignation. [v]

THE PRINCIPLE IS UNIVERSAL

Ordinary ethics seeks to find limits within the sphere of human life and relationships. But the absolute ethics of the will-to-live must reverence every form of life, seeking so far as possible to refrain from destroying any life, regardless of its particular type. It says of no instance of life, "This has no value." It cannot make any such exceptions, for it is built upon reverence for life as such. It knows that the mystery of life is always too profound for us, and that its value is beyond our capacity to estimate. We happen to believe that man's life is more important than any other form of which we know. But we cannot prove any such comparison of value from what we know of the world's development. True, in practice we are forced to choose. At times we have to decide arbitrarily which forms of life, and even which particular individuals, we shall save, and which we shall destroy. But the principle of reverence for life is none the less universal.   [v]

BIRTH AND NATURE OF ETHICS

▣ We have dared to say that ethics is born of physical life, out of the linking of life with life. It is therefore the result of our recognizing the solidarity of life which nature gives us. And as it grows more profound, it teaches us sympathy with *all* life. Yet, the extremes touch, for this material-born ethic becomes engraved upon our hearts, and culminates in spiritual union and harmony with the creative Will which is in and through all.   [v]

THE SOLIDARITY OF LIFE

▣ The important thing is that we are part of life. We are born of other lives; we possess the capacities to bring still other lives into existence. In the same way, if we look into a microscope we see cell producing cell. So nature compels us to recognize the fact of mutual dependence, each life necessarily helping the other lives which are linked to it. In the very fibers of our being, we bear within ourselves the fact of the solidarity of life. Our recognition of it expands with thought. Seeing its presence in ourselves, we realize how closely we are linked with others of our kind. We might like to stop here, but we cannot. Life demands that we see through to the solidarity of all life which we can in any degree recognize as having some similarity to the life that is in us. [v]

THE ETHICS OF THE FLOCK

A flock of wild geese had settled to rest on a pond. One of the flock had been captured by a gardener, who had clipped its wings before releasing it. When the geese started to resume their flight, this one tried frantically, but vainly, to lift itself into the air. The others, observing his struggles, flew about in obvious efforts to encourage him; but it was no use. Thereupon, the entire flock settled back on the pond and waited, even though the urge to go on was strong within them. For several days they waited until the damaged feather had grown sufficiently to permit the goose to fly. Meanwhile, the unethical gardener, having been converted by the ethical geese, gladly watched them as they finally rose together, and all resumed their long flight. [v]

LIFE IS LINKED TOGETHER

I have the virtue of caring for all stray monkeys that come to our gate. (If you have had any experience with

large numbers of monkeys, you know why I say it is a
virtue thus to take care of all comers until they are old
enough or strong enough to be turned loose, several together, in the forest—a great occasion for them—and for
me!) Sometimes there will come to our monkey colony a
wee baby monkey whose mother has been killed, leaving
this orphaned infant. I must find one of the older monkeys
to adopt and care for the baby. I never have any difficulty
about it, except to decide which candidate shall be given
the responsibility. Many a time it happens that the seemingly worst-tempered monkeys are most insistent upon
having this sudden burden of foster parenthood given to
them.   [v]

MUTUAL DEPENDENCE

A friend in Hanover owned a small café. He would
daily throw out crumbs for the sparrows in the neighbor-
hood. He noticed that one sparrow was injured, so that it
had difficulty getting about. But he was interested to discover that the other sparrows, apparently by mutual agreement, would leave the crumbs which lay nearest to their
crippled comrade, so that he could get his share, undisturbed.   [v]

STABLE AND UNSTABLE SOCIETIES

The idea of the rights of man was formed and developed in the eighteenth century, when society was an organized and stable thing. Whatever the fundamental rights
of men are, they can only be fully secured in a stable and
well-ordered society. In a disordered society the very well-

being of man himself often demands that his fundamental rights should be abridged. [vi]

THE RIGHTS OF MAN

🔲 The fundamental rights of man are, first, the right to habitation; secondly, the right to move freely; thirdly, the right to the soil and subsoil, and to the use of it; fourthly, the right to freedom of labor and of exchange; fifthly, the right to justice; sixthly, the right to live within a natural national organization; and, seventhly, the right to education. [vi]

THE RIGHT TO HABITATION

🔲 Man has the right to live where his life has been developed, and not to be displaced. This is a burning point in primitive society. Yet in colonization the right is constantly menaced; often not by ill will in any degree, but by the sheer force of facts. For instance, a large, modern white city grows up round a small, primitive village, or the creation and development of an arterial road on which the very lives of the inhabitants depends, involves living by that road. The future development of the good of the people may necessitate the movement of villages, yet, if it is done without long foresight, careful planning and adequate warning, with provision for the creation of new plantations, and if any violence enters into it, a fatal impression will be created in the mind of the native that he is delivered up to the working of an arbitrary will. Any movement that is ordered must always be on a rational basis and for the future good. [vi]

THE RIGHT TO CIRCULATE FREELY

◰ The right of emigration and immigration is today surrounded by every kind of difficulty. For instance, vast cocoa plantations exercise a very strong economic pull for labor on the plantations of the neighboring territories. To allow that economic pull to have free play would rob neighboring colonies of the essential labor. Therefore there is restriction on movement. In the collection of taxes again, there is a strong temptation to the natives to disappear into the forest and move to another area to escape taxes. So the administration insists that he stay in his own canton. From the state's point of view and from that of the development of the country this is reasonable; but the right to circulate is limited. [vi]

THE RIGHT TO THE SOIL

◰ There is a right to the natural riches of the soil and subsoil; and to dispose of it as one will. But here, again, two very strong factors enter in. First, the development of the value of the whole land by enterprises from without. Few things are more difficult to foresee on a long view than what lands and subsoils should remain in the hand of the native, and how much should be placed in the hands of enterprises that will develop their values.

Again, on the other hand, a chief is offered money to sell his land. The money is put into his hands. He spends it on clothes, and trinkets, and tools and other things for himself and his wives. The land is gone and the money is gone; and his descendants find themselves pariahs—landless laborers. It is, therefore, in the interests of the people themselves to restrict the right of the chief to dispose of his land.   [VI]

THE RIGHT TO FREE WORK

No right is more fundamental or more essential than that of the free disposal by a man of his labor. In the present condition of things, however, we are confronted from time to time by circumstances and conditions that seem to make it essential for the state to demand labor. The state has the right to impose taxes to be collected in money or in kind. Has it also the right to collect service in actual labor? . . . A famine occurs in a certain area to which food must be transported if life is to be saved. The men will not carry that food for simple payment. (Payment, of course, is always made whether labor is forced or not.) Is it not then essential actually to command labor?   [VI]

THE RIGHT TO JUSTICE

Primitive tribal justice has the great quality that it is justice for everybody face to face with his adversary, administered locally and swiftly by the chief. Attempts to administer justice by Europeans, with a judge either infrequently there or at a long distance, not knowing the language or the people individually, and unable to penetrate behind the lives of the witnesses, is often long, slow, difficult and inefficient. Furthermore, the natives' own law (often more severe than ours) has been developed to meet their own conditions. Therefore in order to secure the great need for a settlement on the spot at a man's own door, we must have traveling judges or administrators who will move from place to place giving justice on the spot, in cooperation with the authority of the chiefs. . . . To do away with that authority is to destroy your one intermediary between the administration and the multitude. In Europe the intermediary between government and the people is the office. That process is impossible with primitive peoples. It is always the man that matters. We have to do not with peoples but with tribes; not with organized governments, but with chiefs. [VI]

THE RIGHT TO NATURAL SOCIAL ORGANIZATION

The only way to defend other rights is to develop a new stable social organization. To go back to the very beginning of what I have here said—the rights of man are a direct function of the normal organization of society. We have, therefore, to create a social organization and economic conditions in which the natives can flourish face to face with Western commerce. To do this we need a stable population, possessing houses, fields, orchards, workshops, and the requisite capacity to create and use them. This can only be achieved by the exercise of the right to education. [VI]

THE RIGHT TO EDUCATION

The education so far undertaken has been incomplete —in fact, usually the only educational work yet done has been that contributed by the missionaries. If, for instance, I want (or any man wants) an artisan—someone who can really work skillfully with his hands, a carpenter, for instance—I cannot find any save those educated by the missionary societies. When the modern state talks about doing an educational work among the natives, I say to it: "Do not make phrases; show me your work. How many educators have you in fact exported to your colony?" [vi]

EDUCATION AND THE ESSENTIALS OF LIFE

The work of education among a primitive people must be a blend of the intellectual and the manual adapted to the needs of citizenship in a primitive society. We must send out to such areas not only ordinary teachers, but artisan educators; in fact, a central problem of education there is how to make a craft loved and practiced among primitive peoples. The native is in danger of cutting out the stage between primitive life and professional. That is, he tends to eliminate the stages of agriculture and handicraft. He has a certain antagonism to the use of tools, and a desire to sit in an office with a cigarette in his mouth and a pen in his hand. I am constantly hearing the phrase "I want to be a writer." At my hospital recently I was helping to carry things to the garden, partly in order to create this impression of the dignity of labor. I saw a native in white clothes standing by the fence, and asked him to join in and help. His reply was—"No, I am an intellectual; a brain-worker." I went to a store, run by a native for natives, and could not get a single tool that I wanted, but found masses of silk stockings. We cannot, therefore, build a proper social organization until the native himself is skilled in making the essentials of his life—that is, growing his food and building his habitation. All independence, and therefore all capacity to face economic stress and to secure justice, is rooted there. [vi]

INDEPENDENCE

⧉ The independence of primitive or semi-primitive peoples is lost at the moment when the first white man's boat arrives with powder or rum, salt or fabrics. The social, economic and political situation at that moment begins to be turned upside down. The chiefs begin to sell their subjects for goods. From that point the political work of a state in colonizing is to correct, by its action, the evils developed through unrestrained economic advance.   [VI]

COLONIZATION AND ITS RESPONSIBILITIES

⧉ Independence is not lost by primitive peoples from the moment when a Protectorate or other form of government is proclaimed; but has already been lost in the commercial advance of which the political colonization must be a corrective. The question for us, therefore, is not —"Have we a right there?"—the question is simply one of alternatives. Are we on the one hand, the masters of these folk and lands, simply as raw material for our industries; or are we, on the other hand, responsible for developing a new social order, so as to create the possibility among those peoples of resisting the evils, and of developing themselves a new political organization? We have, I hold, the right to colonize if we have the moral authority to exercise this influence.   [VI]

A New Ethical System Needed

◲ Despite the mounting pressures at the hospital, I still managed to find time to reflect on our civilization and our ethical values and why they were losing their force. But now I had to tackle a more basic question: could a lasting, more profound, and more vital ethical system be brought about? The sense of satisfaction that came with my recognition of the nature of the problem did not last long, however. Month after month went by without my advancing one step toward a solution. Everything I knew or had read on the subject of ethics served only to confound me even more.

In the summer of 1915, I took my wife, who was in poor health, to Port-Gentil on the Atlantic. I brought the meager drafts of my book along. In September, I received word that the wife of the Swiss missionary, Pelot, had fallen ill at their mission in N'Gômô, and that I was expected to make a medical call there.

The mission was 120 miles upstream on the Ogooué

River. My only means of immediate transportation was a small, old steamboat, towing heavily laden scows. Besides myself, there were only a few Africans aboard. Since I had had no time to gather provisions in the rush of departure, they kindly offered to share their food with me.

We advanced slowly on our trip upstream. It was the dry season, and we had to feel our way through huge sand-banks. I sat in one of the scows. Before boarding the steamer, I had resolved to devote the entire trip to the problem of how a culture could be brought into being that possessed a greater moral depth and energy than the one we lived in. I filled page on page with disconnected sentences, primarily to center my every thought on the problem. Weariness and a sense of despair paralyzed my thinking. [VII]

Reverence for Life

At sunset of the third day, near the village of Igendja, we moved along an island set in the middle of the wide river. On a sandbank to our left, four hippopotamuses and their young plodded along in our same direction. Just then, in my great tiredness and discouragement, the phrase "Reverence for Life" struck me like a flash. As far as I knew, it was a phrase I had never heard nor ever read. I realized at once that it carried within itself the solution to the problem that had been torturing me. Now I knew that a system of values which concerns itself only with our relationship to other people is incomplete and therefore lacking in power for good. Only by means of reverence for life can we establish a spiritual and humane relationship with both people and all living creatures within our reach. Only in this fashion can we avoid harming others, and, within the limits of our capacity, go to their aid whenever they need us.

It also became clear to me that this elemental but complete system of values possessed an altogether different depth and an entirely different vitality than one that concerned itself only with human beings. Through reverence for life, we come into a spiritual relationship with the universe. The inner depth of feeling we experience through it gives us the will and the capacity to create a spiritual and ethical set of values that enables us to act on a higher plane, because we then feel ourselves truly at home in our world. Through reverence for life, we become, in effect, different persons. I found it difficult to believe that the way to a deeper and stronger ethic, for which I had searched in vain, had been revealed to me as in a dream. Now I was at last ready to write the planned work on the ethics of civilization.

For two days, I had been busy treating the sick wife of the missionary. When she showed signs of getting better, I sailed downstream to the ocean. A few days later, my wife and I returned to Lambaréné. There, I began to sketch in the volume on my philosophy of civilization. The plan was simple. First, I would give a general view of civilization and ethics as set forth in the writings of the world's great thinkers. Secondly, I would occupy myself with the essence and the significance of the ethics of reverence for life.

[VII]

Human Awareness

◳ The fundamental fact of human awareness is this: "I
am life that wants to live in the midst of other life that
wants to live." A thinking man feels compelled to approach
all life with the same reverence he has for his own. Thus,
all life becomes part of his own experience. From such a
point of view, "good" means to maintain life, to further
life, to bring developing life to its highest value. "Evil"
means to destroy life, to hurt life, to keep life from developing. This, then, is the rational, universal, and basic principle of ethics.

Ethics up to now had been incomplete because it had
held that its chief concern was merely with the relationship
of man to man. In reality, however, ethics must also be
concerned with the way man behaves toward all life. In
essence, then, man can be considered ethical only if life as
such is sacred to him—both in people and in all creatures
that inhabit the earth.

The actual living of this ethic, with its responsibilities

extending toward all living things, is deeply rooted in universal thought. The ethical relationship of man to man is not something in and of itself, but part of a greater concept. The idea of reverence for life contains everything that expresses love, submission, compassion, the sharing of joy, and common striving for the good of all. We must free ourselves from thoughtless existence.

At the same time, we are all subject to the mysterious and cruel law by which we maintain human life at the cost of other life. It is by this very destruction and harm of other life that we develop feelings of guilt. As ethical human beings, we must constantly strive to escape from this need to destroy—as much as we possibly can. We must try to demonstrate the essential worth of life by doing all we can to alleviate suffering. Reverence for life, which grows out of a proper understanding of the will to live, contains life-affirmation. It acts to create values that serve the material, the spiritual, and ethical development of man.

[VII]

The Goal of True Thought

Whereas the thoughtless modern world walks aimlessly about in ideals of knowledge, skills, and power, the goal of true and profound thought is the spiritual and ethical perfection of man. This requires a new ethical civilization that seeks peace and renounces war. Only the kind of thinking dominated by reverence for life can bring lasting peace to our world. All lesser efforts for peace must forever remain unsuccessful.

A new renaissance must come, and it must be much greater than the one that lifted the world out of the Middle Ages. This new renaissance must help mankind to advance from the pathetic sense of reality in which it lives, toward the spirit of reverence for life. Only through a truly ethical civilization can life take on meaning. Only through it can mankind be saved from destruction, from its senseless and cruel wars. It alone can bring about peace in the world.

[VII]

The Only Way to Save Ourselves

⊐ Today, many schools throughout the world are teaching reverence for life. Everything I hear and learn about the growing recognition of reverence for life strengthens my conviction that it is the fundamental truth mankind needs in order to reach the right spirit, and to be guided by it.

For today's generation, this is of a special significance. Compared to former generations, inhumanity has actually grown. Because we possess atomic weapons, the possibility and temptation to destroy life has increased immeasurably. Due to the tremendous advances in technology, the capacity to destroy life has become the fate of mankind. We can save ourselves from this fate only by abolition of atomic weapons.

For years now, the atomic powers have tried to reach an agreement on the abolition of atomic weapons. They have failed. All their suggestions thus far have been impotent to create the mutual trust which is necessary for a total renunciation of atomic weapons.

Trust is a matter of the spirit. It can be born only of the spirit. It can come about only when the spirit of reverence for life rises in all nations. Nations are not conscious of how inhumane they are. If they were, they would not rely on atomic weapons which can annihilate millions upon millions of people in a day.

We must not allow cruel national thinking to prevail. The abolition of atomic weapons will become possible only if world opinion demands it. And the spirit needed to achieve this can be created only by reverence for life. The course of history demands that not only individuals become ethical personalities, but that nations do so as well.   [VII]

Among the Africans

Anyone who has once penetrated into the imaginary world of primitive man, and knows something of the state of fear in which people may live when they believe in taboos, unavoidable curses and active ju-jus, can no longer doubt that it is our duty to endeavor to liberate them from these superstitions.

Everyone who is "at the front" knows how difficult it is to carry on this war. These conceptions have such deep roots in the world-view and traditions of primitive people that they are not easy to eradicate.

In the eyes of the Africans, the fact that individuals still perish by trespassing against their taboos, by curses of which they are the victims, or by magic to which they are exposed is a proof of the truth of their ideas which it is not easy to controvert. It is difficult indeed to make them understand that in these cases the events are determined by psychical conditions.

When natives in all good faith assure us that they have

attained to freedom from such ideas, they are by no means always really so advanced. The ideas are still subconsciously present and with any provocation may come to life again.

In our endeavors for the spiritual liberation of the Africans we find ourselves in a tragic position due to the revival of superstition in Europe. This unexpectedly vindicates primitive superstition. The Negroes who read newspapers know from these that there are also white men who believe in supernatural powers which man employs in his service. They spread the news out here and take us to task about it.

And in addition the Africans are made acquainted with the new forms of superstition across the seas by Europeans who make a trade of offering their services in prospectuses sent by post. By the numerous letters of this kind sent to my male nurses I can form some conception of the extent to which this exploitation is carried on. Probably every one of them—and one and another more than once—has sent his month's wages to Europe to receive in exchange his horoscope or a talisman. Formerly they came to ask me to send their money for them, but since they know I forbid the practice, they apply to someone else.

Some time ago one of my nurses brought me a typed letter in which an astrologer told him that recently, in an hour of meditation, he had felt impelled to concern himself with his case. In this way he had discovered something of great importance to him, which he would communicate in return for a certain sum of money. The Negro stood before me trembling with pride and excitement because a white man at a distance had been thinking about him. When

I explained to him that the man was a rascal who had sent the same letter to many other natives, he could not understand. He believed I grudged him the honor that had come his way and the happiness that lay before him. It is pretty certain that he sent the money secretly.

Various enterprises of this nature in various European countries have the addresses of my black nurses and many other natives of the Lambaréné area.

The fact that in Europe a frivolous game is played with superstition constitutes a grave danger for the prestige of the white man among the Africans.   [VIII]

The Will to Live

⊒ We may take as the essential element in civilization
the ethical perfecting of the individual and of society as
well. But at the same time, every spiritual and every
material step in advance has a significance for civilization.
The will to civilization is then the universal will to progress
which is conscious of the ethical as the highest value for
all. In spite of the great importance we attach to the
triumphs of knowledge and achievement, it is nevertheless
obvious that only a humanity which is striving after ethical
ends can in full measure share in the blessings brought by
material progress and become master of the dangers which
accompany it. To the generation which had adopted a belief
in an immanent power of progress realizing itself, in some
measure, naturally and automatically, and which thought
that it no longer needed any ethical ideals but could advance
to its goal by means of knowledge and achievement alone,
terrible proof was being given by its present position of
the error into which it had sunk.

The only possible way out of chaos is for us to come once more under the control of the ideas of true civilization through the adoption of an attitude toward life that contains those ideals.

But what is the nature of the attitude toward life in which the will to general progress and to ethical progress are alike founded and in which they are bound together?

It consists in an ethical affirmation of the world and of life.

What is affirmation of the world and of life?

To us Europeans and to people of European descent everywhere the will to progress is something so natural and so much a matter of course that it never occurs to us to recognize that it is rooted in an attitude toward life and springs from an act of the spirit. But if we look about us in the world, we see at once that what is to us such a matter of course is in reality anything but that. To Indian thought all effort directed to triumphs in knowledge and power and to the improvement of man's outer life and of society as a whole is mere folly. It teaches that the only sensible line of conduct for a man is to withdraw entirely into himself and to concern himself solely with the deepening of his inner life. He has nothing to do with what may become of human society and of mankind. The deepening of one's inner life, as Indian thought interprets it, means that a man surrenders himself to the thought of "no more will to live," and by abstention from action and by every sort of life denial reduces his earthly existence to a condition of being which has no content beyond a waiting for the cessation of being.

The striving for material and spiritual progress, which characterizes the people of modern Europe, has its source in the attitude toward the world to which these people have come. As a result of the Renaissance and the spiritual and religious movements bound up with it, men have entered on a new relation to themselves and to the world, and this has aroused in them a need to create by their own activities spiritual and material values which shall help to a higher development of individuals and of mankind. It is not the case that the man of modern Europe is enthusiastic for progress because he may hope to get some personal advantage from it. He is less concerned about his own condition than about the happiness which he hopes will be the lot of coming generations. Enthusiasm for progress has taken possession of him. Impressed by his great experience of finding the world revealed to him as constituted and maintained by forces which carry out a definite design he himself wills to become an active, purposeful force in the world. He looks with confidence toward new and better times which shall dawn for mankind, and learns by experience that the ideas which are held and acted upon by the mass of people do win power over circumstances and remold them.

It is on his will to material progress, acting in union with the will to ethical progress, that the foundations of modern civilization are being laid.

In modern European thought a tragedy is occurring in that the original bonds uniting the affirmative attitude toward the world with ethics are, by a slow but irresistible process, loosening and finally parting. The result that we are coming to is that European humanity is being guided by a will-to-progress that has become merely external and has lost its bearings.

The affirmative attitude can produce of itself only a partial and imperfect civilization. Only if it becomes inward and ethical can the will-to-progress which results from it possess the requisite insight to distinguish the valuable from the less valuable, and strive after a civilization which does not consist only in achievements of knowledge and power, but before all else will make men, both individually and collectively, more spiritual and more ethical.

But how could it come about that the modern attitude of the world and life changed from its original ethical character and became nonethical?

The only possible explanation is that it was not really founded on thought. The thought out of which it arose was noble and enthusiastic but not deep. The intimate connection of the ethical with the affirmative attitude toward life was for it a matter of feeling and experience rather than of proof. It took the side of life affirmation and of ethics without having penetrated their inner nature and their inward connection.

This noble and valuable view, therefore, being rooted in belief rather than in thinking which penetrated to the real nature of things was bound to wither and lose its power over men's minds. All subsequent thinking about the problems of ethics and man's relation to his world could not but expose the weak points of this view, and thereby help to hasten its decay. Its activity took effect in this direction even when its intention was to give support, for it never succeeded in replacing the inadequate foundation by one that was adequate. Again and again the new foundations and the underpinning masonry which it had taken in hand showed themselves too weak to support the building.

At bottom I am convinced that the inner connection between the affirmative attitude and ethics, declared to be part of the concept of civilization which had hitherto proved impossible to demonstrate fully, had come from a presentiment of the truth. So it was necessary to undertake to grasp as a necessity of thought by fresh, simple, and sincere thinking the truth which had hitherto been only suspected and believed in although so often proclaimed as proved.

In undertaking this I seemed to myself to be like a man who has to build a new and better boat to replace a rotten one in which he can no longer venture to trust himself to the sea, and yet does not know how to begin.

For months on end I lived in a continual state of mental excitement. Without the least success I let my thinking be concentrated, even all through my daily work at the hospital, on the real nature of the affirmative attitude and of ethics, and on the question of what they have in common. I was wandering about in a thicket in which no path was to be found. I was leaning with all my might against an iron door which would not yield.

All that I had learned from philosophy about ethics left me in the lurch. The conceptions of the Good which it had offered were all so lifeless, so unelemental, so narrow, and so destitute of content that it was quite impossible to bring them into union with the affirmative attitude. Moreover, philosophy could be said never to have concerned itself with the problem of the connection between civilization and attitude toward the world. The modern concept of progress had become to it such a matter of course that it had felt no need for coming to clear ideas about it.

To my surprise I had also to recognize the fact that the

central province of philosophy, into which meditation on civilization and attitude toward the world had led me, was practically unexplored land. Now from this point, now from that, I tried to penetrate to its interior, but again and again I had to give up the attempt. I was already exhausted and disheartened. I saw, indeed, the conception needed before me, but I could not grasp it and give it expression.

While in this mental condition I had to undertake a longish journey on the river. The only means of conveyance I could find was a small steamer, towing an overladen barge, which was on the point of starting. Slowly we crept upstream, laboriously feeling—it was the dry season—for the channels between the sandbanks. Lost in thought I sat on the deck of the barge, struggling to find the elementary and universal conception of the ethical which I had not discovered in any philosophy. Sheet after sheet I covered with disconnected sentences, merely to keep myself concentrated on the problem. Late on the third day, at the very moment when, at sunset, we were making our way through a herd of hippopotamuses, there flashed upon my mind, unforeseen and unsought, the phrase "Reverence for Life." The iron door had yielded: the path in the thicket had become visible. Now I had found my way to the idea in which affirmation of the world and ethics are contained side by side! Now I knew that the ethical acceptance of the world and of life, together with the ideals of civilization contained in this concept, has a foundation in thought.

What is Reverence for Life, and how does it arise in us?

If man wishes to reach clear notions about himself and his relation to the world, he must ever again and again be looking away from the manifold, which is the product of his thought and knowledge, and reflect upon the first, the most immediate, and the continually given fact of his own consciousness. Only if he starts from this given fact can he achieve a rational view.

Descartes makes thinking start from the sentence "I think; so I must exist" (*Cogito, ergo sum*), and with his beginning thus chosen he finds himself irretrievably on the road to the abstract. Out of this empty, artificial act of thinking there can result, of course, nothing which bears on the relation of man to himself, and to the universe. Yet in reality the most immediate act of consciousness has some content. To think means to think something. The most immediate fact of man's consciousness is the assertion: "I am life which wills to live, in the midst of life which wills to live," and it is as will-to-live in the midst of will-to-live that man conceives himself during every moment that he spends in meditating on himself and the world around him.

As in my will-to-live there is ardent desire for further life and for the mysterious exaltation of the will-to-live which we call pleasure, while there is fear of destruction and of that mysterious depreciation of the will-to-live which we call pain, so too are these in the will-to-live around me, whether it can express itself to me, or remains dumb.

Man has now to decide what his relation to his will-to-live shall be. He can deny it. But if he bids his will-to-live change into will-not-to-live, as is done in Indian and indeed in all pessimistic thought, he involves himself in self-contradiction. He raises to the position of his philosophy of life something unnatural, something which is in itself untrue, and which cannot be carried to completion. Indian thought, and Schopenhauer's also, is full of inconsistencies because it cannot help making concessions time after time to the will-to-live, which persists in spite of all negation of the world, though it will not admit that the concessions are really such. Negation of the will-to-live is self-consistent only if it is really willing actually to put an end to physical existence.

If man affirms his will-to-live, he acts naturally and honestly. He confirms an act which has already been accomplished in his instinctive thought by repeating it in his conscious thought. The beginning of thought, a beginning which continually repeats itself, is that man does not simply accept his existence as something given, but experiences it as something unfathomably mysterious. Affirmation of life is the spiritual act by which man ceases to live unreflectively and begins to devote himself to his life with reverence in order to raise it to its true value. To affirm life is to deepen, to make more inward, and to exalt the will-to-live.

At the same time the man who has become a thinking being feels a compulsion to give to every will-to-live the same reverence for life that he gives to his own. He experiences that other life in his own. He accepts as being good: to preserve life, to promote life, to raise to its highest value life which is capable of development; and as being evil: to destroy life, to injure life, to repress life which is capable of development. This is the absolute, fundamental principle of the moral, and it is a necessity of thought.

The great fault of all ethics hitherto has been that they believed themselves to have to deal only with the relations of man to man. In reality, however, the question is what is his attitude to the world and all life that comes within his reach. A man is ethical only when life, as such, is sacred to him, that of plants and animals as that of his fellow men, and when he devotes himself helpfully to all life that is in need of help. Only the universal ethic of the feeling of responsibility in an ever-widening sphere for all that lives —only that ethic can be founded in thought. The ethic of the relation of man to man is not something apart by itself: it is only a particular relation which results from the universal one.

The ethic of Reverence for Life, therefore, comprehends within itself everything that can be described as love, devotion, and sympathy whether in suffering, joy, or effort.

The world, however, offers us the horrible drama of Will-to-Live divided against itself. One existence holds its own at the cost of another: one destroys another. Only in the thinking man has the Will-to-Live become conscious of other will-to-live, and desirous of solidarity with it. This solidarity, however, he cannot completely bring about, because man is subject to the puzzling and horrible law of being obliged to live at the cost of other life, and to incur again the guilt of destroying and injuring life. But as an ethical being he strives to escape whenever possible from this necessity, and as one who has become enlightened and merciful to put a stop to this disunion (*Selbstentzweiung*) of the Will-to-Live so far as the influence of his own existence reaches. He thirsts to be permitted to preserve his humanity, and to be able to bring to other existences release from their sufferings.

Reverence for Life arising from the Will-to-Live that has become reflective therefore contains affirmation of life and ethics inseparably combined. It aims to create values, and to realize progress of different kinds which shall serve the material, spiritual, and ethical development of men and mankind. While the unthinking modern acceptance of life stumbles about with its ideals of power won by discovery and invention, the acceptance of life based on reason sets up the spiritual and ethical perfecting of mankind as the highest ideal, and an ideal from which alone all other ideals of progress get their real value.

Through ethical acceptance of the world and of life, we reach a power of reflection which enables us to distinguish between what is essential in civilization and what is not. The stupid arrogance of thinking ourselves civilized loses its power over us. We venture to face the truth that with so much progress in knowledge and power true civilization has become not easier but harder. The problem of the mutual relationship between the spiritual and the material dawns upon us. We know that we all have to struggle with circumstances to preserve our humanity, and that we must be anxiously concerned to turn once more toward hope of victory the almost hopeless struggle which many carry on to preserve their humanity amid unfavorable social circumstances.

A deepened, ethical will to progress which springs from thought will lead us back, then, out of uncivilization and its misery to true civilization. Sooner or later there must dawn the true and final Renaissance which will bring peace to the world. [IX]

Book Two

The Light Within Us

The Light Within Us

HE BEGINNING of all spiritual life is fearless belief in truth and its open confession.

[V:63]

⧉ Everything deep is also simple and can be reproduced simply as long as its reference to the whole truth is maintained.

[V:7]

⧉ But what matters is not what is witty but what is true. In this case the simple thing is the truth, the uncomfortable truth with which we have to work.

[V:23]

⧉ I intentionally avoid technical philosophical phraseology. My appeal is to thinking men and women whom I wish to provoke to elemental thought about the questions of existence which occur to the mind of every human being.

[O:199]

◨ Always accustomed in French to be careful about the rhythmical arrangement of the sentence, and to strive for simplicity of expression, these things have become equally a necessity to me in German. And now through my work on the French *Bach* it became clear to me what literary style corresponded to my nature. [O:63]

◨ The difference between the two languages, as I feel it, I can best describe by saying that in French I seem to be strolling along the well-kept paths in a fine park, but in German to be wandering at will in a magnificent forest. Into literary German there flows continually new life from the dialects with which it has kept in touch. French has lost this ever fresh contact with the soil. It is rooted in its literature, becoming thereby, in the favorable, as in the unfavorable sense of the word, something finished, while German in the same sense remains something unfinished. The perfection of French consists in being able to express a thought in the clearest and most concise way; that of German in being able to present it in its manifold aspects. As the greatest linguistic creation in French I count Rousseau's *Contrat Social*. What is nearest perfection in German I see in Luther's translation of the Bible and Nietzsche's *Jenseits von Gut und Boese* ("Beyond Good and Evil"). [O:62, 63]

◨ When I look back upon my early days I am stirred by the thought of the number of people whom I have to thank for what they gave me or for what they were to me. At the same time I am haunted by an oppressive consciousness of the little gratitude I really showed them while I was young.

How many of them have said farewell to life without my having made clear to them what it meant to me to receive from them so much kindness or so much care! Many a time have I, with a feeling of shame, said quietly to myself over a grave the words which my mouth ought to have spoken to the departed, while he was still in the flesh.   [M:65]

🔲 In the same way we ought all to make an effort to act on our first thoughts and let our unspoken gratitude find expression. Then there will be more sunshine in the world, and more power to work for what is good. But as concerns ourselves we must all of us take care not to adopt as part of our theory of life all people's bitter sayings about the ingratitude in the world. A great deal of water is flowing underground which never comes up as a spring. In that thought we may find comfort. But we ourselves must try to be the water which does find its way up; we must become a spring at which men can quench their thirst for gratitude.
          [M:66]

🔲 In my first years at Mülhausen I suffered much from a homesick longing for the church at Günsbach; I missed my father's sermons, and the services I had been familiar with all my life.

The sermons used to make a great impression on me, because I could see how much of what my father said in the pulpit was of a piece with his own life and experience. I came to see what an effort, I might say what a struggle, it meant for him to open his heart to the people every Sunday. I still remember sermons I heard from him while I was at the village school.

But what I loved best was the afternoon service, and of these I hardly ever missed a single one when I was in Günsbach. In the deep and earnest devotion of those services the plain and homely style of my father's preaching showed its real value, and the pain of thinking that the holy day was now drawing to its close gave these services a peculiar solemnity.

From the services in which I joined as a child I have taken with me into life a feeling for what is solemn, and a need for quiet and self-recollection, without which I cannot realize the meaning of my life. I cannot, therefore, support the opinion of those who would not let children take part in grown-up people's services till they to some extent understand them. The important thing is not that they shall understand, but that they shall feel something of what is serious and solemn. The fact that the child sees his elders full of devotion, and has to feel something of their devotion himself, that is what gives the service its meaning for him.

[M:44, 45]

There was another incident of my earliest childhood which I remember as the first occasion on which I consciously, and on account of my own conduct, felt ashamed of myself. I was still in petticoats, and was sitting on a stool in the yard while my father was busy about the beehives. Suddenly a pretty little creature settled on my hand, and I watched it with delight as it crawled about. Then all at once I began to shriek. The pretty little creature was a bee, which had a good right to be angry when the pastor was robbing him of the honey-filled combs in his hive, and to sting the robber's little son in revenge! My cries brought the whole household round me, and everyone pitied me. The servant girl took me in her arms and tried to comfort me with kisses, while my mother reproached my father for beginning to work at the hives without first putting me in a place of safety. My misfortune having made me so interesting an object, I went on crying with much satisfaction, till I suddenly noticed that, although the tears were still pouring down, the pain had disappeared. My conscience told me to stop, but in order to be interesting a bit longer I went on with my lamentations, so getting a lot more comforting than I really needed. However, this made me feel such a little rogue that I was miserable over it all the rest of the day. How often in after life, when assailed by temptation, has this experience warned me against exaggeration, or making too much of whatever has happened to me!   [M:3, 4]

On this, my first meeting with an author, there followed a second and greater experience. A Jew from a neighboring village, Mausche by name, who dealt in land and cattle, used to come occasionally through Günsbach with his donkey-cart. As there was at that time no Jew living in the village, this was always something of an event for the boys; they used to run after him and jeer at him. One day, in order to announce to the world that I was beginning to feel myself grown up, I could not help joining them, although I did not really understand what it all meant, so I ran along with the rest behind him and his donkey-cart, shouting: "Mausche, Mausche!" The most daring of them used to fold the corner of their shirt or jacket to look like a pig's ear, and spring with that as close to him as they could. In this way we followed him out of the village as far as the bridge, but Mausche, with his freckles and his grey beard, drove on as unperturbed as his donkey, except that he several times turned round and looked at us with an embarrassed but good-natured smile. This smile overpowered me. From Mausche it was that I first learnt what it means to keep silent under persecution, and he thus gave me a most valuable lesson. From that day forward I used to greet him politely, and later, when I was in the secondary school (the *Gymnasium*), I made it my practice to shake hands and walk a little way along with him, though he never learnt what he really was to me. He had the reputation of being a usurer and a property-jobber, but I never tried to find out whether this was true or not. To me he has always been just "Mausche" with the tolerant smile, the smile which even to-day compels me to be patient when I should like to rage and storm.   [M:8, 9]

All my life I have been glad that I began in the village school. It was a good thing for me that in the process of learning I had to measure myself with the village boys, and thus make it quite clear to myself that they had at least as much in their heads as I had in mine. I was never a victim of that ignorance which afflicts so many of the boys who go straight to a Gymnasium, and there tell each other that the children of the educated classes have more in them than the lads who go to school in darned stockings and wooden clogs. Even today if I meet any of my old schoolfellows in the village or on a farm, I at once remember vividly the points in which I did not reach their level. One was better at mental arithmetic; another made fewer mistakes in his dictation; a third never forgot a date; another was always

top in geography; another I mean you, Fritz Schoppeler—
wrote almost better than the schoolmaster. Even today they
stand in my mind for the subjects in which they were at that
time superior to me. [M:21]

◻ That a deep sense of duty, manifested in even the
smallest matters, is the great educative influence, and that
it accomplishes what no exhortations and no punishments
can, has, thanks to him, become with me a firm conviction,
a conviction the truth of which I have ever tried to prove in
practice in all that I have had to do as an educator.
[M:39, 40]

◻ Then a savior appeared for me in the person of a
new form-master, Dr. Wehmann by name. In the course of
the first few days I saw clearly through the mist of my
dreaminess this fact: our new teacher came with every
lesson carefully prepared; he knew exactly how much of
the subject he wanted to take, and he got through that
amount. He also gave us back our fair-copy exercise books
on the proper day, and in the proper lesson hour. Experience of this self-disciplined activity had a distinct effect
upon me. I should have been ashamed to incur his pleasure,
and he became my model. Three months later when my
form, the Quarta, got its Easter report, I was one of the
better scholars, although my Christmas report had been so
bad that my mother had gone about the whole of the Christmas holidays with eyes that were red from crying. [M:39]

◻ In the education and the school books of today the
duty of humanity is relegated to an obscure corner, as
though it were no longer true that it is the first thing neces-

sary in the training of personality, and as if it were not a matter of great importance to maintain it as a strong influence in our human race against the influence of outer circumstances. [D:26]

⊐⊐ As far back as I can remember I was saddened by the amount of misery I saw in the world around me. Youth's unqualified *joie de vivre* I never really knew, and I believe that to be the case with many children, even though they appear outwardly merry and quite free from care.

One thing that specially saddened me was that the unfortunate animals had to suffer so much pain and misery. The sight of an old limping horse, tugged forward by one man while another kept beating it with a stick to get it to the knacker's yard at Colmar, haunted me for weeks.

It was quite incomprehensible to me—this was before I began going to school—why in my evening prayers I should pray for human beings only. So when my mother had prayed with me and had kissed me goodnight, I used to add silently a prayer that I had composed myself for all living creatures. It ran thus: "O, heavenly Father, protect and bless all things that have breath; guard them from all evil, and let them sleep in peace." [M:27, 28]

⊐⊐ From my mother I also inherited a terribly passionate temper, which she again had inherited from her father, who was a very good man but very quick-tempered. My disposition showed itself in games; I played every game with terrible earnestness, and got angry if anyone else did not enter into it with all his might. When I was nine or ten years old I struck my sister Adela, because she was a very slack opponent in a game, and through her indifference let me win a very easy victory. From that time onwards I began to feel anxious about my passion for play, and gradually gave up all games. I have never ventured to touch a playing-card. I also, on January 1, 1899, when I was a student, gave up for ever the use of tobacco. [M:23]

◧ From experiences like these, which moved my heart and often made me feel ashamed, there slowly grew up in me an unshakeable conviction that we have no right to inflict suffering and death on another living creature unless there is some unavoidable necessity for it, and that we ought all of us to feel what a horrible thing it is to cause suffering and death out of mere thoughtlessness. And this conviction has influenced me only more and more strongly with time. I have grown more and more certain that at the bottom of our heart we all think this, and that we fail to acknowledge it and to carry our belief into practice chiefly because we are afraid of being laughed at by other people as sentimentalists, though partly also because we allow our best feelings to get blunted. But I vowed that I would never let my feelings get blunted, and that I would never be afraid of the reproach of sentimentalism. [M:31]

◧ The thought that I had been granted such a specially happy youth was ever in my mind; I felt it even as something oppressive, and ever more clearly there presented itself to me the question whether this happiness was a thing that I might accept as a matter of course. Here, then, was the second great experience of my life, viz. this question about the right to happiness. As an experience it joined itself to that other one which had accompanied me from my childhood up; I mean my deep sympathy with the pain which prevails in the world around us. These two experiences slowly melted into one another, and thence came definiteness to my interpretation of life as a whole, and a decision as to the future of my own life in particular.

It became steadily clearer to me that I had not the inward right to take as a matter of course my happy youth, my good health, and my power of work. Out of the depths of my feeling of happiness there grew up gradually within me an understanding of the saying of Jesus that we must not treat our lives as being for ourselves alone. Whoever is spared personal pain must feel himself called to help in diminishing the pain of others. We must all carry our share of the misery which lies upon the world.   [M:60, 61]

◳ The formation of drops of rain, of snowflakes, and of hailstones had always been a special puzzle to me. It hurt me to think that we never acknowledge the absolutely mysterious character of Nature, but always speak so confidently of explaining her, whereas all that we have really done is to go into fuller and more complicated descriptions, which only make the mysterious more mysterious than ever. Even at that age, it became clear to me that what we label Force or "Life" remains it its own essential nature forever inexplicable.

Thus I fell gradually into a new habit of dreaming about the thousand and one miracles that surround us, though fortunately the new habit did not, like my earlier thoughtless day-dreams, prevent me from working properly. The habit, however, is with me still, and gets stronger. If during a meal I catch sight of the light broken up in a glass jug of water into the colors of the spectrum, I at once become oblivious of everything around me, and unable to withdraw my gaze from the spectacle.   [M:52, 53]

▤ But how often do I inwardly rebel! How much I suffer from the way we spend so much of our time uselessly instead of talking in serious-wise about serious things, and getting to know each other well as hoping and believing, striving and suffering mortals!   [M:56]

▤ If I meet people to whom it is impossible to open oneself out as a man who thinks, I feel a passionate enjoyment in their society as if I were as young as ever, and if I stumble on a young man who is ready for serious discussion, I give myself up to a joyous exchange of cut and thrust which makes the difference between our ages, whether for good or ill, a thing of no account.   [M:56]

▤ I always think that we live, spiritually, by what others have given us in the significant hours of our life. These significant hours do not announce themselves as coming, but arrive unexpected. Nor do they make a great show of themselves; they pass almost unperceived. Often, indeed, their significance comes home to us first as we look back, just as the beauty of a piece of music or of a landscape often strikes us first in our recollection of it. Much that has become our own in gentleness, modesty, kindness, willingness to forgive, in veracity, loyalty, resignation under suffering, we owe to people in whom we have seen or experienced these virtues at work, sometimes in a great

· 107 ·

matter, sometimes in a small. A thought which had become act sprang into us like a spark, and lighted a new flame within us.

I do not believe that we can put into anyone ideas which are not in him already. As a rule there are in everyone all sorts of good ideas, ready like tinder. But much of this tinder catches fire, or catches it successfully, only when it meets some flame or spark from outside, *i.e.*, from some other person. Often, too, our own light goes out, and is rekindled by some experience we go through with a fellow man. Thus we have each of us cause to think with deep gratitude of those who have lighted the flames within us.

[M:67, 68]

▣ Similarly, not one of us knows what effect his life produces, and what he gives to others; that is hidden from us and must remain so, though we are often allowed to see some little fraction of it, so that we may not lose courage. The way in which power works is a mystery.   [M:68]

▣ To this fact, that we are each a secret to the other, we have to reconcile ourselves. To know one another cannot mean to know everything about each other; it means to feel mutual affection and confidence, and to believe in one another. A man must not try to force his way into the personality of another. To analyze others—unless it be to help back to a sound mind someone who is in spiritual or intellectual confusion—is a rude commencement, for there is a modesty of the soul which we must recognize, just as we do that of the body. The soul, too, has its clothing of which we must not deprive it, and no one has a right to say to another: "Because we belong to each other as we do, I have a right to know all your thoughts." Not even a mother may treat her child in that way. All demands of that sort are foolish and unwholesome. In this matter giving is the only valuable process; it is only giving that stimulates. Impart as much as you can of your spiritual being to those who are on the road with you, and accept as something precious what comes back to you from them.   [M:69]

We must all beware of reproaching those we love with want of confidence in us if they are not always ready to let us look into all the corners of their heart. We might almost say that the better we get to know each other, the more mystery we see in each other. Only those who respect the personality of others can be of real use to them.

I think, therefore, that no one should compel himself to show to others more of his inner life than he feels is natural to show. We can do no more than let others judge for themselves what we inwardly and really are, and do the same ourselves with them. The only essential thing is that we strive to have light in ourselves. Our strivings will be recognized by others, and when people have light in themselves, it will shine out from them. Then we get to know each other as we walk together in the darkness, without needing to pass our hands over each other's faces, or to intrude into each other's hearts.   [M:70]

Our human atmosphere is much colder than it need be, because we do not venture to give ourselves to others as heartily as our feelings bid us.   [M:72]

▣ We must, indeed, take care to be tactful, and not mix ourselves up uninvited in other people's business. On the other hand we must not forget the danger lurking in the reserve which our practical daily life forces on us. We cannot possibly let ourselves get frozen into regarding everyone we do not know as an absolute stranger. No man is ever completely and permanently a stranger to his fellow man. Man belongs to man. Man has claims on man. Circumstances great or small may arise which make impossible the aloofness which we have to practice in daily life, and bring us into active relations with each other, as men to men. The law of reserve is condemned to be broken down by the claims of the heart, and thus we all get into a position where we must step outside our aloofness, and to one of our fellow men become ourselves a man.   [M:71, 72]

▣ The conviction that in after life we must struggle to remain thinking as freely and feeling as deeply as we did in our youth has accompanied me on my road through life as a faithful adviser. Instinctively I have taken care not to become what is generally understood by the term "a man of ripe experience" (*ein reifer Mensch*).

The epithet "ripe" applied to persons always did, and does still, convey to me the idea of something depressing. I hear with it, like musical discords, the words impoverishment, stunted growth, blunted feelings. What we are usually invited to contemplate as "ripeness" in a man is the resigning of ourselves to an almost exclusive use of the reason. One acquires it by copying others and getting rid, one by one, of the thoughts and convictions which were dear in the days of one's youth. We believed once in the victory of truth; but we do not now. We believed in our fellow men; we do not now. We believed in goodness; we do not now. We were zealous for justice; but we are not so now. We trusted in the power of kindness and peaceableness; we do not now. We were capable of enthusiasm; but we are not so now. To get through the shoals and storms of life more easily we have lightened our craft, throwing overboard what we thought could be spared. But it was really our stock of food and drink of which we deprived ourselves; our craft is now easier to manage, but we ourselves are in decline. [M:73, 74]

As one who tries to remain youthful in his thinking and feeling, I have struggled against facts and experience on behalf of belief in the good and the true. At the present time when violence, clothed in life, dominates the world more cruelly than it ever has before, I still remain convinced that truth, love, peaceableness, meekness, and kindness are the violence which can master all other violence. The world will be theirs as soon as ever a sufficient number of men with purity of heart, with strength, and with perseverance think and live out the thoughts of love and truth, of meekness and peaceableness.

The knowledge of life, therefore, which we grownups have to pass on to the younger generation will not be expressed thus: "Reality will soon give way before your ideals," but "Grow into your ideals, so that life can never rob you of them." If all of us could become what we were at fourteen, what a different place the world would be!

[M:77]

◨ Only a person who can find a value in every sort of activity and devote himself to each one with full consciousness of duty has the inward right to take as his object some extraordinary activity instead of that which naturally falls to his lot. Only a person who feels his preference to be a matter of course, not something out of the ordinary, and who has not thought of heroism, but just recognizes a duty undertaken with sober enthusiasm, is capable of becoming a spiritual adventurer such as the world needs. There are no heroes of action, only heroes of renunciation and suffering. Of such there are plenty. But few of them are known, and even these not to the crowd, but to the few.

[O:91]

◨ Three times a week, from eleven to twelve, when the morning lessons were over, I had to take the Confirmation classes for boys, which in Alsace continue for two years. I tried hard to give them as little homework to do as possible, that the lessons might be a time of pure refreshment for heart and spirit. I therefore used the last ten minutes for making them repeat after me, and so get to know by heart, Bible sayings and verses of hymns which they might take away from these classes to guide them throughout their lives. The aim of my teaching was to bring home to their hearts and thoughts the great truths of the Gospel, and to make them religious in such a way that in later life they might be able to resist the temptations to irreligion which would assail them. I tried also to awake in them a love for the Church, and a feeling of need for a solemn hour for their souls in the Sunday services. I taught them to respect traditional doctrines, but at the same time to hold fast to the saying of St. Paul that where the spirit of Christ is, there is liberty.

Of the seed which for years I was thus sowing, some has taken root and grown, as I have been privileged to learn. Men have thanked me for having then brought home to their hearts the fundamental truths of the religion of Jesus as something to be absorbed into one's thought, and having thus strengthened them against the danger of giving up all religion in later life. [O:27, 28]

⧉ Grown-up people reconcile themselves too willingly to a supposed duty of preparing young ones for the time when they will regard as illusion what now is an inspiration to heart and mind. Deeper experience of life, however, advises their inexperience differently. It exhorts them to hold fast, their whole life through, to the thoughts which inspire them. It is through the idealism of youth that man catches sight of truth, and in that idealism he possesses a wealth which he must never exchange for anything else.
[M:75]

⧉ That ideals, when they are brought into contact with reality, are usually crushed by facts does not mean they are bound from the very beginning to capitulate to the facts, but merely that our ideas are not strong enough; and they are not strong enough because they are not pure and strong and stable enough in ourselves.

The power of ideals is incalculable. We see no power in a drop of water. But let it get into a crack in the rock and be turned to ice, and it splits the rock; turned into steam, it drives the pistons of the most powerful engines. Some-

thing has happened to it which makes active and effective
the power that is latent in it.   [M:75]

▤ Ideals are thoughts. So long as they exist merely as
thoughts, the power latent in them remains ineffective,
however great the enthusiasm, and however strong the conviction with which the thought is held. Their power only
becomes effective when they are taken up into some refined
human personality.

The ripeness, then, that our development must aim at is
one which makes us simpler, more truthful, purer, more
peace-loving, meeker, kinder, more sympathetic. That is
the only way in which we are to sober down with age. That
is the process in which the soft iron of youthful idealism
hardens into the steel of a full-grown idealism which can
never be lost.   [M:75, 76]

▤ No one who is always striving to refine his character
can ever be robbed of his idealism, for he experiences in
himself the power of the ideals of the good and the true.
                                                    [M:76, 77]

▤ All acts and facts are a product of spiritual power,
the successful ones of power which is strong enough; the
unsuccessful ones of power which is too weak. Does my
behavior in respect of love effect nothing? That is because
there is not enough love in me. Am I powerless against the
untruthfulness and the lies which have their being all
around me? The reason is that I myself am not truthful
enough. Have I to watch dislike and ill will carrying on
their sad game? That means that I myself have not yet

completely laid aside small-mindedness and envy. Is my love of peace misunderstood and scorned? That means that I am not yet sufficiently peace-loving. [M:76]

◱ Where there is power, there some result or other is produced. No ray of sunlight is ever lost, but the green which it wakes into existence needs time to sprout, and it is not always granted to the sower to live to see the harvest. All work that is worth anything is done in faith. [M:77]

◱ All the kindness which a man puts out into the world works on the heart and the thoughts of mankind, but we are so foolishly indifferent that we are never in earnest in the matter of kindness. We want to topple a great load over, and yet will not avail ourselves of a lever which would multiply our power a hundredfold.

There is an unmeasured depth of truth in that strange saying of Jesus: "Blessed are the meek, for they shall inherit the earth" (St. Matt. v, 5). [M:78]

◱ At the station at Tarascon we had to wait for the arrival of our train in a distant goods shed. My wife and I, heavily laden with baggage, could hardly get along over the shingle between the lines. Thereupon a poor cripple whom I had treated in the camp came forward to help us. He had no baggage because he possessed nothing, and I was much moved by his offer, which I accepted. While we walked along side by side in the scorching sun, I vowed to myself that in memory of him I would in future always keep a lookout at stations for heavily laden people, and help them. And this vow I have kept. On one occasion, however, my offer made me suspected of thievish intentions! [O:176]

On a stone on the river bank an old woman whose son had been taken sat weeping silently. I took hold of her hand and wanted to comfort her, but she went on crying as if she did not hear me. Suddenly I felt that I was crying with her, silently, towards the setting sun, as she was. [E:114]

Anyone can rescue his human life, in spite of his professional life, who seizes every opportunity of being a man by means of personal action, however unpretending, for the good of fellow men who need the help of a fellow man. Such a man enlists in the service of the spiritual and good. No fate can prevent a man from giving to others this direct human service side by side with his life work. [O:93]

Anyone who proposes to do good must not expect people to roll stones out of his way, but must accept his lot calmly if they even roll a few more upon it. A strength which becomes clearer and stronger through its experience of such obstacles is the only strength that can conquer them. Resistance is only a waste of strength. [O:92]

That everyone shall exert himself in that state of life in which he is placed, to practice true humanity toward his fellow men, on that depends the future of mankind. Enormous values come to nothing every moment through the missing of opportunities, but the values which do get turned into will and deed mean wealth which must not be undervalued. Our humanity is by no means so materialistic as foolish talk is continually asserting it to be. Judging by what I have learned about men and women, I am convinced that there is far more in them of idealist will power than ever comes to the surface of the world. Just as the water of the streams we see is small in amount compared to that which flows underground, so the idealism which becomes visible is small in amount compared with what men and women bear locked in their hearts, unreleased or scarcely released. To unbind what is bound, to bring the underground waters to the surface: mankind is waiting and longing for such as can do that.   [O:93, 94]

Create for yourselves an auxiliary task, a simple and, if possible, a secret one. Open your eyes and try to see where a man needs a little time, a little sympathy, a little company, a little care. Perhaps he is a solitary, an embittered, a sick or an awkward man, to whom you can mean something. Perhaps he is an old man, perhaps a child. Who can enumerate all the possible uses of the valuable operating capital called man? He is needed in all parts. Therefore seek you for an opportunity to set your humanity to work. Do not avoid an auxiliary task, in which you give of yourself as man to other men. One is surely destined for you if you but really want it.   [K:254]

I gave up my position of professor in the University of Strasbourg, my literary work, and my organ-playing in order to go as a doctor to Equatorial Africa. How did that come about?

I had read about the physical miseries of the natives in the virgin forests; I had heard about them from missionaries, and the more I thought about it the stranger it seemed to me that we Europeans trouble ourselves so little about the great humanitarian task which offers itself to us in far-off lands. The parable of Dives and Lazarus seemed to me to have been spoken directly of us! We are Dives, for, through the advances of medical science, we know a great deal about disease and pain, and have innumerable means of fighting them; yet we take as a matter of course the incalculable advantages which this new wealth gives us! Out there in the colonies, however, sits wretched Lazarus, the colored folk, who suffers from illness and pain just as much as we do, nay, much more, and has absolutely no means of fighting them. And just as Dives sinned against the poor man at his gate because for want of thought he never put himself in his place and let his heart and conscience tell him what he ought to do, so do we sin against the poor man at our gate.   [E:1]

◩ We and our civilization are burdened, really, with a great debt. We are not free to confer benefits on these men, or not, as we please; it is our duty. Anything we give them is not benevolence but atonement. For every one who scattered injury someone ought to go out to take help, and when we have done all that is in our power, we shall not have atoned for the thousandth part of our guilt. That is the foundation from which all deliberations about "works of mercy" out there must begin.   [E:115, 116]

◩ It was, and is still, my conviction that the humanitarian work to be done in the world should, for its accomplishment, call us as men, not as members of any particular nation or religious body. [E:2]

⊐ On one point he [the native] has an unerring intuition, and that is on the question whether any one white man is a real, moral personality or not. If the native feels that he is this, moral authority is possible; if not, it is simply impossible to create it. The child of nature, not having been artificialized and spoilt as we have been, has only elementary standards of judgment, and he measures us by the most elementary of them all, the moral standard. Where he finds goodness, justice, and genuineness of character, real worth and dignity, that is, behind the external dignity given by social circumstances, he bows and acknowledges his master; where he does not find them he remains really defiant in spite of all appearance of submission, and says to himself: "This white man is no more of a man than I am, for he is not a better one than I am."
[E:89]

⊐ Believing it, as I do, to be my life's task to fight on behalf of the sick under far-off stars, I appeal to the sympathy which Jesus and religion generally call for, but at the same time I call to my help also our most fundamental ideas and reasonings. We ought to see the work that needs doing for the colored folk in their misery, not as a mere "good work," but as a duty that must not be shirked.
[E:115]

⊐ How can I describe my feelings when a poor fellow is

brought me in this condition? I am the only person within hundreds of miles who can help him. Because I am here and am supplied by my friends with the necessary means, he can be saved, like those who came before him in the same condition and those who will come after him, while otherwise he would have fallen a victim to the torture. This does not mean merely that I can save his life. We must all die. But that I can save him from days of torture, that is what I feel as my great and ever new privilege. Pain is a more terrible lord of mankind than even death himself.

So, when the poor, moaning creature comes, I lay my hand on his forehead and say to him: "Don't be afraid! In an hour's time you shall be put to sleep, and when you wake you won't feel any more pain." Very soon he is given an injection of omnipon; the doctor's wife is called to the hospital, and with Joseph's help, makes everything ready for the operation.

The operation is finished, and in the hardly-lighted dormitory I watch for the sick man's awakening. Scarcely has he recovered consciousness when he stares about him and ejaculates again and again, "I've no more pain! I've no more pain!" . . . His hand feels for mine and will not let it go. Then I begin to tell him and the others who are in the room that it is the Lord Jesus who has told the doctor and his wife to come to the Ogowe, and that white people in Europe give them the money to live here and cure the sick Negroes. Then I have to answer questions as to who these white people are, where they live, and how they know that the natives suffer so much from sickness. The African sun is shining through the coffee bushes into the dark shed, but we, black and white, sit side by side and feel that we know by experience the meaning of the words: "And all ye are brethren" (St. Matt. xxiii, 8). Would that my generous friends in Europe could come out here and live through one such hour! [E:62, 63]

Whether we will or no, all of us here live under the influence of the daily repeated experience that nature is everything and man is nothing. This brings into our general view of life—and this even in the case of the less educated —something which makes us conscious of the feverishness and vanity of the life of Europe; it seems almost something abnormal that over a portion of the earth's surface nature should be nothing and man everything! [E:101]

To be prepared for confirmation I was sent to old Pastor Wennagel, for whom I had a great respect. But to him, too, I kept myself closely shut up. I was a diligent candidate, but the good man never suspected what was stirring in my heart. His instruction was in itself excellent, but it gave no answer to a great deal of what my inner self was concerned with. How many questions I would gladly have asked him. But that was not allowed us.

On one point—on that I was quite clear—my ideas differed from his in spite of all the respect I showed him. He wanted to make us understand that in submission to faith all reasoning must be silenced. But I was convinced— and I am so still—that the fundamental principles of Christianity have to be proved true by reasoning, and by no other method. Reason, I said to myself, is given us that we may bring everything within the range of its action, even the most exalted ideas of religion. And this certainly filled me with joy.   [M:42, 43]

▣ I find it no light task to follow my vocation, to put pressure on the Christian Faith to reconcile itself in all sincerity with historical truth. But I have devoted myself to it with joy, because I am certain that truthfulness in all things belongs to the spirit of Jesus.   [O:59]

▣ "As one unknown and nameless He comes to us, just as on the shore of the lake He approached those men who knew not who He was. His words are the same: 'Follow thou Me!' and He puts us to the tasks which He has to carry out in our age. He commands. And those who obey, be they wise or simple, He will reveal Himself through all that they are privileged to experience in His fellowship of peace and activity, of struggle and suffering, till they come to know, as an inexpressible secret, Who He is. . . ."
                                                    [O:56, 57]

▣ The true understanding of Jesus is the understanding of will acting on will. The true relation to Him is to be taken possession of by Him. Christian piety of any and every sort is valuable only so far as it means the surrender of our will to His.   [O:56]

▣ I know that I myself owe it to thinking that I was able to retain my faith in religion and Christianity.

The man who thinks stands up freer in the face of traditional religious truth than the man who does not, but the profound and imperishable elements contained in it he assimilates with much more effect than the latter.

The essential element in Christianity as it was preached by Jesus and as it is comprehended by thought, is this, that it is only through love that we can attain to communion with God. All living knowledge of God rests upon this foundation: that we experience Him in our lives as Will-to-Love. [O:238]

▣ What Christianity needs is that it shall be filled to overflowing with the spirit of Jesus, and in the strength of that shall spiritualize itself into a living religion of inwardness and love, such as its destined purpose should make it. Only as such can it become the leaven in the spiritual life of mankind. What has been passing for Christianity during these nineteen centuries is merely a beginning, full of weaknesses and mistakes, not a full-grown Christianity springing from the spirit of Jesus.

Because I am devoted to Christianity in deep affection, I am trying to serve it with loyalty and sincerity. In no wise do I undertake to enter the lists on its behalf with the crooked and fragile thinking of Christian apologetic, but I call on it to set itself right in the spirit of sincerity with its past and with thought in order that it may thereby become conscious of its true nature. [O:239-40]

▣ In my own life anxiety, trouble, and sorrow have been allotted to me at times in such abundant measure that had my nerves not been so strong, I must have broken down under the weight. Heavy is the burden of fatigue and responsibility which has lain upon me without a break for years. I have not much of my life for myself, not even the hours I should like to devote to my wife and child.

But I had blessings too: that I am allowed to work in the service of mercy; that my work has been successful; that I receive from other people affection and kindness in abundance; that I have loyal helpers, who identify themselves with my activity; that I enjoy a health which allows me to undertake most exhausting work; that I have a well-balanced temperament which varies little, and an energy which exerts itself with calmness and deliberation; and finally, that I can recognize as such whatever happiness falls to my lot, accepting it also as a thing for which some thank offering is due from me.

I feel it deeply that I can work as a free man at a time when an oppressive lack of freedom is the lot of so many, as also that though my immediate work is material, yet I have at the same time opportunities of occupying myself in the sphere of the spiritual and intellectual.

That the circumstances of my life provide in such varied ways favorable conditions for my work, I accept as something of which I would fain prove myself worthy. [O:242]

▣ My mental freshness I have, strange to say, preserved almost completely in spite of anaemie and fatigue. If the day has not been too exhausting I can give a couple of hours after supper to my studies in ethics and civilization as part of the history of human thought, any books I need for it and have not with me being sent me by Professor Strohl of Zürich University. Strange, indeed, are the surroundings amid which I study; my table stands inside the lattice-door which leads on to the verandah, so that I may snatch as much as possible of the light evening breeze. The palms rustle an *obbligato* to the loud music of the crickets and the toads, and from the forest come harsh and terrifying cries of all sorts. Caramba, my faithful dog, growls gently on the verandah, to let me know that he is there, and at my feet, under the table, lies a small dwarf antelope. In this solitude I try to set in order thoughts which have been stirring in me since 1900, in the hope of giving some little help to the restoration of civilization. Solitude of the primeval forest, how can I ever thank you enough for what you have been to me? . . .   [E:100]

⊐ Two perceptions cast their shadows over my existence. One consists in my realization that the world is inexplicably mysterious and full of suffering; the other in the fact that I have been born into a period of spiritual decadence in mankind. I have become familiar with and ready to deal with each, through the thinking which has led me to the ethical and affirmative position of Reverence for Life. In that principle my life has found a firm footing and a clear path to follow.

I therefore stand and work in the world as one who aims at making men less shallow and morally better by making them think.   [O:219]

The truth that the ethical is the essence of religion is firmly established on the authority of Jesus.   [O:58]

⊐ A man is ethical only when life, as such, is sacred to

him, that of plants and animals as that of his fellow men, and when he devotes himself helpfully to all life that is in need of help. [O:158-59]

⊒ Ethics is the activity of man directed to secure the inner perfection of his own personality. [D:94]

⊒ Christianity has need of thought that it may come to the consciousness of its real self. For centuries it treasured the great commandment of love and mercy as traditional truth without recognizing it as a reason for opposing slavery, witch burning, torture, and all the other ancient and medieval forms of inhumanity. It was only when it experienced the influence of the thinking of the Age of Enlightenment that it was stirred into entering the struggle for humanity. The remembrance of this ought to preserve it forever from assuming any air of superiority in comparison with thought. [O:236]

⊒ Late on the third day, at the very moment when, at sunset, we were making our way through a herd of hippopotamuses, there flashed upon my mind, unforeseen and unsought, the phrase "Reverence for Life." The iron door had yielded: the path in the thicket had become visible. Now I had found my way to the idea in which affirmation of the world and ethics are contained side by side! Now I knew that the ethical acceptance of the world and of life, together with the ideals of civilization contained in this concept, has a foundation in thought. [O:156-57]

⊒ Reverence for Life arising from the Will-to-Live that

has become reflective therefore contains affirmation of life
and ethics inseparably combined. It aims to create values,
and to realize progress of different kinds which shall serve
the material, spiritual, and ethical development of men
and mankind. While the unthinking modern acceptance of
life stumbles about with its ideals of power won by discovery and invention, the acceptance of life based on reason sets up the spiritual and ethical perfecting of mankind
as the highest ideal, and an ideal from which alone all other
ideals of progress get their real value.   [O:159-60]

⊐ To affirm life is to deepen, to make more inward, and
to exalt the will-to-live.

At the same time the man who has become a thinking
being feels a compulsion to give to every will-to-live the
same reverence for life that he gives to his own. He experiences that other life in his own. He accepts as being good:
to preserve life, to raise to its highest value life which is
capable of development; and as being evil: to destroy life,
to injure life, to repress life which is capable of development. This is the absolute, fundamental principle of the
moral, and it is a necessity of thought.   [O:158]

⊐ Anyone who comes under the influence of the ethic of
Reverence for Life will very soon be able to detect, thanks
to what that ethic demands from him, what fire glows in the
lifeless expression. The ethic of Reverence for Life is the
ethic of Love widened into universality. It is the ethic of
Jesus, now recognized as a logical consequence of thought.
                                                  [O:232]

⊒ The concept of Reverence for Life has, therefore, a religious character. The man who avows his belief in it, and acts upon the belief, shows a piety which is elemental.
[O:235]

⊒ Through Reverence for Life I raise my existence to its highest value and offer it to the world.

From the mysticism of Reverence for Life spring the drives to create and preserve the values which serve the perfection of man and mankind and the sum of which constitutes culture.   [S:38]

⊒ The will to life that has become thought extends this behavior of Reverence for Life to all the will to life that comes within its range. This behavior makes man affirm life and the world and also makes him ethical. Ethics is not only behavior towards one's fellow men aimed at achieving a human society as happy and well ordered as possible. It is also the experience of a responsibility towards all living things, arising from an inner necessity.
[S:38]

⊒ Living truth is that alone which has its origin in thinking.   [O:223]

⊒ With its depreciation of thinking, our generation has lost its feeling for sincerity and with it that for truth as well. It can therefore be helped only by its being brought once more on to the road of thinking.

Because I have this certainty I oppose the spirit of the age, and take upon myself with confidence the responsibil-

ity of taking my part in the rekindling of the fire of
thought.   [O:224]

▣ Not less strong than the will to truth must be the will
to sincerity. Only an age which can show the courage of
sincerity can possess truth which works as a spiritual force
within it.

Sincerity is the foundation of the spiritual life. [O:224]

▣ Because I have confidence in the power of truth and
of the spirit, I believe in the future of mankind.   [O:241]

▣ It is not through learning about the world that we
enter into a relationship with it but by experiencing it.
Learning about the world can lead man only to a knowledge that everything that appears around him in time
and space is essentially as much a will to life as he himself. The last knowledge turns to experience.   [S:38]

▣ Civilization I define in quite general terms as spiritual
and material progress in all spheres of activity, accompanied by an ethical development of individuals and of
mankind.   [O:198]

▣ How completely this want of thinking power has become a second nature in men today is shown by the kind
of sociability which it produces. When two of them meet
for a conversation each is careful to see that their talk does
not go beyond generalities or develop into a real exchange
of ideas. No one has anything of his own to give out, and
everyone is haunted by a sort of terror lest anything orig-

inal should be demanded from him. [D:20]

▭ It is doubtful whether big cities have ever been foci of civilization in the sense that in them there has arisen the ideal of a man well and truly developed as a spiritual personality; today, at any rate, the condition of things is such that true civilization needs to be rescued from the spirit that issues from them and their inhabitants.

[D:20, 21]

▭ The newest scientific knowledge may be allied with an entirely unreflecting view of the universe. [D:72]

▭ But civilization can only revive when there shall come into being in a number of individuals a new tone of mind independent of the one prevalent among the crowd and in opposition to it, a tone of mind which will gradually win influence over the collective one, and in the end determine its character. It is only an ethical movement which can rescue us from the slough of barbarism, and the ethical comes into existence only in individuals. [D:73]

▭ The final decision as to what the future of a society shall be depends not on how near its organization is to perfection, but on the degrees of worthiness in its individual members. [D:73]

▭ The existing one is maintained by the Press, by propaganda, by organization, and by financial and other influences which are at its disposal. This unnatural way of spreading ideas must be opposed by the natural one, which goes from man to man and relies solely on the truth of the thoughts and the hearer's receptiveness for new truth. Unarmed, and following the human spirit's primitive and natural fighting method, it must attack the other, which faces it, as Goliath faced David, in the mighty armor of the age. [D:74, 75]

ⵡ That is the condition in which we are now, and that is why it is the duty of individuals to rise to a higher conception of their capabilities and undertake again the function which only the individual can perform, that of producing new spiritual-ethical ideas. If this does not come about in a multitude of cases nothing can save us.

A new public opinion must be created privately and unobtrusively. [D:74]

ⵡ Thus we tend to forget our relationship with our fellows, and are on the path towards inhumanity. Whereever there is lost the consciousness that every man is an object of concern for us just because he is man, civilization and morals are shaken, and the advance to fully developed inhumanity is only a question of time. [D:24]

ⵡ As a matter of fact, the most utterly inhuman thoughts have been current among us for two generations past in all the ugly clearness of language and with the authority of logical principles. There has been created a social mentality which discourages humanity in individuals. The courtesy produced by natural feeling disappears, and in its place comes a behavior which shows entire indifference, even though it is decked out more or less thoroughly in a code of manners. The standoffishness and want of sympathy which are shown so clearly in every way to strangers are no longer felt as being really rudeness, but pass for the behavior of the man of the world. Our society has also ceased to allow to all men, as such, a human value and a human dignity; many sections of the human race have become merely raw material and property in human form.

[D:24, 25]

⊐ The normal attitude of man to man is made very difficult for us. Owing to the hurry in which we live, to the increased facilities for intercourse, and to the necessity for living and working with many others in an overcrowded locality, we meet each other continually, and in the most varied relations, as strangers. Our circumstances do not allow us to deal with each other as man to man, for the limitations placed upon the activities of the natural man are so general and so unbroken that we get accustomed to them, and no longer feel our mechanical, impersonal inter- course to be something that is unnatural. We no longer feel uncomfortable that in such a number of situations we can no longer be men among men, and at last we give up trying to be so, even when it would be possible and proper.

[D:23, 24]

⊐ Every being who calls himself a man is meant to develop into a real personality within a reflective theory of the universe which he has created for himself.   [D:93]

⊐ In this way our own age, having never taken the trouble to reflect, arrived at the opinion that civilization consists primarily in scientific, technical and artistic achievements, and that it can reach its goal without ethics, or, at any rate, with a minimum of them. [D:40]

▤ The difficult problems with which we have to deal, even those which lie entirely in the material and economic sphere, are in the last resort only to be solved by an inner change of character. The wisest reforms in organization can only carry them to a little nearer solution, never to the goal. The only conceivable way of bringing about a reconstruction of our world on new lines is first of all to become new men ourselves under the old circumstances, and then as a society in a new frame of mind so to smooth out the opposition between nations that a condition of true civilization may again become possible. Everything else is more or less wasted labor, because we are thereby building not on the spirit, but on what is merely external. [D:60]

▤ If the ethical is the essential element in civilization, decadence changes into renaissance as soon as ethical activities are set to work again in our convictions and in the ideas which we undertake to stamp upon reality. The attempt to bring this about is well worth making, and it should be world-wide.

It is true that the difficulties that have to be reckoned with in this undertaking are so great that only the strongest faith in the power of the ethical spirit will let us venture on it. [D:64]

▤ The idea of the civilized man is none other than that of a man who maintains his humanity under all conditions.

For ourselves it almost means to be civilized men if we maintain ourselves as men under the conditions of modern civilization. [K:266]

◨ The future of civilization depends, therefore, on whether it is possible for thought to reach a theory of the universe which will have a more secure and fundamental hold on optimism and the ethical impulse than its predecessors have had. [D:96, 97]

◨ Let us regard as valid only that which is compatible with humanity. . . . We hold high once more the sacred human rights, not those that the political rulers praise in their speeches and trample in their actions but the true ones. Once more we demand justice, not the one elaborated by lawyers deadened by juridical scholastics or that for which demagogues of all political shades shout themselves hoarse but a justice filled with the value of every human existence. The foundation of law is humanity. [K:261]

◨ When in the spring the withered grey of the pastures gives place to green, this is due to the millions of young shoots which sprout up freshly from the old roots. In like manner the revival of thought which is essential for our time can only come through a transformation of the opinions and ideals of the many brought about by individual and universal reflection about the meaning of life and of the world. [D:101]

◨ The ways along which we have to struggle toward the goal may be veiled in darkness, yet the direction in which we must travel is clear. We must reflect together about the meaning of life; we must strive together to attain a theory of the universe affirmative of the world and of life, in which the impulse to action which we experience as a necessary and valuable element of our being may find justification, orientation, clarity and depth, may receive a fresh access of moral strength, and be retempered, and thus become capable of formulating, and of acting on, definite ideals of civilization, inspired by the spirit of true humanitarianism.   [D:105]

Book Three

Pilgrimage to Humanity

*The world—majesty mask-
ing the dreadful, the absurd
hidden in the rational, joy
embracing suffering.* [1]

Europe and Human Culture*

ONLY an ethical energy can redeem us from our
want of culture. [2] What is culture? Its
essence is the ethical perfecting of individuals
and of society. Every spiritual and material development
possesses a meaning for culture. The will to culture is a
universal will to progress which recognizes the ethical as
the highest value. Apart from all the meaning which we
ascribe to the advancement of knowledge and skills, it is
clear that only a humanity which strives for ethical ideals
can really partake in full measure of the blessings of
material progress. Moreover, only such a humanity can
be master among the perils such an advance brings with it.
For a generation which exhibits and deems fitting for itself
a faith in an immanent, automatic, and naturally realized
process of development, ethical ideals are no longer
needed. But to live by a faith in the competence of knowl-

* Schweitzer's "Kultur" is rendered by "culture" rather than, as is com-
monly the case, by "civilization."

edge and skills alone leads to the frightful consequences of error in which we find ourselves. The only possible escape from the present chaos is for us to be guided by a concept of culture in which the ideals of genuine culture are sovereign.

What is the world-view in which the universal will to progress and the ethical will to progress are united and grounded in one another?

It consists in ethical world-affirmation and life-affirmation.

What are world-affirmation and life-affirmation?

For us Europeans and descendants of Europeans, the will to progress is something so natural and self-evident that we no longer recognize that it is rooted in a world-view and springs from a spiritual act. If we look around us in the world, we immediately perceive, however, that what is so obvious to us is really anything but self-evident. [3] The world-view which prevails among a people determines whether or not the will to progress is present. The world-view of world-negation and life-negation precludes it; that of world-affirmation and life-affirmation promotes it. Among primitives and half-primitives, whose undeveloped world-view is not yet related to the problem of world-affirmation or world-negation, no will to progress is present. Their ideal is the simplest and least troublesome sort of life.

As a result of the fortunes of time and because of a transformation in our world-view, we Europeans are enchanted with the will to progress. [4] The struggle for material and spiritual development which prevails among modern European men arises from the world-view which they entertain. In the Renaissance and religious movements connected with it, man became newly related to himself and to the world. This reorientation awakened in him the need to create spiritual and material values which would promote a higher development of men and humanity. Nevertheless, modern European man is not inspired in the direction of progress simply because he hopes personally to profit from it. On the contrary, he is more preoccupied with the fortunes which will befall coming generations than with his own condition. Enthusiasm for progress infuses him. Impressed by the great experiences which the world has evidently produced and preserved for him by the exercise of practical and dynamic powers, he determines that he will himself become a purposeful and vigorous force in the world. With high confidence he looks forward to new and better times which will dawn for mankind; and he understands that the power of the ideals advanced and practiced by the many conquers and transforms the conditions of life. In this will to material progress, which is united with the ethical, modern culture is grounded. [5]

Under the influence of Christianity, philosophical ethics acquired an enthusiasm which was not up to that time characteristic of it. Conversely, as a result of the impact of philosophical energies, Christian ethics began to reflect on what it should really mean and what it must accomplish. From this felicitous fusion, there arose the conviction that ethics could no longer permit what it had earlier allowed, namely, injustices, cruelties, and the heinous effects of superstition. Torture was to be done away with. The scourge of witchcraft trials was to be eliminated. Humane principles were to take the place of inhuman laws. [6] An endeavor to understand the principles and ends of law accompanied the struggle against illegality and inhumane practices. Jeremy Bentham, for example, raised his prophetic voice against laws which permitted usury, foolish customs barriers, and inhuman colonization.

An era of the sovereignty of the practical and the moral appeared on history's horizon. People began to grasp the concepts of duty and honor by which the human community was later nourished. Without alarm, a profound and felicitous reform in conduct was achieved. The education of men for civilized life was carried forward in nobler ways. The public welfare was elevated as a standard of judgment for governments and for their subjects. At the same time, men began to appreciate that every human being should be able to exercise himself in a manner commensurate with his own dignity and welfare. The war against ignorance was under way. [7]

With the discovery that reason teaches the principle of love, there came a reformation which has no equal in the history of humanity. [8]

Nevertheless, the course of modern European thought reveals a tragedy. By a slow but irresistible process, the union of the ethical and world-affirmation and life-affirmation has been dissolving and threatens to disappear completely. Consequently, European humanity is infused and impelled by a will to progress which is superficial and improperly oriented. [9]

In the nineteenth century, the spirit of realism raised its head. . . . The first important personality in which it was incarnate was Napoleon I. The first significant thinker who acted as its prophet was the German philosopher Hegel.

According to Hegel, men do not find it necessary to transform reality in order to bring it into conformity with ideals established by thought. Progress itself establishes and preserves the correlation in a natural way. In one way or another, the passions of dominant personalities and of nations subserve progress—even war. The notion that ethical idealism is a kind of sentimentalism, with which one can achieve nothing in the world of reality, originated with Hegel. He voices the theory of realism in a phrase, when he writes, "What is rational is real; and what is real is rational." When this formula was written on June 25, 1820, our age was born—an age which continues to move toward world war and which will perhaps one day destroy culture completely.

Hegel ventures to assert that everything subserves progress. The passions of rulers and nations are servants of progress. We can only say that Hegel did not know national passions as we know them; otherwise he would not have dared to write that! . . . Will we be able again to entertain and exercise ideals which can transform reality? This is the question before us today. [10]

A proper understanding of the laws and limits of human thought is required if we are to clear the building site for the construction of a future philosophy. . . . As great and as significant as the progress of natural science has been, the materialistic philosophy bound up with it will be of no help. It will always display the same poverty and the same radical errors. Although some distinguished scientific scholars have recognized this, materialism nevertheless continues to believe that its future is firmly fixed by the development of natural science. . . . For the foreseeable future, materialism will remain the philosophical religion of truncated intellects. Consequently, Feuerbach is destined to be resurrected in many editions and in many periodicals. [11]

Our philosophy incorporates only unstable fragments of an edifying world-view which hovers before it. As a result, our culture remains fragmentary and insecure.

It was disastrous that western thinkers did not confess the unsatisfactory results and the futility of their search for a secure, valuable world-view. Our philosophy became more and more superficial. Thinkers lost touch with the elemental questions which man has posed about life and the world. More and more they found themselves gorged on a diet of pedantic philosophical questions and of the professional manipulation of philosophical technicalities. Instead of producing genuine philosophy, they concocted in a professional and perfunctory manner an impotent brew. Often their maneuvers were versatile and professional, but the results were nevertheless impotence and irrelevance.

This artificial philosophizing failed to grapple with a world-view founded in thought and directed to the service of life. Through it we lost an invigorating world-view and, consequently, culture.

Some signs of self-reflection are beginning, however, to make their appearance. Here and there we discover a recognition that a philosophy must again be sought which will offer men a meaningful world-view. [12]

The mind of mankind must be renewed, if it is not to go down to destruction. [13]

When the thought of future thinkers moves to a deeper, more ethical will to progress, we will be redeemed from our want of culture and its attendant miseries and move toward genuine culture. Sooner or later that true and definitive renaissance which brings peace to the world must dawn. [14]

African Problems

When I am in a boat with Africans who ask what is different in Europe from what it is here, I describe three of the most striking things. At one time or another, most of the Africans connected with the Lambaréné hospital have heard me speak of them. Repetition brings them as new to their ears. They continue to be amazed by them and to comment on them.

First, I tell them that there are forest fires in Europe. This they cannot understand, for even in the dry season here it is so damp that the forest cannot catch fire, no matter what one does to set it ablaze. Even trees which are cut in the dry season and left to dry for months cannot easily be burned. Only the small and middle-sized branches are consumed. The large branches and the great trunks are simply charred.

At the sawmills here, owner and workers smoke their pipes and shake out the glowing embers into the sawdust. It is so damp that there is no danger of fire. The African cannot understand that in Europe a forest fire may be started by someone dropping a burning match.

After they have made their comments on this remarkable event, I tell them that in Europe people row boats for pleasure. This revelation is greeted with unrestrained laughter and a flood of questions. "Who order them to row?" "No one." "Someone must give them a gift for doing it." "No, they do it willingly and for nothing. They often row until they are completely exhausted!"

Their remarks on this matter are apparently endless. Here in Africa, if the men in two canoes are going upstream or downstream together, they may race each other for a short distance. But the idea that people will get into a boat, not wanting to go on a journey or without articles to be transported, simply in order to row is incomprehensible for the African. Furthermore, the idea that they will use their leisure time in this senseless activity is incredible. I do not attempt to make clear to them what sport is. Their life is such that they have to use their physical energies more than they like. Consequently, they cannot understand how people will exert themselves when not forced to do so.

The third thing I tell them is that in Europe a man can marry without having to pay for his wife. This cannot be true, they say. The doctor is having some fun at the expense of the poor black man. [15]

Among primitive people, taboo is extremely important. Taboo means that something must be avoided, lest misfortune or death results. The origin of taboo ideas is a dark matter. Some taboos have significance for all members of a group. Others have a meaning only for certain individuals. Among those of general significance, there are the important taboos to be observed by a man whose wife is expecting a child. The Pahouin taboo forbids him to eat

· 147 ·

meat which has begun to smell (apart from the taboo, the natives readily eat meat which is almost putrid), to touch a chameleon, to fill a hole with earth, to drive nails, to be present at the death of a man or a beast, to have anything to do with a dead body, to step over a procession of driver ants, and to do many other things.

At one time I was upset when Africans absolutely refused to carry the bier at hospital funerals. By presents and pressure, I tried to persuade them, when their turn came. A man would fall on his knees, begging me to release him from the task. Since then I have come to appreciate the inner conflicts my requests produced. Nowadays I use only volunteers for this duty, and they receive a fixed wage for their service. [16]

There is nothing in the life of these people which cannot become the object of a taboo. [17] Some women have the idea that, if their first child is a boy, either they or the child must die. . . . The fact that some Africans die if their taboo is violated can only be explained on the ground that their belief in taboo affects them mentally in a way beyond our ability to imagine. Certain Europeans who have earned the confidence of the Africans can accomplish something in such cases by their spiritual authority. [18] For the African, Christianity is the light which shines in the darkness of fear. It assures him that he is not under the control of nature-spirits, ancestral gods, or fetishes. It testifies that no man exercises any uncanny power over another. It signifies that only God's will is sovereign in all events.

> "I lay in cruel bondage,
> Thou cam'st and mad'st me free!"

The words of Paul Gerhardt's advent hymn express better than any others what Christianity means for primitive man. [19]

▣ Speaking of my work in the primeval forest of Equatorial Africa provides an opportunity to express myself on the difficult problems of colonization among primitive people.

Do we Europeans have the right to impose our rule on primitive and half-primitive people? No, if we desire only to rule and to get material gain from their lands. Yes, if we seriously intend to educate them and to help them realize a condition of well-being. Were it really possible for them to live unto themselves, we could leave them to their own devices. But the fact is that international trade has made its impact on them. Neither we nor they can undo this. Already they have lost their freedom because of it. Their economic and social fabric has been transformed by it. As a result, the chiefs, by use of the weapons and wealth international trade has brought to them, reduce the mass of the natives to servitude and turn them into slaves who are required to work for the export trade in order to enrich the few. Moreover, sometimes people themselves become merchandise to be exchanged for money, lead, gunpowder, tobacco, and liquor, just as in the days of slave trading. In face of the situation produced by the advent of international trade, there is no question of real freedom of self-determination. It is only a question as to whether native peoples are to be left to the mercies, good and evil, of greedy native rulers or to be ruled by officials of European nations.

Many of those who undertook, in our name, to seize

colonial lands were guilty of acts of injustice, violence, and cruelty which were just as offensive as those of the native rulers. A heavy load of guilt, therefore, rests upon us. Not one of the sins committed against native peoples today should be buried in silence or excused. [20]

The tragic fact is that the interests of colonization and those of civilization are not commensurate. On the contrary, they are in many ways at war with each other. It would be best for primitive peoples to be left, while isolated as much as possible from international trade, to work out slowly under perceptive guidance their development from a nomadic or half-nomadic state to the point where they became settled agriculturalists and artisans. This is, however, impossible because they will not restrain themselves before the invitation to earn money by selling to the markets of international trade, and international trade will not refuse to purchase goods from them by exchanging manufactured items. It is therefore extremely difficult to carry forward a colonization which at the same time promotes true civilization. Real wealth for native peoples would be found in their producing, as far as possible, the necessities of life by their own agricultural and handicraft efforts. Unfortunately they think only of producing what international trade will use and that for which it will pay well. With the money they receive, they buy manufactured items and processed foods. Native industry is thus made impossible, and frequently their own agricultural pursuits are jeopardized. This is the unfortunate situation of the primitive and half-primitive peoples who can offer international trade rice, cotton, coffee, cocoa, minerals, timber, and other goods. [21]

The problems of native education are entangled with those of economics and social affairs and they are just as complicated as the latter. Agriculture and crafts are the foundation of culture. Only where they are present do we have the necessary ground for the formation and continued existence of a level of population which can pursue commercial and intellectual interests. But in dealing with the natives among the colonies, we begin—and they demand it themselves—as if reading and writing were the beginnings of culture, not agriculture and crafts. In schools which are organized on the European model, we produce "educated persons," who think themselves above manual labor and want to engage only in commercial and intellectual pursuits. When they are not able to find suitable employment in business or government offices, they sit around as idlers and grumblers. [22]

In a particularly difficult period in our African work, Minköe, a promising helper, left me. He acted as foreman for construction work and for the care of the patients' quarters. He had discovered that this sort of work was beneath him. People had also told him that so talented a young man should not waste away in the role of a handy man and orderly for the doctor. So he determined to attend the "high school" which would open its doors at the nearby Mission Station in November. In order to be adequately prepared for the studies facing him, he must meanwhile give his brain some rest. Thus he left me immediately, while our hands were full of things to do, if we were to complete the necessary work before the advent of the rainy season. While he played the role of intellectual, I had to trouble myself with the business of lumber and bamboo and take his place wielding hammer and saw. . . .

In the middle of September, the first rains fall. The cry then goes up to get all the building timber under cover. Since we have scarcely an able-bodied man in the hospital, I begin, with the help of two faithful workers, to drag the beams and boards. Then I see an African in white clothing sitting by a patient he has come to visit. "Say friend," I call, "won't you give us a little help?" "I am an intellectual —I don't drag timber," comes the answer. "You're lucky," I respond. "I wanted to be an intellectual too, but I didn't make it." [23]

In almost all the colonies, the battle against disease has been launched too late and with too little vigor. We may thank modern medical science and its techniques that it can be carried forward today with some hope of success. It is often contended that we should bring medical aid to the colonies because, without it, the colonies would become worthless. We have here, however, something more important than an economic issue. It is inconceivable that civilized peoples should keep to themselves the means modern science provides for fighting diseases, pain, and death. If there is any ethical sensitivity among us, we cannot do anything else but use the new tools of medicine to serve those in distant lands who are in greater physical distress than we. In addition to the physicians who are sent out by European governments and who can accomplish only a part of what is required, others must go also, commissioned by the human community as such. Those of us who through our experience have come to know what pain and anxiety are must endeavor to extend to others in physical distress the sort of help we have received. We are no longer our own—we are brothers to all who suffer. . . .

By faith in the fundamental truth which is expressed in the concept of the "Fellowship of Those Who Bear the Mark of Pain," I established the hospital at Lambaréné. Above all, it affirms that whatever good we do for colonial peoples is not charity but atonement for the great suffering we have brought them from the first days that our ships found their ways to their lands. As we face them today, colonial problems cannot be solved by political measures alone. European and African must encounter one another in a new ethical spirit. Only then will understanding be possible.

Let us strive to create this spirit. It will make world politics a fountain of blessings for the future. [24]

The Story of My Life

〓 I was born on January 14, 1875, at Kaysersberg in Upper Alsace, the second child of pastor Ludwig Schweitzer, who served a small evangelical congregation there. My grandfather on my father's side was a school teacher and organist at Pfaffenhofen in Lower Alsace. Three of his brothers were of similar calling. My mother, Adele, whose maiden name was Schillinger, was the daughter of the pastor of Mühlbach in the Münster Valley (Upper Alsace).

A few weeks after my birth, my father came to Günsbach in the Münster Valley. There I lived a very happy childhood with my three sisters and a brother, troubled only by my father's frequent illnesses. Later his health improved. Indeed, while a robust seventy years of age, he ministered to his parish during the war, under the fire of the French guns which looked down on the Valley from the Vosges mountains and which took their toll of the houses and inhabitants of Günsbach. He died at an advanced age in 1925.

· 154 ·

My mother was run down by cavalry and killed on the road between Günsbach and Weierim-Tal in 1916.

When I was five years old, my father began to instruct me on grandfather Schillinger's old piano. While he had no great technical ability, he improvised beautifully. When I was seven I surprised my school teacher by playing on the harmonium some hymns for which I supplied my own harmonies. At eight I began to play the organ, although my legs were scarcely long enough to reach the pedals. I derived my love for the organ from my grandfather Schillinger, who had busied himself with organs and organ-playing. My mother told me that he was noted for improvising excellently. . . . I first took the place of the organist for the service at Günsbach when I was nine years old.

I attended the village school at Günsbach until the autumn of 1884. After that I was in the *Realschule* . . . at Münster for a year. During this time I took private lessons in Latin in order to prepare for the Fifth Form of the Gymnasium. In the autumn of 1885, I entered the Gymnasium at Mülhausen in Alsace. [25]

When I look back upon my youth, I am moved by the thought of all the people I have to thank for what they gave to me or meant to me. Yet I am plagued by the consciousness that, while I was young, I did not really show them proper gratitude. How many have departed this life without my having expressed to them what it meant for me to receive kindness and care from them. Often I have shamefully and quietly uttered words of gratitude over the graves of those to whom I should have spoken while they were still living.

For this reason I believe I can say that I was not ungrateful. I early awakened from that youthful thoughtlessness which reckoned the goodness and care I received from people as something self-evident. [26]

On June 18, 1893, I passed the final examination. At the end of October, I enrolled in the University of Strasbourg. It was then in its prime. Chained by no traditions, teachers and students strove to realize the ideal of a modern university.... I attended lectures in the faculties of theology and philosophy. [27, 28]

In the year following April 1, 1894, I discharged my responsibilities for military service. [29]

The years of study at Strasbourg passed quickly. At the end of the summer of 1897 I stood for the first theological examination. [30]

On the advice of Theobald Ziegler, I next undertook the dissertation for the degree of doctor of philosophy. At the end of the semester, in a chat under an umbrella on the University steps, he indicated that my research should be in the religious philosophy of Immanuel Kant. This pleased me very much. Near the end of October, 1898, I traveled to Paris in order to study philosophy at the Sorbonne and to continue organ studies under Widor. [31]

The doctoral research did not suffer damage either from my devotion to art or from my social obligations, because my health permitted extensive studies at night. Sometimes I played for Widor in the morning without having been to bed. [32]

In the middle of March, 1899, I returned to Strasbourg and presented my finished work to Theobald Ziegler. He expressed strong agreement with it. My degree would be awarded at the end of July.

In the summer of 1899, I was in Berlin and invested my time chiefly in philosophical studies. My desire was to read the major works of ancient and modern philosophy. I also heard the lectures of Harnack, Pfleiderer, Kaftan, Paulsen, and Simmel. While at first I only occasionally went to Simmel's lectures, later I became a regular attendant. . . . In Berlin, I spent much time with Karl Stumpf. His psychological studies of feeling for tone were of great interest to me. . . . With the exception of Egidi, the Berlin organists were somewhat disappointing. They tried more for outward virtuosity than for true plasticity of style, which Widor emphasized heavily. And how dull and dry was the sound of the new Berlin organs in comparison with the instruments of Cavaillé-Coll in St. Sulpice and Notre Dame.

Professor Heinrich Reimann, organist at the Kaiser Wilhelm Memorial Church, to whom I brought a letter of introduction from Widor, hired me as his substitute when he was away. Through him I came to know some Berlin musicians, painters, and sculptors.

At the home of the widow of Ernst Curtius, a well-known Hellenist, I got to know the academic world. She kindly introduced me as a friend of her step-son. . . . Even today I reckon it a striking piece of good fortune to have been able in her home to get to know the leaders of Berlin's intellectual life at that time.

Berlin's intellectual life impressed me more than that of Paris. In the latter—world-city though it was—the intellectual life was fragmented. A person had to be completely accustomed to it before he could make a judgment about the values existing in it. On the other hand, in Berlin the intellectual life was centered in its highly organized university, which was itself a living organism. [33]

At the end of July, 1899, I returned to Strasbourg and received my doctor's degree. Ziegler and Windelband agreed that in my oral examination I did not perform as well as they expected from my dissertation. The dissertation appeared in 1899 as a book with the title *The Religious Philosophy of Kant from the "Critique of Pure Reason" to "Religion within the Bounds of Reason Alone."*

Theobald Ziegler suggested that I undertake the duties of *Privat-dozent* in philosophy. I decided, however, for the theological assignment and remained in Strasbourg from then on. The task of correcting the proofs of my doctor's dissertation was scarcely complete when I set to work to achieve the theological Licentiate. [34]

On December 1, 1899, I secured an appointment as preacher at the Church of St. Nicholas in Strasbourg. First I was a so-called *"Lehrvikar."* When I passed my second theological examination, I became a curate.

This second theological examination, which was conducted by elderly clergymen, I passed on July 15, 1900, only with great difficulty. Since I was preoccupied with the dissertation for the Licentiate, I had neglected to refresh my knowledge of the different departments of theology on which this examination was given. [35]

My afternoon sermons, which I conceived as devotionals rather than as sermons, were so short that at one time certain groups in the congregation complained to Mr. Knittel, who held the post of "Inspector in Spiritual Matters." He had to summon me before him on this issue, but he was as embarrassed about it as I was. When he wanted to know what he was to say to those who felt themselves aggrieved,

I responded that he should tell them that I was only a poor curate who stopped talking when he discovered he had nothing else to say about the text. [36]

Three times a week after classes, I conducted from eleven to twelve o'clock the confirmation classes for boys. I tried to give them the least possible outside work so that the sessions we had together would be periods of untroubled renewal of spirit and heart. The last ten minutes of the sessions I devoted to having them repeat after me and commit to memory biblical texts and verses of hymns which they could take with them through life for guidance. I conceived the goal of my instruction to be that of inserting in their hearts and minds the truths of the Gospel and of making them religious in such a way that later they would resist the temptations of irreligion. I also sought to awaken in them a love for the church and a sense of need for the Sunday hour of meditation. I taught them respect for the traditional doctrines, but at the same time to hold to Paul's principle that where the spirit of Christ is present, there is freedom. . . . In the course of these religious studies, I became aware of how much of a residue of the school teacher was left in me from my ancestors. [37]

One distinct advantage of my position was that it left me adequate time for scientific work and music. . . . In this simple way the stream of my life flowed during the years which were so critical for my creative work. I worked at length and with unbroken concentration but without haste.

Since I had neither time nor money, I did not travel much. . . . When my savings allowed, I made the pilgrimage to Bayreuth when it was a festival year. [38]

On July 21, 1900, my work on the problem of the Las

Supper earned for me the degree of Licentiate in Theology. A second work, *The Secret of the Messiahship and the Passion*, secured for me in 1902 the position of *Privat-dozent* at the University. [39]

On March 1, 1902, I delivered my inaugural address before the Strasbourg theological faculty. It was on the Logos doctrine in the Gospel of John. [40] My lectures began in the summer semester of 1902 with a course on the Pastoral Epistles.

It was some conversations with students which moved me to my study of the history of research on the life of Jesus. They reported that they had not learned anything about previous research on this topic in their studies. . . . [41] My *Quest of the Historical Jesus* appeared as early as 1906. [42] While I was involved in this research, I completed in French my book on J. S. Bach. . . . During 1903 and 1904, I invested all my free time in the study of this musician. [43]

It was, indeed, a bold undertaking for me to write a book on Bach! While I had read some in the history and theory of music, my studies were not those of a professional. I had no intention of turning up new material on Bach and his times. As a musician, I simply wanted to talk to musicians about Bach. I intended briefly to treat what had been handled too cursorily in previous works, namely, the essential meaning of Bach's music and the proper way of rendering it. Consequently, the biographical material in the book is merely introductory. [44]

It delighted me that the book met with recognition in Germany as an introduction to Bach research. . . . In

Kunstwart, von Lüpke asked about a translation. But when I undertook the job, I was soon convinced that I would not be capable of satisfactorily translating myself. . . . So, I put the French Bach aside and determined to produce a new and better German one. The publisher was amazed to discover that the 455-page book grew into one of 844 pages. [45]

The German edition appeared at the beginning of 1908. From it the English translation was made. . . . [46]

In connection with the work on Bach, I published in the autumn of 1905, before my medical studies began, an essay on organ building.

It was from my grandfather Schillinger that I derived the interest in organ building, which, even when I was a boy, moved me to learn all about the insides of organs. [47]

Slowly attention was drawn to the idea of a reform of organ-building which I advanced in my essay. At the Congress of the International Music Society at Vienna in 1909 . . . there appeared for the first time a section on organ building. Some colleagues and I worked out "International Regulations for Organ Building," which attempted to wipe out the blind admiration for purely technical improvements and called for carefully built organs of beautiful tone. As years passed, I began to understand more and more that the good organ must unite the tone qualities of the old instrument with the technical advances in the new one. Twenty-two years after its appearance, my essay on organ building was able to be republished, without change, as containing the acceptable principles of reform in this field.

With the addition of an appendix on the present state of the organ building industry, it appeared as a jubilee edition. [48]

I have given much time and energy to the struggle for the true organ. Many a night I have spent over organ plans which had to be approved or revised. And I have undertaken many a journey in order to study the question of restoring or rebuilding an organ. . . . How often were these many letters, journeys, and conversations in vain, because the people involved decided for the factory organ, whose plans looked so fine on paper!

The hardest fights were those in behalf of preserving old organs. . . . The first old organ which I saved—with much trouble—was the excellent work of Silberman at St. Thomas' in Strasbourg.

My friends used to say, "In the South he rescues old Africans, in the North old organs." [49]

▤ On Friday, October 13, 1905, I dropped some letters into a mailbox on the Avenue de la Grande Armée in Paris. They were addressed to my parents and to my friends. In them I said that I was going to become a medical student at the beginning of the winter semester and that I would later go as a doctor to Equatorial Africa. . . . The plan I now set in motion had been with me for a long time. Its origin was to be found in my student days. It was incomprehensible to me that I should lead a happy life when so many people around me were struggling with suffering and grief. . . . On a bright summer morning in the Whitsuntide holiday in 1896 at Günsbach, I awoke with the thought that my good fortune was not to be taken as something self-evident. . . . In peaceful reflection, while the birds were singing, I decided before I got up that I would be justified in devoting myself until I was thirty to science and art in order to give myself thereafter to direct services to humanity. . . . It was not yet clear to me what the exact nature of the activities I thus planned would be. I left it to circumstances to determine them. But one thing was certain. However insignificant it might appear, the goal must be a direct service of humanity. [50]

One morning in the autumn of 1904 I found on my writing table one of the green-covered magazines in which the Paris Missionary Society reported each month its activities. . . . My eye fell on an article with the title "The Needs of the Congo Mission." When I finished reading the article, I serenely began my work. My search was over. [51]

Several months later, I spent my thirtieth birthday like the man in the parable who wants to build a tower and estimates whether he has the resources to complete the job. I finally decided to realize my plan for service to humanity through work in Equatorial Africa. [52]

What seemed most senseless to my friends was that I wanted to go to Africa as a physician, not a missionary. This meant at thirty years of age a long, difficult period of training. I had no doubt myself that the project would require an exceptional effort. . . . I wanted to be a doctor so I could serve without having to talk. . . . My calling as theological teacher and preacher was certainly a source of satisfaction to me. This new calling appeared to me, however, to be a matter of putting the religion of love to work rather than of talking about it. [53]

At the beginning of my medical course, I was hard pressed by financial problems. Later my situation improved because of the success of my German *Bach* and because of concert fees I earned. In October, 1911, I took the state medical examination. . . . On December 17, I took my last examination under Madelung, the surgeon. When I left the hospital to step into the cold darkness outside, I had difficulty appreciating that the tremendous effort of medical training was now behind me. Over and over, I had to assure myself that I was not dreaming but awake. As we walked along, Madelung's voice seemed to fall in from a great distance: "Only because of your good health were you able to finish that task." [54]

Even while I was busy with my medical studies, I was making preparations for the journey to Africa. Early in 1912, I resigned from my teaching duties at the University and from my post at St. Nicholas'. . . . To give up preaching and teaching represented a very great personal loss. . . . Finally I also gave up my residence on St. Thomas Embankment in order that with my wife—Helen Bresslau, daughter of the Strasbourg historian, whom I married on June 18, 1912—I might spend my last months in my father's parsonage at Günsbach. . . .

I spent the spring of 1912 in Paris studying tropical medicine and purchasing things for Africa. [55]

When I was sure I could summon the means for founding a small hospital, I made a definite offer to the Paris Missionary Society to come and serve at my own expense as a mission doctor at Lambaréné in its mission field on the River Ogowé. . . . About a year later, I had secured the funds necessary for the trip to Lambaréné and for the operation of the hospital during its first year. Some wealthy friends permitted me to think that they would again give help when my funds were exhausted. [56]

In February, 1913, the seventy crates were prepared and sent as freight to Bordeaux. [57] On the afternoon of Good Friday, 1913, my wife and I left Günsbach. In the evening of March 26, we embarked at Bordeaux.

LAMBARENE

At Lambaréné the missionaries cordially received us. Unfortunately they had not been able to construct the small buildings of corrugated sheet-iron in which I was to begin my medical work. The necessary workers had not been hired. . . . At first I had to make use of an old chicken house which stood next to our residence. In late autumn I was able to move into a corrugated-iron building with a palmleaf roof down by the river. Only eight meters long and four meters wide, it contained a small consulting room and an even smaller dispensary. Eventually there appeared around this unit a string of large bamboo huts for the native patients. The European patients were put up in the mission establishment and in the doctor's house.

From the first days, before I even had time to unpack the medicines and instruments, I was beset by patients. [58] The choice of Lambaréné as the site for the hospital proved to be wise. Native patients could be brought to me by canoe on the River Ogowé from distances of two hundred or three hundred kilometers upstream and downstream. The chief diseases I had to cope with were malaria, leprosy, sleeping sickness, dysentery, frambesia, and phagedenic ulcers. I was startled by the number of cases of pneumonia and heart disease which came to me. There were also many urinary diseases to be treated. Surgery was demanded chiefly by hernia and elephantiasis tumors. Among the natives of Equatorial Africa, hernias are much more common than among Europeans. In the absence of medical treatment, many suffer painful deaths each year due to strangulated hernia, from which they could have been saved by timely surgery. My first surgical case was of this kind.

During my first weeks it became clear that physical suffering was even greater among the Africans than I had supposed. How glad I was that, in spite of all objections, I had persevered in my plan to serve here as a doctor! . . .

At the beginning of my service, I was greatly troubled because I could not find natives to serve as interpreters and orderlies. The first one who proved to be of any help had formerly been a cook. . . . He remained with me in spite of the fact that I could not pay him as much as he received in his former work. Moreover, he gave me some very good advice about dealing with Africans. On one point, which seemed most important to him, I could not follow through. He told me to refuse to treat the persons whose lives I was not likely to save. Repeatedly he pointed to the example of the fetish doctors, who turned aside such cases so that their reputations would not be jeopardized. . . .

Since my wife had been trained as a nurse, she was able to render service in the hospital. She did so courageously, caring for the dangerously ill. In addition, she handled the supply of linen and bandages and took care of the instruments in the dispensary. She made the preparations for the operations and administered the anesthetics. . . . It was a tremendous achievement for her to spend these hours in the hospital, while managing the complicated affairs of an African household.

Within a few months the hospital was providing daily accommodations for forty patients. Beyond this, it was also necessary to furnish lodging for their companions who brought them to the hospital and would stay in order to take them back home.

While the work itself was hard enough, it did not weigh upon me as heavily as the care and responsibilities it entailed. . . .

Insofar as it was possible, I required that my African patients express their gratitude for the help they received in some concrete fashion. Repeatedly I reminded them that the benefits they received from the hospital were the result of sacrifices by many Europeans and that they, in turn, must help keep it going. Eventually I was able to establish the custom of having them pay for the medicines with money, bananas, poultry, or eggs. Of course, what I received was much less in value than the actual cost of the services and medicines. It was, however, a measure of help in supporting the work of the hospital. With the bananas I could feed the patients whose supplies were exhausted. If the bananas gave out, I could buy rice with the money. . . . Of course, I did not demand gifts from the very poor and the very old—and among primitive peoples to be old is to be poor.

The real savages had quite a different interpretation of a gift. When they left the hospital cured, they asked one from me, because now I was their friend. [59]

⊒ Preaching brought me considerable pleasure. It was a splendid experience to be able to present the messages of Jesus and Paul to persons to whom they were entirely new. The native teachers from the Mission School acted as translators, rendering each of my sentences immediately into the language of the Galoas or the Pahouins or both.

The small amount of free time I had during my first year at Lambaréné was invested in the last three volumes of the American edition of Bach's organ music.

For my organ playing, I had the splendid piano with pedal attachment, built especially for the tropics, which the Paris Bach Society had given to me as a gift for my years of service as their organist. At first I was not in the mood to practice, for I had envisaged my African service as meaning the end of my career as an artist. Thus, I thought it would be easier to reconcile myself to this situation if I allowed my fingers and feet to lose their dexterity. But one evening as I was playing a Bach organ fugue, in a melancholy mood, the thought struck me that I could use my free hours in Africa for improving and deepening my technique. Immediately I conceived the plan of taking up in succession and learning in detail and by heart compositions by Bach, Mendelssohn, Widor, César Franck, and Max Reger, even if I had to spend weeks or months on a given piece. [60]

⊒ My wife and I had now spent our second dry season in Africa. We were beginning to plan a return home at the beginning of the third when we heard, on August 5, 1914, that war had broken out in Europe. [61]

Fortunately, my medicines and dressings did not run out. On the last ship to arrive before the outbreak of war I had received a great supply of materials. [62]

Our health is not excellent, but it is not really bad. Tropical anemia has, of course, set in. It exhibits itself in intense fatigue. Although the walk from the hospital to my residence is but four minutes, it exhausts me. And we sense in ourselves another of its symptoms, namely, great nervousness. . . .

In spite of the anemia and fatigue, I have been able to preserve my mental alertness. If the day has not been too much of a physical strain, I can spend two hours after supper on my work on ethics and culture in the history of human thought. . . . My desk stands before the lattice door which leads out on the veranda. Here I am able to get as much of the evening breeze as possible. The palms rustle lightly as the crickets and toads join in loud music. Harsh and strange cries issue from the forest. My faithful dog, Caramba, growls gently to make his presence known. A small dwarf antelope lies at my feet under the desk. In this solitude, I summon the thoughts which have been within me since 1900, in order to give some help in the restoration of culture. Solitude of the primeval forest!—how can I ever express my gratitude for what you have meant to me? [63]

We spent the rainy season of 1916-17 on the coast because my wife's health had suffered from the sultry air at Lambaréné. A timber merchant permitted us to use a house at Chienga near Cape Lopez at the mouth of one of the branches of River Ogowé. It had been the home of an employee. Because of the war, it was empty. As an expression of my gratitude, I joined his African workmen in rolling okoume logs to shore so that, in the long period they might have to wait before being shipped to Europe, they might not fall victims to the bore-worm. Often it took hours to roll one of these two- or three-ton logs onto the shore. The work had to be done, therefore, at high tide. While the tide was out, I worked on my manuscript on philosophy of culture, if my time was not required by patients. [64]

In September, 1917 . . . the order came that we were immediately to be taken by ship to Europe and placed in a prisoner-of-war camp. Fortunately, the ship was several days late. With the aid of the missionaries and some Africans, we therefore had time to pack our medicines, instruments, and belongings in cases for storage in a small building of corrugated iron. . . .

Two days before our departure I had to operate on a strangulated hernia in the midst of packed and half-packed cases.

As we were being taken aboard the river steamer and while the natives were calling out farewell from the shore, the father superior of the Catholic mission came aboard. With an authoritative gesture, he waved aside the African soldiers who moved to prevent his coming to us. "You shall not leave this land without my thanking you both for all the good that you have done for it," he said. We were never to see him again. Shortly after the war he went down in the Bay of Biscay with the *Afrique*, the very ship which took us to Europe. [65]

When in the middle of July, 1920, I left Swedish soil,

where I had been so generously treated, I resolved again to take up my work at Lambaréné. Up to this time I had not dared to think of it. [66]

On February 4, 1924, I departed from Strasbourg. This time my wife could not come with me because of her health. . . . At the hospital site there stood only a small corrugated-iron building and the hardwood frame of one of the big bamboo huts. During the seven years I was away, all the other buildings had decayed or been broken down. . . . First we had to repair the rotten and leaky roofs of the doctor's residence and the two hospital buildings which still stood. I next rebuilt the fallen hospital buildings. This work took many months. It was so exhausting that I could not, as I had planned, give my evenings to revisions of the manuscript, *The Mysticism of St. Paul*, which was begun in 1911 and which I had now brought a second time to Africa.

The round of my life was physician in the mornings and master builder in the afternoons. Just as in my first venture here, no workers were available. All the labor was consumed by the flourishing timber trade, which revived after the war.

I had to make do with a few "volunteers" who came to the hospital as companions for the patients or were convalescents. They worked with no enthusiasm and, if it suited them, they found it convenient to disappear on their work days. . . .

The number of patients kept increasing. As a result, in 1924 and 1925 I sent to Europe for two doctors and two nurses.

In the autumn of 1925, the hospital was for the most

part rebuilt. . . . Then a severe famine set in, because throughout the territory the cultivation of foods had been neglected for the cutting of timber. At the same time, we were afflicted by a terrible epidemic of dysentery. These two events kept my helpers and I busy for many months. We had to make numerous trips in our two motorboats, *Tack sa mycket* and *Raarup* (one a gift from Swedish friends, the other from Jutland friends), in order to secure rice wherever possible, if nothing else was available for our hospital's inmates. [67]

The dysentery epidemic proved to me that it was necessary to move the hospital to a larger site. It could not be placed on the mission property, because all the land at my disposal there was shut in by water, swamp, or steep hills. The buildings which could be placed on it would be adequate for the fifty patients and their attendants for whom we had earlier provided, but not for the hundred and fifty who now required our care. . . . The dysentery epidemic also demonstrated something else—the danger to the hospital because of its lacking an isolation ward for infectious cases. Since I could not separate dysentery patients from the others, the whole hospital was being infected. It was a frightful time!

The lack of room for the mentally ill was another serious disadvantage. . . .

With great reluctance, then, I forced myself to move the hospital to a site three kilometers up the river where it could be expanded at will. Trusting in the support of friends of my work, I replaced the old bamboo huts, whose roofs were always needing repairs, with corrugated-iron structures on piles. . . .

As soon as the building site was cleared, I began to prepare the surrounding land for cultivation. What a joy it was to win fields from the forest!

Year after year since then, we have struggled to produce a Garden of Eden around the hospital. Already we have hundreds of young fruit trees growing. . . . [68]

The fact that I had earlier rebuilt the old hospital rather than immediately building a new one was no real setback. We had acquired many experiences which were now invaluable to us. [69]

On January 21, 1927, when some of the buildings were complete, we transferred the patients to the new hospital. On the last trip that evening, I brought the mentally ill to the new site. Their caretakers never stopped telling them that in the new hospital they would be housed in cells with wooden floors. The old ones had floors of damp earth. . . . For the first time since I began work in Africa, my patients were provided for in a humane fashion! . . .

By the middle of the summer, I completed several more wards. Now I had a hospital in which, if necessary, I could provide for two hundred patients and their companions. [70]

On my third arrival at Lambaréné (at the end of 1929), I found other building projects awaiting me. During a dysentery epidemic, which was coming to an end as I arrived, the wards had been found inadequate. . . . The cells for the mentally ill had to be taken by the dysentery cases. Now quarters for the former had to be constructed. The new cells were made stronger. They were also constructed so as to allow more sunlight and more air to come in. After that I had to build a large ward with individual beds for the very ill, an airy and secure room for food supplies, and rooms for the African orderlies. With the help of our African carpenter, Monenzali, I completed these projects in a year's time, while continuing, of course, my work in the hospital. . . .

Around Easter, 1930, my wife returned to Europe because the climate was making inroads on her health. . . .

Nowadays the hospital is known throughout an area hundreds of kilometers from the site. Some patients spend weeks traveling to the hospital for operations. Through the kindness of friends in Europe, the hospital has an operating room with all the necessary equipment. They have also seen to it that our dispensary contains an adequate store of medicines and drugs, including the special ones required for treating colonial diseases. Furthermore, we are able to feed the many patients who are too poor to buy their own food. So, now it is fine to be at work in Lambaréné, especially since we now have enough doctors and nurses to carry forward the work without having to work to exhaustion. How can we adequately thank the friends of the hospital for making this work possible?

Since the hospital work, while difficult, is no longer "beyond our power," I am fresh enough in the evenings to devote myself to intellectual endeavors. Of course, this must be interrupted, sometimes for days and weeks, when I am so full of anxiety over surgical cases and serious medical cases that I cannot think of anything else. [71]

◲ Satisfactions have come my way. I am called to the service of mercy. My work has been successful. I received much love and kindness from others. I have faithful helpers who make my duties theirs. My health permits the most strenuous kind of work. I possess a temperament which gives me stability and an energy which expresses itself with calmness and deliberation. Finally, whatever good fortune befalls me, I can recognize it as such and receive it as something for which I must bring an offering of thanksgiving.

I am deeply moved by the fact that I am a free man in a time when oppressive lack of freedom is the misfortune of so many. Moreover, I am deeply grateful for the fact that, though my immediate work is material, I have the opportunity to invest myself in the sphere of intellectual activities. [72]

IN THE SECOND WORLD WAR

◲ On January 12, 1939, left Lambaréné after a two-year stay in order to travel to Europe, where I intended to spend a few months. From the beginning, it was impossible to feel any real joy about the period of relaxation before me. The reports of the course of political events in Europe called forth too great an anxiety and sorrow. In all the ports in which we stopped, we saw warships which symbolized the menace of war. What reports or rumors came over the loudspeakers on the deck and in the dining room or were passed on in conversation were not such as to dispel apprehension—they simply reinforced it.

Upon landing at Bordeaux, I decided to forego the European sojourn and in twelve days to return to Africa by the same ship on which I arrived. The few days I was able to spend in Alsace, I used in ordering supplies for the hospital. If war should really come, I must be at my post and be in charge at the hospital in the difficult situations which it would bring.

I again sailed into the River Ogowé on March 3, 1939. As we sailed between the wooded banks which loomed before us, I asked myself what would happen before I again came down the river to the sea. In the next months, I used all the hospital funds to purchase a supply of medicines, drugs, and other necessities. Some I bought in Africa; others had to come from Europe. Fortunately, almost all the supplies arrived before the outbreak of war. [73]

◨ In March, 1940, the passenger boat *Brazza*, which had been running between Bordeaux and Equatorial Africa, was torpedoed in the vicinity of Cape Finisterre. The boat went down so quickly that only a few passengers were rescued. Many of those who died were from our region. . . . With the sinking of the ship, we lost our last consignment of materials from Europe. . . .

The startling events of May and June, 1940, convinced all of us that the war had really broken out and that it would not yield to the former in frightfulness but really surpass it.

In the fighting between the troops of General de Gaulle and those of Vichy which occurred in October and November, 1940, in the vicinity of Lambaréné, our hospital escaped damage. For this we had to thank both the location of the site as well as the respect of the contending forces. The hospital is not at Lambaréné itself but four kilometers upstream, and it is separated from it by a wide stream perhaps five hundred meters across. The crews of the airplanes on both sides were ordered not to bomb the hospital. It therefore became a place of refuge for both Europeans and Africans. We secured ourselves from stray gunfire by strengthening the walls of our houses which faced Lambaréné with heavy corrugated iron. Fortunately, we had enough of it available. [74]

The road which leads from Leopoldville to Brazzaville runs from Cape Town, through Lambaréné, to Algeria. There is a ferry over the arms of the Ogowé. About five hundred meters upstream from the hospital, the northern stretch of the road leading to the Cameroun and Nigeria begins. . . . One must be in control of this road in case it is too dangerous or too difficult to transport troops from south to north or from west to east by sea. [75]

In the summer of 1941, my wife arrived at Lambaréné. She had gone from France to Lisbon. From there she sailed on a Portuguese boat to the colony of Angola at the mouth of the Congo. Traveling through the Belgian Congo, she arrived at Lambaréné on August 2. [76]

⧉ During 1944 we became conscious of how really tired we were. This exhaustion is the result of our long work in the hot, damp equatorial climate and of continuous overexertion in excessive work. We have to draw upon our last reserves of energy in order to be able to perform the tasks our work demands. Not to become ill, again to be able to go to work—this is our daily concern. How clear it is to all of us that, if someone is forced to give up, there is no possibility of another taking up his work. Substitutes can no longer come to our rescue. . . . Nevertheless, we remain erect.

While we are always exhausted, our work continues to exact more of us. A large measure of the additional work is due to the continually increasing number of European patients who must be hospitalized. . . . The real cause of these cases of ill health is, next to the tropical climate, diet deficiencies. . . .

In the shipments of medicines which we received from America, Europe, and Switzerland, there were arsenic, iron, and liver preparations which we need in the struggle against anemia. Thus many Europeans who come to us exhausted and pale leave the hospital in a somewhat satisfactory condition. [77]

Among the African patients we find, as before, many with phagedenic ulcers. . . . Heart difficulties are frequently met among the natives. Usually they come to us first when the malady has developed to the point where they have difficulty breathing or have dropsy. The excellent equipment which we received from Switzerland makes it possible for us to give help in most cases, even to those who come to us so late.

Many African patients come to us with rheumatism and sciatica. . . . Not infrequently there are stomach ulcers among the Africans. . . .

Tuberculosis is found here. The cases of lung tuberculosis have as a rule an uninterrupted, unfortunate course. Among cases of bone tuberculosis, we often see illnesses of the breast vertebra, which frequently respond well to treatment. There is also intestinal tuberculosis among the Africans. . . .

There are far fewer cases of sleeping sickness now than in the early years, because a government health program is directed at it in our region. . . . As in the early days, we have to cope with leprosy among the natives. . . . Recently there has appeared a real hope of coming medically to grips with it. [78]

Although we are constantly on the run, we are always preoccupied and oppressed by what we fear will come to pass. We feel ashamed that we have enough to eat here, while millions at a distance suffer from hunger. The news of those who are in prison camps, of the abuse of the Jews, and of the suffering which is endured by displaced people fills us with horror. . . . We know that we must seize courage from one another daily in order to go forward in the face of depression with the work which is given us to do. It continually strikes us as incomprehensible that we are called to a work of mercy, while others are condemned to suffering or must commit deeds which result in injury or death. This blessing daily gives us new energy for our tasks and makes them precious to us. [79]

The news of the war's end came at midday on Monday, May 7. . . . In the afternoon, the hospital bell was rung and the community gathered to hear the good news. Later, in spite of great fatigue, I had to drag myself to the plantation to see how the work there was progressing.

Only in the evening did I have an opportunity to reflect on the significance of the end of hostilities in Europe and what it must mean to many men to be able, after some years, to experience their first night without fear of bombardment. [80]

Considering the great impoverishment which has set in everywhere but is not always visible, doubt invades us as to whether from now on the further extension of our work will be possible.

We have faith, however, that the friends of our work will remain true to it under the coming difficult conditions. One thing is certain—this work is necessary, as necessary in the future as it has been in the past. Those of us who know how much physical suffering exists here and how much the hospital does for the many who suffer venture to ask our friends: "Help, that we may continue to help them in the future." [81]

IN THE UNREST OF THE TIME

In 1921 I had the pleasure of playing the organ at the first performance of Bach's St. Matthew Passion at the Orféo Català. It was the first time that this work was performed in Spain.

I resigned my two positions in Strasbourg in April, 1921, to support myself by my organ playing. In order to work undisturbed on my *Philosophy of Culture,* I moved with my wife and child—a daughter born to us on my birthday, January 14, 1919—to my father's parsonage in Günsbach. In Strasbourg, where I frequently spend long periods of time working in the library, I rented an attic room. . . .

My work was, of course, frequently interrupted by journeys. I received invitations from different universities to lecture on the philosophy of culture or on the problems of primitive Christianity. I also had to deliver lectures about the hospital at Lambaréné in order to raise funds for carrying on the work there. By organ concerts, I provided for the support of my family and myself during the years I would be in Africa.

In the autumn of 1921, I was in Switzerland. In November I went from there to Sweden. Leaving Sweden at the end of January, I went to Oxford in order to deliver the Dale Memorial Lectures in Mansfield College. After that I lectured in the Selly Oak College at Birmingham . . . and at Cambridge. I also gave a series of organ concerts in England. [82]

For the most part, my audience was made up of missionaries or those preparing for mission work, that is, Christians who would have to vindicate Christianity before other world religions, especially Buddhism and Hinduism. In my lectures, I tried to clarify what was unique and peculiarly profound about Christianity. [83]

From the Lectures in England: You and I desire to preach the Christian gospel in the world. Consequently, it is essential that we be clear why it is for us the highest wisdom. Why do we think it to be the leaven which will leaven the thought, will, and hope of all humanity?

In our time, it is especially necessary that our thinking be clear on this issue. Today men are making a searching examination of religiosity in the world generally. . . . Is simple Christianity really the deepest expression of man's religious yearnings? Now do not expect me to voice an apology of the kind we generally meet before such a question—an apology which contends that Christianity contains truths which are above all reason and which, therefore, do not have to be made commensurate with reason. This looks to me like a retreat to a mountain fortress, which is excellent for defense, but from which one cannot launch a vigorous offensive.

From my youth I have been convinced that all religious truth must be conceived as truth which can necessarily be understood. In the field where ideas struggle with one another and where religions enter into contest with one another, Christianity cannot plead for special treatment. It must be in the thick of the battle of ideas, trusting in the power of its inherent truth. [84]

When you preach the gospel, beware of proclaiming it as the religion which explains everything. I imagine that in England, as on the Continent, many thousands of men despair of Christianity because they have seen and experienced the abominations of war. In face of the inexplicable, the religion which they believed to be the explanation of everything collapsed.

For ten years before my departure for Africa, I taught boys in the confirmation classes of St. Nicholas' in Strasbourg. After the war, some of them came to me and thanked me for teaching them clearly that religion was not a formula for explaining everything. Whereas many in the trenches, not being prepared for the inexplicable, had thrown Christianity over, they were able to hold to it.

When you preach, therefore, lead men away from the desire to know everything to the one thing that is necessary, namely, the desire to be in God, through which we become other than the world and through which we are redeemed from the world, standing beyond all riddles. "If I have

only you, I ask nothing from heaven and earth." "All
things work together for good to them that love God."
These insights are the peaks of Ararat, where men may find
refuge when the flood of the inexplicable sweeps over all
else. [85]

In the middle of March, 1922, I returned to Sweden
from England in order to give more concerts and lectures.
Scarcely had I returned, when I left again to present lectures and concerts in Switzerland.

In the summer of 1922, I was able to work undisturbed
on the *Philosophy of Culture.*

In the autumn I went back to Switzerland. After that I
lectured on ethics at Copenhagen at the invitation of the
theological faculty there. There were also organ concerts
and lectures in various towns in Denmark.

In January, 1923, at the invitation of Professor Oscar
Kraus, I lectured at Prague on the philosophy of culture. . . .

Early in 1923 the first two volumes of the *Philosophy of
Culture* were finished. They appeared in the same year.
[86]

*From the Preface of the Second Volume, "Culture and
Ethics"*: My subject is the tragedy of the western world-
view.

Even as a student I was surprised that the history of
thought was presented always as a history of philosophical
systems, not as a history of the struggles to achieve a world-
view. Later, when reflecting on the cultural movement in
which I stood, I was struck by the strange and unyielding
relations which exist between culture and world-view. I felt
impelled to direct to western thought the question as to

what it had sought and what it had achieved as regards a world view. What remains of our philosophical achievements, when they are stripped of their sham scholarship? What do they offer us when we ask for the basic sustenance we need in order to live as vital, profound, and humane persons?

Thus I gave myself to an unsparing analysis of western thought. [87]

In this book I have written, therefore, about the tragedy of the search for a world-view. I have here also moved along a new path to a proper world-view. . . . It is my faith that, if the requisite revolution is to occur, we must exercise ourselves as thinking men.

A new renaissance must come—one much greater than that into which we stepped out of the Middle Ages. It must be a renovation in which mankind discovers that the ethical is the highest truth and the highest practicality. In it mankind must experience liberation from that impoverished understanding of reality by which it has up to now been chained.

As a humble herald of this renaissance, I proclaim a faith in a new humanity, casting it as a torch into the darkness of our age. I dare to do this, because I believe I can offer a philosophy of life as a firm foundation for the movement to humanity, which until now has subsisted only as a noble sentiment. This philosophy of life is a result of elemental thinking and encompasses a generally intelligible world-view. It and the movement of humanity it stimulates achieve a new power of attraction and persuasion. Moreover, its worth can now be assessed by testing its conclusions in an energetic and consistent manner against reality. [88]

From the vain endeavor to unite a knowledge of the world and ethics into a world-view, human thought must turn to the task of drawing forth the world-view of ethics. [89]

How magnificent life was in those years! When I went to Africa, I was ready to make three sacrifices: to abandon the organ; to forsake teaching, in which I had invested my heart; and to give up my financial independence, relying for the rest of my life on help from friends.

I had begun to make these sacrifices. Only my close friends knew how difficult it was for me.

But now the miracle which came to Abraham as he prepared to sacrifice his son occurred for me. I too was spared from making the sacrifice. I was permitted to continue my work on the organ, because the Paris Bach Society gave me a piano with pedal attachment, built for the tropics, and because my health won a victory over the tropical climate. . . . When I returned to Europe, I did so, not as one who had degenerated into an amateur, but as an artist in full possession of his powers. Moreover, I discovered that I was more esteemed as an artist now than before.

In place of the teaching duties at Strasbourg University, which I had forsaken, there were many lectures for me to give in various universities.

Having lost my financial independence for a season, I was now able to win it back by organ and pen.

To be relieved of the necessity of making the three-fold

sacrifice was an encouraging experience which, in all the trials that fell upon me, has kept me strong and ready for every effort and for every renunciation. [90]

◫ The future of humanity depends upon each person striving, in whatever situation he finds himself, to manifest true humanity to men.

In any moment of inactivity, great values are left unrealized through neglect. Whenever they are willed and enacted, they constitute a wealth which should not be underestimated. Our humanity is not so materialistic that it will always be expressed in idle talk. As I have come to know men, it has become clear to me that many more idealistic desires are present among them than become visible. Just as the waters of the visible stream are small in comparison to those which flow underground, so is also the discernible idealism among men in comparison with that which is unreleased or just barely expressed in their hearts. [91]

Goethe

From the Goethe Prize Address, Delivered
at Frankfort-am-Main, August 28, 1928

⊐ At the end of my days as a student, I reread by chance
the description of the *Harzreise* in the winter of 1777. It
struck me as wonderful that this man, whom we consider
an Olympian, made his way through November mists and
rain in order to visit and to try to bring spiritual help to a
pastor's son who was in spiritual distress. Again I discovered in the Olympian a profoundly simple man. I
learned to love Goethe. Thus, when I had to render help to
some man in the course of my life, I said myself, "This is
your Harzreise."

When life's way led me to undertake a work far removed
from my natural talents and distant from the vocation for
which I had prepared, Goethe the comforter provided the
words to help me. Even those who best understood me found
fault with my decision to study medicine. I was not really
prepared for this, they said. It was quixotic. I reflected that
this venture would not perhaps have appeared so quixotic
to the great man who permitted his Wilhelm Meister to

become a surgeon in order to serve, although he was not prepared for it. And it struck me as something significant for all of us that Goethe, in his endeavor to understand human destiny, permits Faust and Wilhelm Meister to end their lives in thoroughly humble activities, through which they achieve humanity in the fullest sense.

As I began to prepare myself for this new vocation and service, I met Goethe again. In preparation for my medical career, I had to study natural science. I did it as a student but he as a man of research. How remote the natural sciences were from the intellectual achievements I planned before I entered my practical work! Then I remembered that Goethe had come back into the natural sciences from intellectual activities. It disturbed me that he lost himself in the natural sciences at the time when so much of what moved within him should have been given its final form. Now I was required to devote myself to the natural sciences, although my preoccupation had formerly been with intellectual matters. By this fortune I was, however, required to sound the depths of my nature. I discovered why Goethe surrendered himself in loyalty to natural sciences. It is a distinctive gain and an occasion of enlightenment for anyone immersed in intellectual work to confront facts which are to be reckoned with, not because he has imagined them, but simply because they exist. All thinking is strengthened when, forsaking preoccupation with imagined entities, it must work its way through reality. And when I experienced this "necessity of working one's way through reality," I was able to view the man who had made this movement before all of us.

When my trying student days had passed and I ventured

forth as a doctor, I met Goethe again. This time I conversed with him in the primeval forest. I had thought that I would go there as a doctor. In my early years, I let those who, in my opinion, were fitted for or hired for manual labor do it. Soon, however, I recognized that this could not be. Either they did not put in an appearance or they were not qualified to handle the job well. Therefore, I undertook work which was quite different from my medical duties. But the worst was yet to come. In the last months of 1925, a great famine threatened the hospital. In order to protect against such a threat in the future, I set to work establishing a plantation for the hospital. I directed the clearing of the site myself. . . . For weeks and months I stood in the jungle, harassed by obstinate workers, trying to turn forest into fruitful land. When I was overwhelmed with despair, I thought of Goethe, who had his Faust busy at the end redeeming the land from the sea in order that men might live and find nourishment there. In the dark primeval forest, Goethe stood beside me as a smiling and understanding comforter.

One other thing I owe to Goethe; and I must mention it. A deep concern for justice infused him. At the turn of the century, theories arose which contended that what was to be achieved should be done without regard to the right and without regard to the fate of the men affected by the change. I did not know how these theories, which had their impact on all of us, were to be met. It was a most meaningful experience, then, to find in Goethe the ardent desire to do what had to be done without sacrificing the right. Whether in Europe or Africa, I read the last pages of *Faust* at Easter, and I am deeply moved by them. They tell of Faust's last guilty act in which he determines to get rid of the hut which stands in his way by a slight, well-intentioned act of violence. He says he is tired of justice. But the well-intentioned act becomes a frightening deed by which lives are lost and by which the hut goes up in flames. The addition of this episode at the end of *Faust* gives us an insight into Goethe. How deep was his concern for justice and how profound his longing to accomplish things without injuring others!

My final, enduring experience of Goethe resulted from the vital way in which he participated in the life of his time, its thoughts and its events. The currents of the time moved through the stream of his consciousness. This is the striking thing about, not only the young Goethe and the mature Goethe, but also the old Goethe. When the mail coach used to creep along the road and the industrial age seemed only a shadow before most of us, the industrial age was already present for him. He was busy with the problems of the replacement of human labor by machines. If he is no longer master of his material in *Wilhelm Meister's Travels*, it is not because he no longer possesses the creativity he once had but because the material has developed into something immeasurable and intractable. He is trying to infuse this material with his whole experience and his deep concern for the future. Among the men of his time, he attempts to be a person who comprehends the coming new era and will match his powers with it. This is what deeply impresses one about the old Goethe.

In such encounters as these, I came to know Goethe intimately. He does not fill one with enthusiasm. In his work he advances no new, inspiring theories. He offers us what he has experienced in thought and action and what he has transformed into a higher reality. Only in personal experience do we come near to him. Only through an experience commensurate with his do we find him a friend instead of a stranger. We thus feel ourselves united to him in reverent friendship.

Before us, Goethe lived through the anxieties and labors of this era. The conditions of modern life have become more chaotic than even he could foresee with his clear vision. Our strength must be greater than that of the circumstances of our life, if we are truly to become men, men who understand their situation and are a match for it.

Goethe's spirit places upon us three obligations. We must contend with the conditions of modern life so that men, who are about to have their humanity strangled by their work, may be able to preserve and enhance their spiritual lives. We must contend with men so that, in a time when external things make so great an impact on their lives, they can find the way to inwardness and persevere in it. And we have to wrestle with ourselves and with everyone else so that, in a time of confusion and inhumanity, we can remain true to the great humane ideals of the eighteenth century, translating them into the concepts of our day and advancing their realization.

In his own life and in his own calling, each must undertake this task in the spirit of the great child of Frankfort, whose birthday we celebrate today in his birthplace. He does not recede from us with the passage of time but moves closer. As we move forward, we recognize Goethe more clearly as a man who, by a deep and comprehensive experience, was concerned for and worked for his age. We too must become persons who understand our time and are a match for it.

Goethe accomplished all these things with the priceless gifts which fortune here laid in his cradle. Our obligation is to act like men who have received only one small pound but who want to be faithful in our stewardship. Let it be so! [92]

⊐ɪ For Goethe, while the ethical is a universal value, it finds expression in an individual or concrete way. He himself sought to express this in living to the achievement of nobility. For him the true good was to impart truth, purity, and peace. One cannot deny that this was his aspiration and that it was achieved only in a limited degree. Whoever has probed his life is struck by the way in which he persevered in bringing to fulfillment the truth, sincerity, and peacefulness rooted in him. Never did Goethe react in kind to the many open and concealed hostilities which he met. He went his way amid all these assaults quitely and peacefully.

The tremendous purity! He always goes his way. He is reproached for not having enough understanding of active love or for lacking enthusiasm. But whereas the light of active love shows itself by a feeble gleam, it burns inwardly by a deep flame. He possessed a love which was peculiarly his own. [93]

Resignation is part of Goethe's world-view. A person should not act in the interests of the results but simply from an inner necessity. He once expressed this thought beautifully with reference to a parable of Jesus. The true man who has a work to do is like the man in the parable who sows seed about him without observing where and how it falls. This is how he understands the parable. [94]

Although Goethe left behind him no completed world-view, he remained true to himself. He gave us, however, a confession of faith in a view of life which he, finite man that he was, tried to realize in his life.

The greatness of a thinker rests in the unity of life and thought which he has achieved. We find this in Goethe. . . . No one who comes to Goethe goes away empty-handed. He takes away something of value for his life. [95]

To men of all times, Goethe's prophetic message is: "Strive for true humanity!"

Johann Sebastian Bach

The peculiar thing about Bach is that he did not try to gain recognition for his greatest works and he did not ask the world to become acquainted with them. Hence the spirit of consecration which surrounds his works. In his cantatas, we sense a kind of virginal charm which we do not meet in other art-works. The gray volumes of the old Bach Society speak a moving language. They tell us of something that will not be lost, because it is true and great and was created not in order to gain recognition, but because it had to be created.

Bach's cantatas and passions are not merely the offspring of the Muse. They are also the children of leisure,* in the honorable and profound sense which this term had in times gone by when it signified the hours of life which a man used for himself and himself alone.

* . . . sind nicht nur Kinder der Muse, sondern auch Kinder der Musse . . .

Bach was not aware of the uniqueness and greatness of his work. . . . He stands perhaps highest among creative artists. His creative energies expressed themselves without self-consciousness, as do those in nature. They are, therefore, as elemental and enriching as the latter. [96]

The master's artistic activity and personality are rooted in his piety. If he is to be understood at all, it must be from this perspective. For him, art was religion. It had no concern with the world and success in worldly affairs. It was an end in itself. According to Bach, religion is included in the definition of art in general. All great art, even if it is called secular, is really religious from his point of view. For him the tones do not fade away—they rise as an ineffable praise to God. [97]

In his inner being, Bach belongs to the history of German mysticism. [98]

Viewed from without, Bach's life seems a scene of conflict and bitterness. In reality, it was, however, peaceful and serene. [99]

As death neared, he dictated to Altnikol (who became his son-in-law in 1749) a chorale fantasia on the melody "Wenn wir in höchsten Nöten sein," and told him to head it with the opening of the hymn "Vor deinen Thron tret ich allhier," which is sung to the same melody. In the manuscript, we can see all the pauses the sick man had to make. The drying ink is more watery from day to day. The notes written at twilight, with the windows curtained, are scarcely readable.

With the veil of death descending, Bach wrote this piece in a dark room. It is unique among his creations. No description can do justice to the perfection of its contrapuntal art. Each segment of the melody is presented in a fugue, in which the inversion of the theme figures each time as the counter-theme. The flow is so natural that after the second line we are not conscious of the art but are completely caught up in the spirit which speaks through these G major harmonies. The storms and confusions of the world no longer penetrated the curtained windows. Around the dying master the harmonies of the spheres sounded. No sorrow invades the music. The peaceful quavers move on the far side of all human passion. Over the whole shines the word "Transfiguration." [100]

In contrast to the Bach of those guardians of the grail of pure music, I present the Bach who is a painter and poet in music. He sets forth in vital clarity all the emotional and pictorial content of the text. Above all he is intent on interpreting the pictorial in lines of tones. He is really more of a tone painter than a tone poet. His art is closer to that of Berlioz than to that of Wagner. If the text tells of shifting mists, of raging winds, of rushing rivers, of waves that rise and fall, of falling leaves, or bells that ring to register death, of firm faith or of weak faith, of the proud who are exalted, of Satan's threats, or of angels from heaven's heights—Bach makes us see and hear all these in his music.

Bach commands a language of sound. His music is a vehicle of recurring rhythmical motives, voicing peaceful happiness, living joy, intense pain, or misery sublimely met.

The drive to express poetic and pictorial thoughts is the essence of music. Music is an invitation to the creative imagination of the hearer to make alive the feelings and the visions from which it derived. But this can only come to pass, if he who speaks in the language of sound possesses the mysterious capacity of rendering thought clearly and vividly. On this point, Bach is the greatest among the great.

His music is poetic and pictorial because its themes are born of poetic and pictorial ideas. From these themes, the composition is developed, an architectural structure of lines of tones. The pictorial and poetic music reveals itself as Gothic architecture in sound. The greatest thing about the elemental vitality, majestic plasticity, and structural perfection we find in Bach's music is the spirit which permeates the whole. In this music a soul which seeks for peace amid the world's unrest and has, indeed, already tasted this blessing permits others to share its experience. [101]

Even to his death, he deviated only in the most limited way from his poetic interpretation of music and from his language of tones. The language of the cantatas is the same as that of the *Orgelbüchlein*. [102]

The *Orgelbüchlein* is not only of significance in the story of the development of the chorale prelude, but it is itself one of the greatest events in music. Never before had anyone expressed the texts in pure music in this way. No one afterwards attempted to do so by such simple means. . . . The *Orgelbüchlein* is, therefore, the dictionary for Bach's language of tones. [103] Suddenly it appears, complete and perfect. [104] If we are to understand what is expressed in the themes of the cantatas and passions, we must begin with it. Until the significance of the *Orgelbüchlein* was perceived, the fundamental character of Bach's music remained dark and debatable. [105]

Bach's music is Gothic. In such architecture, the over-all plan is born of a simple motive, reveals itself in rich detail rather than rigid line, and comes alive through the vividness and clarity of the details. So it is with Bach's music. The impression it makes on the listener depends upon the player's communicating the encompassing plan and the details together in a clear and living manner.

If we replace this double architectonic dynamic by the unary emotional dynamic, such as we have in Beethoven's works, we have simply done our best to make Bach unintelligible, mixing the great and the small nuances into one. [106]

〓 The Brandenburg concertos are the purest revelation of Bach's polyphonic style. Neither on the organ nor on the clavier could he have worked out the architectonic structure of a piece with such vitality. The orchestra alone permits absolute freedom in the employment and grouping of obbligato voices. . . . We see before us what the philosophy of all ages depicts as the elemental mystery of existence, namely, the self-unfolding of the idea, in which it creates its own opposite, struggles to overcome it, and proceeds thus until it returns to itself, having traversed the whole of existence. One experiences the same incomprehensible necessity and mysterious satisfaction when he follows the theme of one of these concertos, from its opening in the *tutti*, through its puzzling struggle with its opposite, to its self-realization in the final *tutti*. [107]

Are the Brandenburg concertos suitable for our concert halls? . . . These works are destined to become popular possessions in the same sense as the Beethoven symphonies are. [108]

◨ The declamatory unity of tone and word in Bach is like that in Wagner. In the latter it is self-evident since the verbal phrase is musically conceived, the music adding only the intervals. In Bach, the unity is displayed in a more inspiring manner. The tones give the words more vitality. The music purges them of lowly connotations. They are revealed in their true form. This miracle occurs repeatedly in the cantatas and the passions. As a result, we take it as a commonplace. As we penetrate deeply into Bach, however, we repeatedly experience the ever-new and ever-greater astonishment which a thoughtful man feels in those daily events which are at the same time the greatest wonders. [109]

◨ The effect of Bach's music rests, not in the perfection of the presentation, but in its spirit. Mendelssohn, Schelble, and Mosewius, who were the first to resurrect the cantatas and passions, were able to do so because they were profound and feelingful men as well as musicians. Only he who sinks himself in Bach's emotional world, who lives and thinks with him, and who is as simple and modest as he, can rightly bring Bach's music to the listener. If the director and the performer are not consecrated in thought and mood, they cannot communicate effectively to the hearer. There is something cold about the music. It is drained of its best power. Perhaps now more than ever before, we need that "one necessary thing" of which Mosewius spoke in 1845, when he was trying to interest the world in Bach's cantatas. This understanding must prevail. Then Bach can help our time achieve that spiritual unity and depth which it needs so desperately. [110]

Bach is an objective artist. The work of the objective artist is not impersonal; it is superpersonal. It is as if he felt but a single impulse, namely, to display definitively in a unique perfection what he finds in life. It is not he who lives—the spirit of the time lives in him. All the artistic movements, desires, creations, aspirations, and errors of his own generation and of the previous ones are comprehended and worked out in him.

In this respect, the greatest German musician can be compared only with the greatest German philosopher. Kant's work reveals the same impersonal character. He is only the intellect in which the philosophical ideas and problems of his time move to a conclusion. He uses without embarrassment the previously established scholastic terminology, just as Bach took over without examination the musical forms which his time offered him.

Bach is clearly not a single, concrete personality; he is a universal personality. He shared in the musical development of three or four generations. If we look at the story of this family, which had such a striking position in Germany's artistic life, we feel that everything which moves there must be actualized in something complete. It appears self-evident that one day a Bach must come in whom all those other Bachs will live again and forever and in whom the portion of German music incarnate in this family will find its fulfillment. Johann Sebastian Bach is, to use Kant's language, a historical postulate.

Any path we take through the poetry and music of the

Middle Ages leads to him. [111]

Bach is an end. Nothing comes from him. Everything simply leads to him. To recite his true biography is to reveal the nature and development of German art, which is fulfilled and perfected in him. It relates also the strivings and failures of that art. This genius was no individual spirit but a corporate spirit. Centuries and generations have worked toward this end, before whose greatness we stand transfixed in reverence. Whoever has studied the history of this time and perceives its end recognizes that it is the realization of spirit before it objectified itself in a single personality. [112]

Nowhere as well as in the *Well-Tempered Clavichord* do we come to understand that, for Bach, art was religion. He does not delineate natural psychic phenomena as Beethoven does in his sonatas. He does not exhibit a striving or struggling for a good. On the contrary, he reveals the reality of life as it is felt by a spirit which recognizes itself as superior to life and in which the conflict of emotions, the wildest grief, and the unrestrained cheerfulness are but aspects of a strong, triumphant core of being. This is the spirit of the sorrow-laden E flat minor prelude of the First Part and the carefree, vital prelude in G major of the Second Part. Whoever has felt this marvelous peace has understood the mysterious spirit which has here translated its world-view into the secret language of tone. He will thank Bach as one renders thanks to those great spirits who reconcile men with life and bring them peace. [113]

The Unknown One*

⊒ Only those to whom it has been disclosed that all help, improvements and benefits must be directed to the creation of a new spirit really understand the nature of work in our time. Work which is not done to this end is a road to uncertainty! The spirit in which we work is the spirit of Jesus. [114]

⊒ *To the participants in the Conference of the International Society for Free Christianity in Bern:*

Lambaréné, Sunday, August 10, 1947
Let me say how sorry I am not to be able to be present

* In the rich spiritual life of this remarkable man [Schweitzer], the character and ethics of Jesus is the dominant note. Jesus' personality and life-view are his, even though the metaphysics of the Nazarene is far different from his own. Though it is certain that Schweitzer's ethical achievement is the most praiseworthy of all the many activities which constitute his inner life . . . , it is also certain that the similarity of his motives to those of Jesus, which he often accents, is the most noteworthy aspect of his psychological personality. (Oscar Kraus, *Albert Schweitzer* [Prague, 1929], p. 51.)

at the Conference. For different reasons, it is impossible for me to travel to Europe now. Nevertheless, I am with you in thought this day.

In this Conference, do not hide from the fact that you serve an unpopular cause! Liberal Christianity is as unpopular today as it ever has been, because the dominant spirit of our time attempts to smother liberal religious thinking. On the other hand, it is a timely cause—as timely as ever—because it is a necessity for the spiritual life of our age. Only through a renewal of ethical and religious thought can the spirit arise which imparts to mankind the knowledge and power necessary for the pilgrimage from darkness and strife to light and peace. Liberal Christianity has the magnificent responsibility of communicating and upholding the conviction that thought and religion are not incompatible but belong together. Every deep piety is reflective; every really deep thought is reverent.

The greatest spirits among men have endeavored to unite thought and religion, because they judged it necessary for the spiritual welfare of man. In a time which must achieve reverence for spiritual truth, we carry on this effort. For us, the nuclear doctrine of Christianity is the kingdom of God. Only a Christianity which is animated and ruled by the idea and the intent of the kingdom of God is genuine. Only such a Christianity can give to mankind what it so desperately needs.

As we speak for liberal Christianity and expect men to arrive at religious positions by their own thinking, we have before us the image of Jesus, who insisted that one should not, in the name of religion, place on men's shoulders improper and heavy burdens. We also hold to the words of

Paul: "Where the spirit of the Lord is, there is liberty."

May your liberal Christianity prove effective in spirit and deed in accomplishing its task in our day. May we all stay awake to the necessity of working to the end that our piety becomes deeper and more vital and that the power of Jesus' spirit flows through us. Our ideal is not merely liberal Christianity but the most profound Christianity. [115]

▣ "Autumn has arrived in church dogmatics, because the sun of the kingdom of God no longer sheds its light there."

In ancient and medieval times, Christians had no faith in progress. They had no will to progress; they did not even entertain the idea that things could move ahead and upward. They did not sense that they were in an unnatural situation inasmuch as their faith and piety were founded on the idea that the kingdom of God was an event in the distant future. It was self-evident that the only possible attitude toward things concerning this kingdom was a passive one.

Things are different with modern men who have been influenced by the spirit of life-affirmation and world-affirmation. To them it is obvious that the kingdom of God is an ethical and spiritual event which is to be conceived as developing in this world and which requires the ethical efforts of believers for its realization. [116]

Those who have the courage to let the texts of Matthew and Luke mean what they say must agree that Jesus' view of the kingdom of God belongs in the framework of late

Jewish eschatology. He did not spiritualize it. As a matter of fact, he used it as a means for expressing his powerful and profound ethic of love.

Of course, it is hard for us to admit that Jesus, who is uniquely an expression of God's spirit and is the supreme revealer of religious and spiritual truth, did not stand above his time in the manner in which his universal significance suggests he should have.

Men of every age would prefer to find in Jesus a highest kind of religious knowledge which is unchanging and simple to acquire. But now we see that he shared the views of an age which are for us untrue and unacceptable. . . . Can he any longer be an authority for us?

I have suffered much from having to advance a truth which must be offensive to Christian faith.

For me, however, Jesus remains what he was. Not for a minute did I have to struggle for my faith that in him we find the highest spiritual and religious authority. Nevertheless, he was in error in expecting an early coming of a supernatural kingdom of God. We cannot make such a hope ours. . . .

We must assume a limitation of knowledge in Jesus. We cannot suppose that, although he possessed a knowledge of nature and its happenings equal to that acquired, or possible of acquisition, by modern science, he simply refrained from using it. The historical Jesus partook in a normal manner of the outlook of his time. There was no pretense here on his part. The limitations of his knowledge were realities. Anything else would be an interpretation which did him an injustice.

· 205 ·

If Jesus understood the world and its occurrences in terms of the outlook of his day, then his interpretation of the coming of the kingdom of God must be similar to that of late Judaism.

Anyone who studies the way in which progress is achieved in history sees clearly that something entirely new does not easily establish itself. If perchance it does succeed in getting a footing, it is likely to seem unnatural and questionable. Thus, even if Jesus had held a completely spiritualized interpretation of the kingdom of God and its coming, his preaching about it would have been very difficult to believe. . . .

Now Jesus did spiritualize the conception of the kingdom of God insofar as he subjected it to his ethic of love. In time, then, this ethic brought about a renovation of the concept of the kingdom of God. . . .

The fact that Jesus conceived the realization of the kingdom in a way that was refuted by fact does not call into question his authority as a unique revealer of spiritual insights. It only refutes the conventional interpretation of his authority and personality. Under the influence of Greek metaphysics, faith ascribed to him a divinity and a divine inerrancy to which he made no claim. . . . He is so great that the revelation that he belonged to his age cannot harm him. He remains our spiritual lord.

All attempts to escape the fact that Jesus entertained a conception of the kingdom and its early coming which was unfulfilled are flights from the truth. So are also all attempts to avoid the fact that this conception is inappropriate for us. In this respect, truth is the essence of the spiritual life. A faith which shuns obvious facts is an impoverished faith. . . .

The modern conception of the kingdom of God and its coming creates a spiritual situation which is like that of Jesus, his companions, and the Christians of the first generation. Now, after many centuries, there is a vital concern with the question of the kingdom. Men generally are changing their minds about its interpretation.

For modern faith, the beginning of the kingdom is discovered in Jesus and in the spirit which entered the world with him. . . .

We cannot believe, as did men of a former age, that the kingdom comes of itself at the end of time. For mankind today, it is a question of realizing the kingdom or perishing. The tragedy of the human situation requires us to invest ourselves earnestly in its realization.

This is the beginning of the end for mankind. Will men use the powers given into their hands by the knowledge and techniques of modern science for creative or destructive purposes? As long as man's capacity for destruction was limited, we could hope that reason would place limits on disaster. We cannot be so optimistic today. Our only hope is that the spirit of God will triumph in its wrestling with the spirit of the world.

The last petition of the Lord's Prayer once again possesses its original meaning in relation to us. It is a prayer for deliverance from the dominion of evil powers in the world. For us, these powers are not embodied in angelic beings revolting against God. No, they are at work in the minds of men, and they are no less real because they are present there! The first believers placed their hope solely on the kingdom, anticipating the end of the world. We do so also, but expect the end of the race.

The spirit shows us the signs of the time and interprets for us their meanings.

The belief in the kingdom of God is the most difficult demand Christian faith makes of us. We are asked to believe in what seems impossible, namely in the victory of the spirit of God over the spirit of the world. Our trust and hope is invested in the miracle which the spirit can produce.

But the miracle must occur in us before it occurs in the world. We dare not hope that by our efforts we can create the conditions of the kingdom in the world. We must certainly work for it. But there can be no divine kingdom in the world, if there is not one first of all in our hearts. The beginning of the kingdom is to be found in our determination to bring our every thought and deed under the dominion of the kingdom. Nothing will come to pass without inwardness. The spirit of God will only contend against the spirit of the world when it has triumphed over that spirit in our hearts. [117]

It is as if I were under commission to impart to men the message that piety is independent of the traditional forms of faith. (*In a letter of the year 1954.*)

The Sermon on the Mount is the unassailable charter of liberal Christianity. By the authority of Jesus, the truth that the essence of religion is ethical is established.

Moreover, due to the withering of the late Jewish eschatological world-view, Jesus' religion of love has been freed from the dogmatism in which it was clothed.

The mold into which the casting was poured is shattered.

Now we are free to let the religion of Jesus come alive in our thought in its direct spiritual and ethical character. We know that much which is valuable has been carried to us in ecclesiastical Christianity, garbed in Greek dogmas and kept alive by the piety of many centuries. We, therefore, hold to the church in love, reverence, and gratitude.

But while hers, we are men who appeal to the words of Paul, "Where the spirit of the Lord is, there is freedom," believing that we serve Christianity better by our devotion to Jesus' religion of love than by submitting to all the articles of faith. If the church possesses the spirit of Jesus, there is ample room in her for every form of Christian piety, even for that which will be free. [118]

The victory of a liberal interpretation of religion does not by any means depend on whether it finds support in history but only on whether it maintains and develops its sense for truth and reality and proceeds on the path which leads to its goals. . . . The time is coming when, after a period in history in which men were preoccupied with the religious spirit unto itself, both thought and history are awarded their proper places and reconciled with one another in the assessment of religion. This can come to pass only if we become conscious of our real relationship to the past and of our freedom from it. Moreover, we must recognize that religion is founded not only on tradition and its significance but also, and indeed much more so, on the spirit. Only the spirit makes it possible to contend against authoritarian religiosity and to achieve through knowledge and deed, the victory of liberality of mind in its noblest and deepest sense. [119]

I have remained old-fashioned in my method insofar as

I present thoughts in their historically conditioned forms. It seems to me that today our ways of examining religious issues are so multifarious and so often shot through with dazzling virtuosity that the resulting confusion has very little relation in the long run to historical religious knowledge or to our religious life. Still, I am persuaded that the abiding spiritual significance which the religious thought of the past has for us finds its greatest worth and vigor when we enter into that piety as it really was, not as we interpret it for ourselves. A Christianity which does not dare place historical truth in the service of spiritual truth is not internally sound, even if it appears outwardly strong. The reverence for truth as such, which must be a part of our faith if it is not to be impoverished, includes a respect for historical truth. [120]

▰ Instead of struggling for the triumph of the ethical spirit of God, by which the individual, the community, and religious groups would be infused with a spirit which sustained them, mankind is surrendering the world to the dominion of the spirit of thoughtlessness, being satisfied with the stagnation or retreat of culture and abandoning the endeavor to rise to the heights of humanity. Those who see the course of events and are not so stunned by it that they cannot be urgently anxious about the future of the world are prepared to understand and appreciate what, apart from all the strangeness of his speech, the historical Jesus had to say to us. They comprehend with him, who in the thought forms of his day experienced a similar anxiety and despair, that we are redeemed from our present unfortunate, irreligious situation by a vital hope and desire for the kingdom of God. In such a faith and hope and in an unconquerable moral spirit, we find steadfastness, freedom, and peace. As in the case of Jesus, by this faith and the vital energy which flows from it, we spread abroad the conviction and commitment that the highest good is focused in the kingdom of God and that for it we must live.

The crucial thing is the enthusiastic and the heroic in the world-view which proceeds from the will to and faith in the kingdom of God. It is a spirit of vigorous heroism which is not impaired but rather strengthened by the circumstances of life. In a religion there is as much understanding of the historical Jesus as there is a possession of a feelingful faith in the kingdom of God. Where this relationship is broken or undiscerned, there remain only empty words and formulas. We possess only as much of him as is yielded in us through the testimony of the kingdom of God.

It is a question of understanding the will to will. . . .

His words translate themselves in a form which must be received in our framework of ideas. Many of them which seem strange at first glance become true for us in a deep and eternal sense, if we do not attempt to repulse the power of the spirit which speaks through them.

Moreover, what modern sensibilities generally feel to be offensive in him is no longer an occasion of disturbance, if he is known by the will to will. He had repudiated work, possessions, and many other things which we reckon as ethical goods. For him, they were not good in themselves, because they were outside the bounds of the kingdom of God. For us, however, relations have shifted, so that what once lay in the shadows now marches along in the light. Furthermore, we put them into the service of the kingdom and remain in harmony with it, because we consider the kingdom as the measure of all moral values. [121]

▰ We must return to the point where we can again perceive the heroic in Jesus. [122]

There came a man to rule the world. He ruled to the ends of blessing and destruction, as history testifies. He destroyed the world into which he was born. . . . That he continues to reign as the unique master and single truth in a world whose continuation he had denied is the elemental phenomenon of the antithesis between spiritual and natural truth which lies at the foundation of all life. In him, it became history. [123]

The names by which men expressed their recognition of Jesus as an authoritative ruler—Messiah, Son of Man, Son of God—have become historical parables for us. If he himself used these titles, it was a qualified expression of the fact that he understood himself as a master and ruler. We can discover no designation which really expresses what he is for us.

He comes to us as one unknown, nameless, just as in an ancient time, by the lakeside, he came to those men who knew him not. He speaks the same word to us: "Follow me!" He places us at the tasks which he must fulfill in our time. To those who obey him, wise or simple, he will reveal himself in the labors, conflicts, and miseries they will experience in communion with him. As an ineffable mystery, they shall come inwardly to know who he is. [124]*

* The characterization which Schweitzer gives of Jesus completes the portrait of Schweitzer himself. (O. Kraus, *op. cit.*, p. 51.)

Reverence for Life

What is reverence for life and how does it originate in us? If one clearly understands himself and his relations with the world, he must ever reflect on the novel which is fashioned from the many, perceptible elements of his consciousness and on the primal, immediate, and continually given elements of consciousness. Only in this way can he arrive at a rational world-view. . . . The immediate facts of human consciousness testify: "I am life which wills to live in the midst of life which wills to live." In every instant in which he reflects on himself and on the world about him, man senses himself as a will to live in the midst of wills to live.

As in my will to live there is a desire for a wider life and for the mysterious exaltation of the will to live which we call pleasure—and also a dread of annihilation and of the mysterious encroachment on the will to live which we call pain—so it is also in the will to live around me, whether it comes to clear expression or remains dormant. [125]

If a man affirms his will to live, he acts naturally and honestly. He simply enacts in conscious thought what he has already accomplished in instinctive thought. The beginning of thought comes when a man senses his existence as something unfathomably mysterious, not as something objectively given. Life-affirmation is the spiritual act in which a man begins to live reflectively and begins to give himself to his life with reverence in order to realize its true value. Life-affirmation is a deepening and an exaltation of the will to live. [126]

Reverence for life gives the fundamental principle of morals, namely, that the good consists in the preservation, enhancement, and exaltation of life and that the destruction, injury, and retardation of life is evil. [127]

The ethics of reverence for life is the ethics of Jesus, philosophically expressed, made cosmic in scope, and conceived as intellectually necessary.

The great error of earlier ethics is that it conceived itself as concerned only with the relations of man to man. The real question is, however, one concerning man's relations to the world and to all life which comes within his reach. A man is ethical only when life, as such, is holy to him, that is, the lives of plants and animals as well as the lives of men. Moreover, he is ethical also only when he extends help to all life that is in need of it. Only the universal ethics of the ever-expanding sense of responsibility for all life can be grounded in thought. The ethics of the relation of man to man is not something unto itself. It is only a particular application of universal ethics.

The ethics of reverence for life, therefore, includes within itself all that can be called love, devotion, compassion, joy, and endeavor.

The world is a dreadful spectacle of the will to live contending against itself. One existence asserts itself at the cost of another. One destroys another. [128]

All living creatures stand under this law of the self-estrangement of the will to live. Man repeatedly discovers that he can only preserve his life or certain other lives at the cost of annihilating yet other forms of life. If he holds to the ethic of reverence of life, he injures or destroys life only under a necessity which cannot be escaped. Never does such a man annihilate living forms from thoughtlessness. Insofar as he is a free being, he seeks out every opportunity of partaking of the blessedness of advancing and assisting life and of protecting it from misery and destruction. [129]

I am most pleased by the new means of treating sleeping sickness. Whereas before I had to stand by and watch this painful disease run its course, now I can contribute to the preservation of life. Even so, every time I have under the microscope the germs which cause this illness, I cannot avoid reflecting that, in order to preserve life, I have to destroy other life.

I will buy from the Africans a young fish eagle which they have caught on a sandbank. But then I have to decide whether to let it starve or daily kill so many small fish in order to keep it alive. I decided for the latter course. Every day, however, I am oppressed by the fact that I am responsible for the sacrifice of one life for another. [130]

The ethics of reverence for life arises from real thinking and brings men into a real and continuous relationship with reality.

At first glance it appears as if reverence for life may be something too general and unlively to be made the content of a living ethics. A thinker does not need to concern himself about whether his expressions sound lively enough but only whether they are true and properly express life. Whoever falls under the influence of the ethics of reverence for life will come to feel the fire which glows in what he might have considered unlively expressions. The ethics of reverence for life is the world-wide ethics of love. It is the ethics of Jesus.

It is also objected that it ascribes to the natural life too great a value. To this we can reply that the fault of previous ethics is to be found in its not having recognized life as such as mysteriously valuable. All spiritual life exists in the context of the natural world. Reverence for life permits the fusion of the natural life and the spiritual life. The man in the parable of Jesus did not save the soul of the lost sheep; he saved the whole sheep. By the energy of reverence for natural life, reverence for spiritual life is awakened.

The ethics of reverence for life seems especially strange because it makes no distinction in value between the higher and the lower forms of life, between the more worthwhile and the less worthwhile forms of life. It is fundamental to it to omit such distinctions.

To undertake to legislate on matters of value among living beings entails having to judge whether they seem to stand, according to our feeling, nearer to or farther from us men. This means that we are really using a completely subjective standard. Who of us knows what significance attaches to other living beings in themselves or in relation to the world?

If one makes such a distinction, it follows that there are worthless forms of life. To injure or destroy them means nothing. Among such worthless beings, we may find included, depending upon the circumstances, species of insects or primitive peoples.

To the truly ethical man all life is holy, even that which appears to us from the human standpoint as the lowest. He makes distinctions only under the force of necessity, namely, when he finds himself in situations where he must choose which life he must sacrifice in order to preserve the other. He knows that he must bear the responsibility for the sacrificed life. [131]

Since I was devoted from my youth to the protection of animal life, it was a special joy to me to recognize that the universal ethics of reverence for life, which so often is reckoned as sentimentalistic, is a duty which no thinking man can evade. When will it come to pass that public opinion no longer puts up with popular amusements which entail mistreating animals?

The ethics of reverence for life is also thought not to be "reasonable," but irrational and enthusiastic. It marks out no intelligently determined boundaries for the sphere of obligation but places upon man the responsibility for all life which is within his reach and compels him to extend help to it. [132]

Reverence for life is an inexorable creditor!

The movement of reverence for life includes the movements of world-affirmation and life-affirmation as well as the ethical. It is directed to the creation of values and to the enhancement of progress which serve to develop to a higher degree the material, spiritual, and ethical status of men and humanity. While unreflective world-affirmation and life-affirmation staggers around among ideals of and passions for knowledge, techniques, and power, reflective affirmations set up the spiritual and ethical fulfillment of man as the highest goal, from which all other ideals of progress derive their real value.

In ethical world-affirmation and life-affirmation we come upon a cardinal point which permits us to distinguish between real culture and unreal culture. An unspiritual cultural darkness loses its power over us, when we are infused by the spirit of the ethical. We dare to look truth in the face, observing that the development of knowledge and techniques makes the achievement of real culture more difficult, not easier. The problem of the correlation of the spiritual and the material is solved for us. We know that we all must wrestle in the interests of humanity over the relations among men and must be concerned to bring the almost hopeless battle in which many find themselves due to unspiritual social relations to a felicitous end. [133]

World-affirmation and life-affirmation in themselves can only produce an incomplete and imperfect culture. But, if they are profound and ethical, the will to progress which proceeds from them possesses the requisite insight for distinguishing the more valuable and the less valuable and there results a culture which not only exhibits an advance in knowledge and techniques but one which will above all bring to men and mankind spiritual and ethical benefits. [134]

▨ Two things cast their shadows over my life. One is the thought that the world is inexplicably mysterious and full of misery. The other is that I have been born in a time of the spiritual decadence of mankind. I am, however, competent for handling both through the ethics of world-affirmation and life-affirmation which proceeds from the idea of reverence for life. In this way my life has been given firm foundation and clear direction.

So I live and work in the world as one who, through thought, tries to promote inwardness and moral improvement among men. Reverence for life produces in me an unrest which the world does not know, but from it I receive a blessing which the world cannot give.

I am completely opposed to the spirit of this age, because it promotes the neglect of thought. . . .

Today there is not only a neglect of thought but an actual distrust or deprecation of it. The organized political, social, and religious groups of our time are bent on inducing the individual to take up uncritically ready-made beliefs rather than inviting him to work out for himself by thought his own convictions. A man who thinks for himself and therefore is free is a troublesome and strange being. There is no assurance that he will fit comfortably into their organizations. All organized groups today find their strength, not so much in the spiritual values of their ideas or of the people who are their members, but in achieving the highest possible degree of unity and exclusiveness. In this they find their strongest power and surest defense.

Throughout his life, modern man is the object of influences which are directed to the end of robbing him of trust in his own power of thought. The spirit of spiritual dependence, to which he is to surrender, is imbedded in everything he reads and hears. It is incarnate in the people he deals with. It lurks in the groups and associations of which he becomes a member. It threatens him in all the circumstances of his life. From all sides and in many ways, pressure is applied to convince him that the truths and trusts which he needs for life have already been manufactured by organizations which have rights over him. The spirit of the age never lets him become his own man. It strangles freedom. Again and again, beliefs are forced upon him in the same way in which commercial establishments which have sufficient money can put pressure on him through high-powered advertising to buy their shoe polish or soap tablets.

The spirit of the age forces modern man to doubt his own capacity for thought in order to make him submit to authority. He cannot resist these insistent influences, because he is overworked, distraught, and anxious. The many constraints within whose domain it is his lot to work conspire to make him believe that he is incapable of thinking for himself.

The continually increasing, huge mass of knowledge which he faces shatters his self-confidence. He can no longer assimilate all the new discoveries being proclaimed. Although he does not understand them, he must take them as matters of fact. Given this situation in face of scientific truth, he is confirmed in the feeling that in matters of thought his judgment is not to be trusted.

Thus the circumstances of modern life deliver modern man over as a victim to the authoritarian spirit of our time.

The seed of skepticism has germinated. Modern man no

longer possesses spiritual self-confidence. Behind his mask of self-assurance, there is really a profound lack of self-confidence. Although he has tremendous abilities in material matters, he is intellectually stunted, because he does not use his capacity for individual, free thinking. It is incomprehensible that our age, which has distinguished itself by its many achievements in knowledge and skills, could have descended to such spiritual depths that it abandoned thinking. [135]

In order to move from the meaninglessness, which has made us captives, to meaningfulness, there is no other way than that each come back to himself and that all of us reflect about the way in which our will to work and to progress is derived from a meaning which we ascribe to our life and to all life about us. . . . This self-reflection on the ultimate and the elemental is the unique, reliable standard. Only in the measure that work is justified on the ground of the meaningfulness of my life and other lives are my intentions and deeds meaningful and valuable. . . .

How much of a mockery it is when people are beset by so many troubles, when the passions of nations have reached such proportions and intensity, when unemployment, poverty, and hunger are so prevalent, when power deals so shamelessly and senselessly with the powerless, when mankind will flee any way from the right—how much of a mockery it is to advance anything so odd as a return to reflection on the meaning of life. But only from such reflection can the strength come which is able to do something to rectify these derangements and distresses. Apart from such reflection, one is destined to use doubtful and inadequate standards.

When in the spring, the gray of the pastures gives way to green, it is due to the millions of new young shoots which sprout up from the old roots. The renewal of thought which is essential for our time can be achieved only when the many reshape their sensitivities and ideals as a result of reflecting on the meaning of life and on the meaning of the world. [136]

The beginning of all valuable spiritual life is courageous faith in the truth and an open confession of it. . . .

Simple reflection on the meaning of life has a value in itself. If such reflection should again arise among us, the ideals rooted in vanity and passion which now flourish among the masses would wither and die. How greatly we could improve our present condition, if we would all give three minutes each evening to gazing in meditation into the infinite world of stars above or if we would reflect on the meaning of life and death as we partake in a funeral rather than engaging in thoughtless conversation as we follow behind the coffin! The ideals which rise from folly or passion and guide those who make public opinion and direct public affairs would have no more power over men, if they began to reflect about the infinite and finite, existence and decay, and thus learned to distinguish between true and false standards. [137]

Although the paths along which we travel toward the goal still lie in darkness, the direction we must go is clear. [138]

World Peace

◿ Modern men generally contend vigorously that reason and morality are not to be read into national perspectives. . . . [139] It seems clear that in all of its movements nationalism concerns itself with the morbid working of the imagination of the masses rather than with things as such. It is resolute in advancing *Realpolitik*. It does not really represent a selective, scientific interpretation of internal and external politics, but exhibits an egoistic and enthusiastic spirit. The *Realpolitik* of nationalism is a dogmatic, idealized, and emotionally overexaggerated view of unilateral territorial and commercial interests. It fights for its claims, without having made an intelligent assessment of their real value. As if to call into question the worth of millions, modern states burden themselves with armaments by the billions. Out of concern for defense and the expansion of trade, such high taxes are imposed that the nation's ability to compete is more seriously threatened than its foes.

Realpolitik is, as a matter of fact, *Irrealpolitik,* because it makes the simplest questions unanswerable through the introduction of popular emotions. It puts commercial interests in the shop-window, while it keeps in stock the grandiose ideas of nationalism. . . . It is significant for understanding the diseased nature of *Realpolitik* to see that it seeks to conceal its real interests in every way by glittering ideals. The war for power is the war for right and for culture. The egoistic community of interests among the people is presented as friendly and congenial. Moreover, if an earlier period of history in the state appears to have been an era of enmity and strife, the façade of congeniality is built across the past. [140]

▱ *From the conclusion of the speech on the occasion of receiving the Nobel Peace Prize in Oslo on November 4, 1954:* Today we await the first sign of the work of the spirit to which we must entrust ourselves. It consists in nothing else than that all nations begin to make reparation, as far as possible, for what they did to others in the last war. Many thousands of prisoners and displaced persons are still waiting to return to their homes. Others, unjustly judged by foreign authorities, wait for acquittal. These and many other injustices still require rectification.

In the name of all those who strive for peace, I venture to ask all peoples to take the first step along a new path. Not one will have to sacrifice a part of the authority and power he needs for self-preservation and defense.

Thus, if we make a beginning in the liquidation of the terrible war behind us, some measure of trust may arise among nations. Trust is the working-capital for all undertakings, without which nothing of real value can be accomplished. It provides the condition for beneficial developments in all spheres.

In the creative atmosphere of trust, the equitable adjustment of the problems which arose from the two wars can be made.

I believe that I voice the thoughts and hopes of millions of men who live in anxiety and in fear of future wars. May my words reach those who live on the other side of the barrier in the same anxiety as we do. May they receive my words in the sense in which they are offered.

Let those who hold the fates of peoples in their hands be careful to avoid everything which may worsen our situation and make it more perilous. Let them take to heart the marvelous words of the Apostle Paul: "As much as lies in you, be at peace with all men." They have meaning, not only for individuals, but also for nations. In their endeavors to preserve peace among themselves, may nations go to the uttermost limits of possibility, so that the human spirit may have time to develop, to grow strong, and to act! [141]

The rise of a reflective, profound, ethical will to progress will turn us from our lack of culture and from its attendant miseries to genuine culture. Sooner or later the true, conclusive renaissance must dawn which brings peace to the world. [142]

Reverence for life includes an elemental concept of responsibility to which we must surrender ourselves. In it

there are energies which compel us to a revision and en-
noblement of our individual, social, and political views and
actions. [143]

One's world-view is, therefore, the germ cell of all
conceptions and convictions which are determinative for the
behavior of individuals and of groups. [144]

Book Four

Philosophy of Religion

Preface

⊒ The present treatise seeks its justification in the following. It does not aim to be a work on Kant's philosophy of religion and it does not intend to pronounce a judgment. Rather, its purpose is to provide an opportunity for Kant to be heard once more after all the books that have been written about Kant's philosophy of religion. Therefore, this treatise offers, in the main, a critical analysis of Kant's thoughts in so far as they have some bearing on the problem of a philosophy of religion. This undertaking is not superfluous, but whether it has scientific significance is not for the author to decide.

For the present we have to avoid only one misunderstanding. The following analysis of those sections in the main works of Kant dealing with the philosophy of religion to some extent distorts the usual picture of Kant's philosophy of religion in some of its characteristics. It gains in wealth of ideas but, in turn, loses unity and completeness. The different stages of development in Kant's philosophy of religion will be drawn in bolder strokes than is usually the case. However, it would be wrong to assume that this presentation of Kant's philosophy of religion will displace the image drawn within the framework of general investigations of the philosophy of religion because it may be found to be more in keeping with the historical development of the various features. You really can no longer analyze and describe the Kantian philosophy of religion which has given direction to the development of the philosophy of religion in the 19th century, for it has already been portrayed in a masterly fashion by Kuno Fischer. We might define it as the philosophy of religion of Kant, oriented to the basic concepts of the *Critique of Practical Reason.* However, Kant's philosophy of religion, as it appears in our analysis of those of his writings which concern themselves with the philosophy of religion, has exercised hardly any influence on the 19th century. What value, then, does this portrayal have?

From the outset, it would seem that the interest in pointing up the true situation, which has been covered up by the state of things in their historic effectiveness, is very mild. Nevertheless, quite a different significance can be attached to such an undertaking, provided one reasons as follows. Kant's philosophy of religion has passed through a sizeable evolution. This development is necessarily orderly. If, now, we were able to recognize the laws of this development, would it, then, not be reasonable to assume that these laws will prove to be identical with the laws to which the philosophy of religion was subjected in the 19th century? The problem stated differently is whether the development of Kant's philosophy of religion is not in a certain sense a preformation of the development of the philosophy of religion in the 19th century.

A. SCHWEITZER

Strassburg, December 1899

Introduction

⊐₁ Kant's philosophy of religion is an attempt to construct, with the aid of his own formulation of the moral law, a philosophy of religion on the basis of critical idealism as developed in the *Critique of Pure Reason*. To the extent that all writings following the *Critique of Pure Reason* refer in some way, be it more or less directly or obliquely, also to the significance of critical idealism for a philosophy of religion, a presentation of the Kantian philosophy of religion must, therefore, include that critique in its consideration. The question now before us is whether we should set down the individual trends of thought in the various writings indiscriminately in a general schematism of Kant's philosophy of religion such as would result from a combination of a philosophy of religion with critical idealism and, at the same time, utilize these individual characteristics in sketching a unified picture, or, whether the trends of thought in the philosophy of religion in the different writings, each considered by itself, already do represent sketches with respect to which it is a question whether they can be joined together in a unified picture. Attention to the latter possibility recommends itself easily in planning and executing an investigation into Kant's philosophy of religion for the sake of making as few assumptions as possible in the presentation. For, if the investigation proceeds along the path first mentioned and thoughts are detached from their intimate contexts without regard to the latter to be incorporated in the general plan of Kant's philosophy of religion, the presupposition is already implied that Kant's philosophy of religion does have a unified infrapattern into whose structure every thought respecting the philosophy of religion in the postcritical writings may be fitted.

Apart from this merely theoretical consideration still other circumstances speak in favor of the adoption of the second method. Some indications, indeed, point to the fact that a unified presentation of Kant's philosophy of religion must meet with difficulties if one does not choose to master all propositions concerning the philosophy of religion in accordance with the blueprint and the ideas contained in the *Critique of Practical Reason*. These difficulties appear as soon as one pursues one of the main concepts of Kant's philosophy of religion in respect to its occurence and significance in the course of the different Kantian treatments similar to what P. Lorentz did in the case of the concept of postulate in that he pointed out the variations, number, arrangement and formulation of the postulates.

No matter with what concept of Kant's philosophy of religion one starts, all sorts of circumstances and problems may be singled out—without going into an investigation of how the thoughts are intertwined—as supporting a call for first devoting in such a presentation of Kant's philosophy of religion a special investigation to the individual trends of thinking in the different writings before proceeding to bring them together into a unified whole. This method is more circuitous and difficult than the one ordinarily employed . . . but it is amply compensated for by the fact that such an investigation is most intimately connected with the objective underlying every consideration of Kant's philosophy of religion, that is, the answer to the question whether or not critical idealism has succeeded in supporting a philosophy of religion. . . . Hence, the pattern for the investigation we are about to commence is justifiably established and presented as having its roots in the ultimate concern of every investigation of Kant's philosophy of religion.

The Sketch of a Philosophy of Religion
in the *Critique of Pure Reason*

THE DESIGNATION of "sketch of a philosophy of religion" for that section of the *Critique of Reason* in which moral and religious interests are detectable in Kant's thinking is justified by the kind of presentation Kant makes. On pp. 605 ff.* of the canon of pure reason there is, indeed, a somewhat sketchy presentation of the thoughts which appear in a purely side-by-side arrangement, without exhibiting the unity of the *Critique of Pure Reason*. The concept of the postulate, the definition of religion, the comprehensive justification of the autonomy of the moral law, and the related and deeply probing treatment of the problem of freedom have not been attained here. The whole section merely forms the conclusion of the critical investigation concerning the limits of human knowledge; it treats the practical use of pure reason, in distinction from the speculative use. Nevertheless, it is just by

* Schweitzer's page references are to the Ph. Reclam edition, K. Kehrbach, editor.

virtue of this close connection with the investigations of critical idealism that this sketch of a philosophy of religion becomes valuable for the portrayal of the philosophy of religion in critical idealism.

The section of the *Critique of Pure Reason* dealing with the philosophy of religion offers, though perhaps only in outlines, the most consistent presentation of Kant's philosophy of religion in so far as it is the philosophy of religion of "critical idealism." Is it, then, correct to say that the development of the thought in this sketch of a philosophy of religion corresponds to the projected philosophy of religion of critical idealism as announced in the investigations of the *Critique of Pure Reason?* Is the outline of the sketch of a philosophy of religion identical with the outlines of a philosophy of religion in the transcendental dialectic in so far as the latter intends to lay the groundwork for a sketch of a philosophy of religion?

The practical use of reason leads us into the realm of morals and religion. Critical idealism furnishes the matter for the transcendental hypotheses which demonstrate the possibility of the ideas of reason. Thus, in the interrelationship of transcendental hypotheses with the assumptions of reason for practical purposes, there lies, at the same time, the relation of critical idealism to the philosophy of religion which is based on it. The ideas which are realized in the practical realm are prepared for this task by the instrumentality of critical idealism. They have moved into a sort of position of equilibrium, from which reason, employed practically, then pulls them toward its own realm. This relationship is also expressed in Kant's terminology;

he speaks, in this connection, of a *theoretical* (speculative) and a *practical* use of pure reason, yet does not distinguish —as he does later in the *Critique of Practical Reason*— between the two. This terminological distinction is grounded in a difference in thinking.

Very instructive is a footnote in the second edition of the *Critique of Pure Reason* where Kant connects the psychological, cosmological, and theological ideas with the ideas of God, freedom, and immortality, after developing them in the sequence of their later dialectical treatment: "Metaphysics has only three ideas as the true object of its search: God, freedom and immortality, understood so that the second concept in combination with the first should lead to the third as the necessary conclusion. Everything else with which this science occupies itself serves it only as a means to attain these ideas and their reality. It needs them not for the sake of natural science, but in order to transcend nature. Insight into them would make theology, morality, and (by combining the two) religion, and, hence, the highest aims of our existence dependent merely on the speculative faculty of reason, and nothing else. In a systematic presentation of these ideas, the order, as given, would be the most appropriate one, being synthetic. However, in the preliminary treatment which is necessary, the analytical presentation which reverses this order will be more appropriate, so that we may, proceeding from what experience presents us with immediately—that is, from psychology to cosmology and, hence, to the knowledge of God—realize our grand design" (p. 290). This passage is most important for the problem confronting us.

With the treatment of the problem of freedom we have reached the point where the positive exposition of the sketch of a philosophy of religion begins to clearly stand out from the outlines of our transitional thinking. We have presented the latter up till now in their most general formulation so as to be able to survey the thinking by which the *Critique of Pure Reason* arrives from its critical labor at those sections which have reference to the practical realization of the three ideas of God, freedom and immortality.

Let us summarize the essential points of the investigation thus far. The keynote of the transitional thoughts comes to the fore in Kant's use of language. By the expressions "pure reason in theoretical usage" and "pure reason in practical usage," he is indicating that at this juncture the absolute unity of reason is much more strongly than at any time later the presupposition of his thinking. At the same time, we are given to understand that his thoughts about the philosophy of religion advance here on the presupposition that the "ideas" which reason realizes in its practical use are absolutely identical with the ideas to which reason in its theoretical employment had been driven as it advanced of necessity from the conditioned to the unconditioned. Overcoming skepticism is the point from which the transitional thoughts we have noted start. With this, we have expressed the basic thought of the sketch of the philosophy of religion in the transcendental dialectic. This now obligates us to clearly expound how, from the number of the ideas treated, the three ideas have developed which are realized later practically, that is, how they specifically attained a practical religious value.

Kant is cautious and reticent when he applies the term "idea" to the individual subjects treated in the cosmological discussions. On p. 345, he specifically speaks of four cosmological ideas: "There are, therefore, not more than four cosmological ideas, according to the four headings of the categories." The linguistic expression regarding the term idea is pursued consistently only for the concept of freedom. (The reasons for and the significance of this fact will occupy us shortly.) Kant remains consistent, however, in his thought heralded by the designation "system of cosmological ideas," in that he retains the cosmological ideas in systematic connection in those sections where, from the standpoint of the practical use of reason, interest in the thoughts treated in the cosmological dispute is illuminated. The clearest expression of this systematic connection may be found in those lines which designate the decisive turning point at which the cosmological ideas move into the spotlight of reason in its practical use.*

What interest does reason have for the "thesis" in question in the cosmological dispute? "First of all, a certain practical interest which every right-thinking person shares heartily if he looks out for his real advantage. That the world has a beginning, that my thinking self is of a simple and, therefore, indestructible nature, that this self is, at the same time, free in its spontaneous actions and beyond natural necessity, and that, finally, the whole order of things which constitute the world are derived from some original Being from whom everything borrows its unity and purposeful connection—these are so many foundation stones of morality and religion."

* These lines, which are of decisive importance, are found on p. 385.

In order to appreciate the entire significance of these lines, one must again and again remind oneself of the fact that we are dealing here with a section in which Kant stresses only the practical value of the cosmological thoughts, not that of the problems treated generally in the dialectic. Here we are merely concerned with the "system of cosmological ideas." All four antinomies are represented, all four are evaluated practically, and all four stand in that particular context in which they had been treated previously dialectically. Simultaneously with this practical evaluation they were subjected to a deflection from their generality in the direction of their formulation with reference to the knowing subject.

What significance do the antinomies have for the ethical and religious view of the world of the knowing subject which sees through their dialectical appearance?

The first antinomy is most thoroughly opposed to this new orientation: "The world has a beginning in time and is, furthermore, limited in regard to space" (p. 354). Even in the dialectical treatment, this first antinomy looks somewhat strange. One has the impression that the dialectic would not suffer if this antinomy had been kept from us. Its subordinate place appears at the instant the transcendental ideas move toward the realm of reason in its practical use. It loses half of its scope in that it only retains its temporal character while it has lost its connection with space. "That the world has a beginning, . . . is a foundation stone of morals and religion" (p. 385). In this abbreviated form, where the stiltedness of the connection of the first cosmological idea with the thought of the conclusion is clearly apparent, we see that the first cosmological idea is dragged onto the new field only because of its systematic connection with the rest of the ideas. The mutilation which it suffers thereby, and the unaccustomed atmosphere of the practical use of reason, accelerate its inevitable end. Exhausted, it collapses. In what follows, not even its demise is announced. It is the fate of every artificial existence.

In the practical ramifications of the cosmological antinomies which extend through several sections (pp. 382-451), the main interest is taken up by the idea of freedom which is treated therein. The central position which this idea occupies in Kant's philosophy in general and in his philosophy of religion in particular comes clearly to the fore. Nowhere has any idea been so fully prepared with respect to its practical realization as the idea of freedom has been in this case. This is already indicated in the frequent use of the word "idea" in application to the concept of freedom treated here, while, for the rest, the application of this term to the theses of the "system of cosmological ideas" remains rather limited. It is quite characteristic for the correctness of the previous investigation that Kant refers to freedom in this connection now as a "transcendental idea," and then again as a "cosmological idea," without indicating that the latter designation really ought to stand in a subordinate relationship to the former. This idea of freedom is the only one which Kant developed to the point where it is about to experience its practical realization. It is exactly that idea which is discussed mainly in the *Critique of Practical Reason*. Thus, at the end of this investigation concerning the scheme of a philosophy of religion in the dialectic, it remains for us to briefly call to mind the preparation which the practical realization of the idea of freedom receives in the transitional sections of the second main portion of the second book of the dialectic in order to be able to decide, as we pass on to the sketch of the philosophy of religion, whether and to what extent the treatment and realization of the idea of freedom given on pp. 608 and 609 correspond to the anticipatory discussion which Kant offers us with regard to this problem.

The preliminary discussion of the practical realization of the idea of freedom takes place on pp. 428 to 445. In every respect, the discussions in these pages set forth the culmination of Kant's presentation of the dialectic. The whole investigation progresses in a highly effective crescendo.

First of all, Kant brings clarity to the problem that is raised here. What is the relationship between the idea of freedom in practical reason and the transcendental or cosmological idea of freedom when reason is used theoretically? By the first-mentioned, Kant understands "the independence of spontaneity from being necessitated by the promptings of sensibility" (p. 429). The last-mentioned has reference to the decision as to "whether causality in conformity to the laws of nature is the only causality or whether we have to assume an additional causality through freedom to explain it" (p. 368). If one were to adhere to the definition given here it would appear as if there were two ideas of freedom independent of each other of which the former does not depend on the latter for realization. However, on p. 385 the practical idea of freedom is already understood as that form which "the cosmological idea of freedom" assumes in its transition to the field of the practical use of reason. This relationship is again attested to on p. 429, and the circumstance is emphasized. And it is in this that Kant's thinking advances—that in this linkage of the two, the difficulty of the realization of the practical idea of freedom rests. "It is extremely noteworthy that the practical concept of freedom is based on this transcendental idea of freedom, and that the transcendental idea of freedom constitutes the really difficult factor in the practical concept, a circumstance which has surrounded the problem of its possibility ever since" (p. 429). We could designate this proposition as fundamental in Kant's treatment of the problem of freedom. Thus, the possibility of solving this difficulty is a matter solely for transcendental philosophy (p. 430). In all this, the insight of critical idealism into the character of the world of appearance offers the only starting point from where removal of the difficulty may be begun, "for if appearances are things-in-themselves, freedom cannot be salvaged" (p. 431). Hence, the cosmological idea of freedom can be presented by means of critical idealism in conjunction with a general "necessity" (p. 434), provided this connection can be justified at all. That the "cosmological idea of freedom" is treated here with a view to the practical idea of freedom is evident from the fact that the problem of the connection between freedom and the law of causality is no longer put in relationship at all with appearances, as it was in the third cosmological antinomy, but is related to the relationship of human action with the causality of appearances as was done on p. 385. Kant's statement here attains wonderful clarity: "Man is one of those appearances of the sensuous world and, hence, also one of the natural causes whose causality must be subject to empirical laws. As such, man must, therefore, also have an empirical character, just as all other things in nature. Man alone, who otherwise knows nature merely through his senses, knows himself also in mere apperception and, to be sure, in actions and inner determinations which he cannot count among the sense impressions at all. He is, let us acknowledge, on the one hand, a phenomenon for himself, but, on the other hand—and that in view of certain faculties—a mere intelligible object because his actions cannot be counted as receptivity of sensibility" (pp. 437 and 438). The kind of necessity expressed by the "ought" permits us to look upon the case as possible in itself that reason, in view of appearance, does possess causality (pp. 438 and 439). Concerning the actuality or possibility of this practical freedom, nothing can be stated if we consider it in its indissoluble relation to the transcendental idea of freedom. Only the fact "that nature is at least not struggling against the causality of freedom, was the only thing we were able to accomplish, showing which was what we had solely and merely in mind" (p. 445).

[*] The scheme of a philosophy of religion in the transcendental dialectic consisted in procuring—as concerns the practical use of reason—practical reality for the speculative ideas of pure reason in so far as we are persuaded that its significance concerns the practical use of reason. The idea of freedom corresponds to the third cosmological idea. It has reference to "whether causality according to the laws of nature is the only one from which the appearances

of this world can *in toto* be derived, or whether it is possible to assume, in addition, a causality through freedom." (cf. *Critique of Pure Reason*, p. 368). For a rational being, the problem thus stated holds interest because it depends for its solution on whether his actions may be explained only by the general law of causality according to the mechanism of nature into which they are, as phenomena, incorporated, or whether he can consider these same actions as a space-time explanation of intelligible facts which are free in so far as they concern the intelligible cause of our volition. The idea of freedom which tends toward practical realization—and so all we have said up to now may be summarized—is the transcendental idea of freedom which rests upon the relationship of the intelligible and the phenomenal world which critical idealism has demonstrated as possible.

This brief survey of the attempts which the Kantian philosophy of religion undertook for the purpose of realizing the moral idea of freedom with the aid of the presuppositions of critical idealism, shows that these attempts treat progressively more and more in depth all of the formulations which the problem of moral freedom can assume in continuous series, beginning with the sketch of a philosophy of religion, which has not even grasped yet the problem in its difficulty, to the investigation of the radical evil, where the problem turns out to be insoluble. For these formulations demand the investigation, with progressive understanding in depth, of the moral law in one form or another. Corresponding to this bolder appearance of the purely ethical interest of the problem of freedom, the idea of transcendental freedom recedes more and more in any combination of the transcendental and the practical ideas of freedom. Thus, in view of the problem of freedom, we have characterized the development of Kant's philosophy of religion as a progressive emphasis on the ethical element and a progressive recession of the material which critical idealism assembles for the structure. It is the idea of freedom which forms the basis of all statements in this connection. A displacement in the treatment of the idea of freedom has in its train the displacement of all thought relationship and the giving of a different coinage to all concepts rooted therein.

After this preview, which was necessary for an insight into the peculiarity and significance of the treatment of the idea of freedom in the practical use of reason given in the sketch of a philosophy of religion, we are resuming the train of thought of this sketch. In view of the practical use of reason in the trinity of ideas, the place of the idea of freedom, corresponding to the cosmological questions, has been taken by the idea of a practical reason which extends only to the field of human action. The idea of freedom which has thus been displaced returns later on in the thinking of this investigation, in that it displays a practical and moral interest in a general reference to the totality of appearances. It appears on the scene as "the practical idea of a moral world" (p. 612). Already, the introduction to this "practical idea of a moral world" has shown its affinity to the idea of a practical freedom. Its starting point is, namely, the fact of the moral law. "I assume that there are really pure moral laws which determine entirely *a priori* (without regard to empirical reasons, such as happiness) our commissions and omissions, that is, the use of freedom in general in a reasonable being, and that these laws make absolute demands (not merely hypothetical ones by presupposing other empirical ends), and hence are to all intents and purposes necessary" (p. 611).

 In what follows (on p. 612), all the difficulties of the practical realization of the idea of freedom in the moral application return once again. If the moral law manifests itself as the principle in the events of human actions, they, as free actions, must demonstrate "a special kind of systematic unity, that is, the moral one" as a practical reality, "while the systematic unity of nature could not be proven according to the speculative principles of reason" (p. 612). The use of the term "principle" in these few lines bears witness to the difficulty which meets us here. First of all, Kant talks about "principles of the possibility of experience, not in the speculative, but in a certain practical, that is, the moral use of reason." Next, he is concerned with a "systematic unity of nature according to speculative principles of reason." Then, he is concerned with the "causality of the moral principles of reason." At last he speaks of "principles of pure reason in its practical, but especially in its moral use" (p. 612). The difficulties assert themselves much more strongly than on pp. 608 and 609. The solution remains the same. The realm of human actions is delineated from the realm of natural events and reduced to the free causality of reason, "because reason possesses causality, to be sure, in view of freedom in general, but not in view of nature as a whole, and moral principles of reason can produce, to be sure, free actions, but not natural laws."

In the present sketchy treatment of the idea of a practical realization of the moral concept of God, its real content is covered up by the concept of happiness which, obscured by the way in which it usually occurs in another train of thought, clouds the insight into the peculiarity of the thought connections that meet us here. The great importance which is to be attributed to the distinction of these two trains of thought in the investigation of Kant's philosophy of religion requires that we trace their outlines in this sketch of the philosophy of religion where they met us first in a still undeveloped form side by side, so as to gain an insight into their differences. The middle term, which seemingly equates them, is the concept of happiness. What is its place in the realization of the idea of God (p. 613 ff.)? In this case, the concept of a moral world is brought into relation with moral mankind in whom acting humanly and morally is thought of as the causal principle of happiness. In this concept of the moral world a perfect ethics is identical with a perfectly achieved happiness. The moral world is a "system of morality which is its own reward" (p. 613). The ethical onus of the individual person in the moral world thus interpreted has, therefore, as object procuring one's own and at the same time others' happiness by achieving perfect ethics. It is exactly for the purpose of maintaining the justification of the ethical onus thus understood, in spite of the anticipation that not all members of humanity who are meant to belong to the moral world will act in that way, that Kant proceeds toward the realization of the concept of God.

We are at the end of the first part of our investigation.

It is true, we have only dealt with the first two sections of the canon of pure reason which contains the sketch of a philosophy of religion, and it remains to investigate only the third section "Concerning Opinion, Knowledge and Faith" (pp. 620 to 628). However, this section is of less importance for an insight into Kant's philosophy of religion since, compared with the two first sections, it does not present any advance in thought at all. It offers thoughts which are lacking in correct and precise delineations. Its investigation holds interest for an understanding of Kant's philosophy of religion only if and when we attack the general question as to what relation the sketch of the philosophy of religion (the conclusion of which constitutes this third section) has to the scheme of a philosophy of religion in transcendental dialectics and to the entire critical undertaking in general. In view of the above quotation the significance of this section, "Concerning Opinion, Knowledge and Faith," rests on the fact that the thoughts contained therein have already occurred in a much clearer and deeper form in the transcendental dialectic. The entire critical undertaking of the dialetic has, as we all know, the one objective of destroying opinion and purifying knowledge. The scheme of a philosophy of religion in the dialectic seeks to explain the scope, justification, and nature of faith in so far as it is not merely compatible with purified knowledge, but is also required by it. Thus, this third section of the canon of pure reason looks like an anachronism. It becomes understandable as being justified only when one carves out the sketch of a philosophy of religion, the canon of pure reason, out of the great critical opus, and seeks to understand it purely in itself, without its connection with the scheme of a philosophy of religion of transcendental dialectics.

These brief remarks are meant merely to explain why we are not devoting a more extensive investigation to this third section of the sketch of a philosophy of religion. The problem for which it has meaning at all concerns the relationship of the sketch of a philosophy of religion to the transcendental dialectic. In the discussions thus far this problem has always been recognized as the main one and presented as such. Nevertheless, if, at the conclusion of the analytical discussions of Kant's presentation, we wish to decide the questions which have emerged in the course of the investigation, the main problem referred to above cannot be settled first.

Now that we are at the end of the quite onerous investigation, the whole situation appears to us as a system of concentric circles. The problem as to what, on the whole, the general character of Kant's philosophy of religion is in the *Critique of Pure Reason* represents the outer circle. The circle closely following inside has reference to the distinction between the scheme of a philosophy of religion in the dialectic and the scheme of the sketch of a philosophy of religion. Pursuing the narrowing-down process of the investigations further, we were first searching more deeply for the essence of the scheme of a philosophy of religion in the transcendental dialectic. Then we analyzed the arrays of thought in the sketch of a philosophy of religion. The circles became smaller and smaller. Within the sketch of a philosophy of religion itself two different thought-structures separated out. Our analytical investigation pursued their differentiation in so far as the fluctuating outlines permitted it. This undertaking, which forms the conclusion of the analytical investigation in general, presents itself as the innermost circle in the system of concentric circles. The path in the analytic investigations went from the outermost circle to the innermost one. In our concluding investigations and in the unified summarization of the thoughts dealt with, we shall go in an opposite direction and run from the inner to the outer circles.

We did arrange the two trends of thought of the sketch of a philosophy of religion side by side and attempted to draw them in sharp outlines. Oftentimes these outlines were drawn more sharply than Kant's fluctuating sketchy type of presentation seemed to permit. This procedure, however, could be justified by the fact that this sharply drawn side-by-side arrangement was made because of the following grand development of Kant's philosophy of religion. In the sketch of a philosophy of religion, the two great trains of thought which appear later in Kant's philosophy of religion are found side by side in a somewhat confused state. The train of thought characterized by us as "the first one" is wound up by the presentation of the "moral theology" in the *Critique of Judgment* and in *Religion Within the Limits of Reason Alone*. It is distinguished by virtue of the fact that our ethical interest in continuing our existence, be it in the form of a "future life" or as "immortality," recedes somewhat into the background, and in place of it, interest in our terrestrial existence assumes greater validity. The latter fact manifests itself in the greater depth to which the problem of ethical freedom is subjected in discussion. To this must be added the predominance of the ethical element in the formulation of the concept of God. The progress of the *Critique of Judgment* and of *Religion Within the Limits of Reason Alone,* compared with the first train of thought of the sketch of a philosophy of religion, rests upon the understanding of the ethical law, which becomes gradually and progressively deeper.

Let us now summarize the thoughts which pertain to the sketch of a philosophy of religion as we ponder them as a whole. They are interconnected by the tripartite disposition which is to be found on p. 610. Concerning freedom, it is asserted that the question as to transcendental freedom has nothing to do with practical freedom. This is possible only if we constantly keep in mind the more comprehensive concept of the practical use of pure reason which the sketch of a philosophy of religion presupposes. The wider scope of this concept is based on a comprehension of the facts of the moral law which has not yet attained the highest degree of ethical profundity. Correspondingly, also the ethical element often recedes, to our surprise, in both questions in which the theoretical and the practical interest of pure reason touch each other. Neither the formulation of the question as to the existence of God nor that as to our continued existence allows the moral interest to come to the fore sufficiently. Great significance is attributed in the sketch of a philosophy of religion to the teleological trends of thought by means of which the conviction as to the existence of God and of a future life is established to such an extent that we gain the impression at the conclusion of the third section that the moral certitude was only meant to neutralize certain inevitable fluctuations in doctrinal faith concerning these two questions.

In this summary the way has now been prepared for the decision regarding the problem on hand, that is, whether and in how far the development of thought in the sketch of a philosophy of religion corresponds to the scheme of a philosophy of religion in transcendental dialectics. The basic thoughts of the latter are still in our mind. The scheme rests on the unity of pure reason in its theoretical and practical use. Thus, we are supposed to procure for the "three" ideas the practical interest of the transcendental, or (according to p. 385) cosmological, ideas the right to exist in the realm of practical reason. This is to take place in this manner so that theoretical reason may guide the transcendental idea in question through all phases up to its limits where it is ready to transcend it (using a passport which documents its origin in the land of critical idealism) and to settle down in the realm of the practical use of pure reason. We were able to pursue the different phases as they move from the widest formulation of a transcendental idea to the definitive, practical, and moral form of one of the ideas in the scheme of three ideas only with respect to the development of the idea of freedom. It alone is being groomed for practical realization for us to see. Thus, it is above all characteristic for the scheme of a philosophy of religion in transcendental dialectics.

The basic thought behind this scheme concerning the idea of freedom rests upon the idea "that it is upon the transcendental idea of freedom that the practical concept of it is based and that the transcendental idea constitutes properly the difficult factor in the idea of freedom, a problem which has for a long time surrounded the question as to the possibility of freedom" (p. 429). All that this critical preparation of the practical idea of freedom by means of the transcendental idea of freedom is able to accomplish is to demonstrate that "nature at least does not run counter to causality from freedom" (p. 445).

The detailed investigation of the treatment of the problem of freedom in the sketch of a philosophy of religion on pp. 608 and 609 has shown that in this decisive problem the scheme of the philosophy of religion in transcendental dialectics has been completely broken down. The question as to transcendental freedom has been totally severed from the problem of practical freedom, while the development of transcendental dialectics on pp. 428 to 445 remains steadfast in the union of both in spite of the fact that it is precisely in this combination that the difficulty of the whole problem lies.

The final sentence with which the treatment of the idea of transcendental freedom finishes on p. 445 contains something pointing to the future: "That nature, at least, is not incompatible with causality through freedom, was the only thing we were able to accomplish and it was this and this alone we had in mind" (p. 445). Why this modesty and yet this confidence? Because now nothing stands in the way of practical freedom, in spite of its entanglement with the transcendental idea of freedom. But now we behold the spectacle that at the point where practical freedom steps on the scene it rejects all connection with the transcendental idea of freedom because the latter has nothing to do with anything practical!

God, freedom and a future life are designated now as "objects" (twice on pp. 604 and 605), now as "cardinal propositions" (p. 607), now as "problems" (p. 607) in the sketch of a philosophy of religion in the first section where they appear in this triune number. After freedom has been eliminated from this triad "because this problem does not belong to reason in its practical use" (p. 609), only "two problems remain" (p. 609). These two are designated in what follows ordinarily as problems (pp. 610 and 619), as concepts, as doctrines (p. 624), or as articles of faith (p. 627). The term "idea" occurs sixteen times, twice on p. 610, twice on pp. 611, 612, 613, three times on pp. 614 and 615, twice on pp. 616 and 617, and on pp. 619, 620, and 625. Of these, a number of passages have reference to the moral law in general. "Judging morality as to its purity and consequences is done according to ideas, adhering to its laws, according to maxims" (p. 615). "The moral law . . . is a mere idea" (p. 615). "In the practical idea moral disposition and happiness are united" (p. 616).

A second group of passages connects the term idea with the concept of a moral world. "The moral world is a mere, yet practical idea which can in actuality have an influence on the world of the senses in order to shape it as much as possible in accordance with it" (p. 612). (What is designated here as "practical idea" is something totally different from what is otherwise understood by "idea of pure reason for practical use.") "Morality and happiness are inseparably connected only in the idea of pure reason" (p. 613). "The system of a morality which is its own reward is only an idea" (p. 613). "The moral law can rest on mere ideas of pure reason and may be known *a priori*" (p. 611). "I call the idea of such an existence . . . which is the cause of all happiness in the world in so far as it stands in exact ratio to morality, the ideal of the highest good" (p. 614). "The world must be conceived as having sprung from an idea . . . if it is to be consonant with the moral use of reason which rests absolutely on the idea of a highest good" (p. 617).

We have arrived at the end of the final summation of our investigation. The main problem as to whether the sketch of a philosophy of religion, the moral-theological culmination of Kant's great critical opus, really presents the basic outlines of the philosophy of religion of critical idealism had to be denied because the development of the sketch of a philosophy of religion makes no reference at all to the scheme of a philosophy of religion in transcendental dialectics and does not presuppose any acquaintance with it at all. Hence, this sketch has, in the presentation of the philosophy of religion of critical idealism, as it is usually given in connection with the *Critique of Practical Reason*, no rightful place. However, if one considers Kant's philosophy of religion as a whole, taking account of the development which it has undergone up to *Religion Within the Limits of Reason Alone*, the sketch of a philosophy of religion does occupy an eminent place. It points to what is to come and contains the entire future development, as it were, in a nutshell. It combines trains of thought which are at odds with each other because their undeveloped form does not yet permit such a unification. Later on these two trains of thought develop fully and clearly and become distinct. They are kept together only by virtue of Kant's profound moral genius. In this way, research into Kant's philosophy of religion turns into a presentation of its development.

The *Critique of Practical Reason*

⊐ The main problem remains the same as for the investigation into the sketch of a philosophy of religion. It is concerned with whether and in how far Kant's composition on the philosophy of religion, as we have dealt with it here, does correspond in its development to the scheme of a philosophy of religion in transcendental dialectics. The solution of this problem seems to assume, in the case of the *Critique of Practical Reason,* a more positive formulation than in respect of the sketch of a philosophy of religion. In the *Critique of Practical Reason* we really get an idea triad. The discussion concerning freedom demonstrates the sincerity and depth which the transcendental dialectic seems to demand. Furthermore, the three ideas stand in an organic connection with each other. And yet, precisely at the decisive moment, this agreement has not been maintained. To be sure, the result in the *Critique of Practical Reason* is the same as is likewise to be expected in the development of the scheme of a philosophy of religion in the transcendental dialectic. Still, the method displays a characteristic difference. According to the scheme of a philosophy of religion in the transcendental dialectic, the fact of the moral law serves to realize in practice the ideas which appear problematic in the field of the theoretic use of reason. In the *Critique of Practical Reason* the moral law generates by itself demands which constitute the possibility of the highest good. After practical reason has, from an inner necessity, attributed reality to these demands in practice, it realizes, in order to confirm, as it were, the correctness of its procedure, that these practically realizable magnitudes which belong to the possibility of the highest good are identical with the ideas which in the realm of theoretical reason were regarded as problematic.

One must not parallel the sketch of a philosophy of religion and the *Critique of Practical Reason* if one has in mind posing and solving the problem of freedom. Both have as little in common with each other as does the problem of freedom in practical use with the problem of transcendental freedom in the sketch of a philosophy of religion. While the latter starts entirely with a separation of both problems of freedom, and finds the solution in the fact that it presupposes this separation as self-evident, the *Critique of Practical Reason* has— in view of the problem of freedom —in common with the scheme of a philosophy of religion in the transcendental dialectic the fundamental presupposition that it assumes the two kinds of freedom as being in insoluble connection with each other. Furthermore, the *Critique of Practical Reason* shares with the transcendental dialectic the circumstance that the treatment of the problem of freedom turns into a profound struggle of ideas where one comes face to face not only with Kant the philosopher, but Kant the profoundly moral person.

As we investigate the realization of the idea of freedom in the *Critique of Practical Reason,* we witness the following peculiar spectacle. In seizing upon the problem (cf. p. 113), the presentation starts with the scheme of a philosophy of religion as laid down in the *Critique of Practical Reason.* The treatment proper and the realization of the idea of freedom (pp. 114-127) take place in the shape of a double polemic, first against empiricism (p. 114), then against the false teachers of metaphysics. The empiricists are charged with not recognizing the importance of the transcendental idea of freedom in practical freedom; the latter are charged with discrediting the idea of transcendental freedom because of their shortsightedness and, thus, of putting the moral idea of freedom in jeopardy against their will. In that the interest of the investigation is concentrated on the transcendental idea of freedom (according to the polemic tendency of the presentation), the scheme of a philosophy of religion in transcendental dialectic becomes operative spontaneously, as it were. After realizing the idea of freedom, this section concludes with a remark which embraces the scheme of a philosophy of religion of the *Critique of Practical Reason* and seems to presuppose that the realization of the idea of freedom has presently come about in accordance with it!

Let us look back upon the road travelled by us in our

investigation. The problem presented itself in view of the possibility of judging every individual act morally. The solution was made possible by virtue of the knowledge offered by critical idealism, according to which the individual act is to be looked upon as a phenomenon within the mechanism of nature, but as free in view of its intelligible character so far as the subject judging his own actions is concerned. The insight into the ideality of space and time (p. 118) served to lift every individual act out of its causal nexus (according to which it seemed necessary and apart from the realm of moral responsibility) and to remove it into the mode of viewing the appearance of freedom of a noumenon, whereby it could be judged morally in the self-consciousness of a rational being. The same reflection was then utilized on p. 120 in order to be able to explain the fact that we feel repentance over a past deed by lifting it out of the sequence of the causal nexus and judging it, freed, as it were, of the time relation, according to the absolute spontaneity of freedom—always, however, presupposing the identity of the acting and the judging subject!

Beginning with p. 120, this identity is cancelled while reflection trained on the double nature of the actions remains intact. With this, however, an entirely new approach is initiated. Up till then, actions were pursued in their two-sidedness in line with phenomena as well as in the intelligible sphere. In the center, and uniting both, stood the moral consciousness of the acting subject. From then on Kant emphasizes, aside from the two-sided nature of every individual act, also the orderly connection of the acts among themselves. If the actions appear in the world of phenomena—"which, on account of the uniformity of be-havior, announce their natural connection"—in an orderly connection, then the question is whether the problem of freedom must not also lift the individual act out of this connection in order to be able to judge it morally. It is of decisive importance that the investigation abandons the presupposition of the identity of the judging subject and, at the same moment, the subject that is judged. In this re-flection, the unity of judgment of an act is to be concentrated on only in so far as it manifests itself as a phenomenon under the mechanism of nature and as an intelligible act under the law of freedom. However, by virtue of the fact that all these preliminary presuppositions are uncon-sciously abandoned, one after another, the problem which we investigated became quite a different one, unnoticed. The resulting displacement becomes most pronounced in the displacement of the middle term which united the intelli-gible and the empirical mode of reflection. Previously, it had been the knowledge the intelligible self has of the moral law. Now, the place of the intelligible self, which is at the same time conscious of the moral law, has been taken by the moral character in so far as it expresses itself in regular acts which, on account of their uniformity of be-havior, indicate a connection with nature. Earlier, the question was: How can I think of an act which, as phenom-enon, is subsumed under the mechanical laws of nature, as having been effected at the same time under freedom, in so far as judging it is required, which the moral law urges upon me through my conscience? The answer is as follows: By virtue of the fact that space and time, in which this has taken place in conformity with the causality of phenomena so far as I understand and know it, have no application to my intelligible self and, consequently, my act also, in so far as it is merely an expression of my disposition which concerns the moral law, is to be judged by me not according to natural necessity (which would be proper to it as a phenomenon), but according to the absolute spontaneity of freedom.

Moral consciousness demands that every deed, in order to be able to be judged as moral, be looked upon as free. That the act which is judged morally is free, and is to be understood as a free effect of the subject from which it proceeds, is the presupposition which is at the basis of every moral judgment. With the progressive insight into the mechanism of nature, with the expansion of the concept "natural event" even into the realm of human actions, this presupposition has been shaken. With it also the moral law falters, since it has to turn out to be an illusion if freedom cannot be salvaged. Our moral consciousness rises in indignation against such a situation. With all means of science, with the expenditure of the greatest acumen to understand the nature of what happens, it seeks to find ways and means whereby the action to be judged morally may be lifted out of the course of natural events and understood as free. In that it attempts to understand scientifically the presupposition of every moral judgment, the epistemological problem attains its profound moral significance by which alone it legitimizes itself as belonging to "philosophy" in the more pregnant Kantian sense. At the same time, the epistemological problem, when perfectly grasped by critical idealism, exhibits a form which not only does not resist being related to the scientific justification of the pre-supposition of our moral judgment, but even demands it itself. In the reconciliation of contradictions by the trans-cendental idea of freedom, even the contradictions of the practical idea of freedom seem to find their solution. Critical idealism brings about an understanding of the same events as, on the one hand, those effected by nature's mechanism and, on the other, those traceable to a free in-telligible ground, by proving the ideality of space and time and thus providing an insight into the nature of the causal-ity of the phenomenal world. Hence it may be combined with the scientific justification of the presupposition of our moral judgment in so far as the latter also endeavors to sever an act from nature's mechanism. Our actions are phe-nomena, and solely as phenomena do they stand in connec-tion with the mechanism of nature. As phenomena, they permit themselves, therefore, to be dissociated from the mechanism of nature and, being traced back to our "intelli-gible self," understood as free. As a result of the combina-tion with critical idealism, the problem of freedom has assumed also the presuppositions of the methods of investi-gation of critical idealism. In the formulation urged upon us by our consciousness of moral responsibility, the prob-lem of freedom has been reduced to a form which exhibits advantages on all counts over the method of investigation of critical idealism.

In posing the problem of freedom, the moral subject starts with himself: How can I present every one of my actions as free to myself in order not to be obliged to under-stand the moral law which expresses itself in my conscience as an illusion? Not until the question has been answered does the subject pass on to the analogous mode of judging with reference to other subjects. In this manner, the posing of the problem of freedom in its most natural form harbors the main presuppositions of the method which critical idealism uses in its investigations (provided critical idealism wishes to establish contact with the realm of the practical use of reason)—in other words, the identity of the knowing and the acting subject and the isolation of action with reference to the subject in so far as only thus the double mode of looking at the act as intelligible and as phenomenon suggests itself as a matter of course. For, as soon as the subject externalizes itself, the identification of act and appearance is no longer possible, since there exist only appearances then, but no longer any acts. Should one, nevertheless, wish to apply this designation, with all its consequences, to a series of phenomena, this can only happen on the basis of a conclusion arrived at by analogy, which deems itself justified in reducing a series of appearances to an intelligible subject and, of necessity, understanding that intelligible subject also as a unity of a knowing and an acting subject. The moral law urges us to take this step because it has reference to the mutual relationships between moral beings and has no meaning apart from the presupposition of a plurality of moral beings. The moral law can be satisfied with the conclusion by analogy, in asserting the existence of other moral beings apart from the subject which experiences the moral law in himself, a conclusion in which a number of appearances are referred, as acts, to an intelligible, moral subject. Critical idealism is meant to be the foundation for this method, although in this point it is flatly opposed to such a procedure, since in general it allows for only one subject, the knowing subject, the "intelligible self," apart from which—or better, for which—there are only phenomena. The problem as to a plurality of knowing subjects does not occur to it at all; for the knowing subject (whatever it might be) which, in going through the thought processes of critical idealism, understands all events as phenomena, is for itself "the knowing subject" in regard to which there is only one world of phenomena and by which appearances are comprehended solely as acts if it comprehends itself as an acting subject. The moral and practical reason which is united with this intelligible subject as a knowing subject necessarily urges on to the establishment of a plurality of intelligible subjects in respect to which certain areas of phenomena are to be understood as acts. At the same time, however, with these acting subjects it establishes knowing subjects in that it has to present these subjects in analogy to its own intelligible self, which it understands as a unity of a knowing and an acting self. However, when this is accomplished the idealistic and critical presuppositions are dissolved.

Thus, a profound antagonism becomes noticeable when the method of investigation of critical idealism is conjoined with the tendencies of practical and moral reason. This antagonism, however mighty it is, slumbers so long as the practical, moral problems present themselves in a form commensurate with the methods of investigation used by critical idealism. This is the case, as was stated above, with the problem of freedom, so long as it regards the act in its relation to nature's mechanism and presents it as free for the purpose of moral self-judgment. This is the form in which it makes its first appearance in moral reflection. It unconsciously contains the presuppositions which allow the method of investigation used by critical idealism to be applied to itself.

It is in this manner, then, that the solution of the problem of freedom develops within the framework of critical idealism. In the grave struggle to lay the foundation for the possibility of a moral *Weltanschauung* with respect to the problem of freedom which we experience with Kant, critical idealism truly does what is expected of it. It offers the possibility of comprehending human actions—in so far as they present themselves to the knowing subject in their twofold nature as either appearances or intelligible actions —as acts of the subject which are free moral judgments.

The struggle now seems at an end, the problem of freedom settled safely. With profound moral earnestness, Kant, with a view to moral judgment, ventures to apply the scientifically acquired presupposition for freedom to a case in which the moral judgment could charge itself with harshness and injustice if the assumption of freedom were not scientifically backed. At that very moment, however, he pulls from under the formulation of the problem of freedom the presuppositions with which it had operated unconsciously thus far. With one stroke, it changes its complexion; the goal already in sight flees far off, and the path trod thus far ends at a gaping precipice in whose abyss the problem of freedom perceives its true image. Frightened, it steps back. Moving once again in the realm of critical idealism, it regains its former appearance while the true image of itself which it saw appears as a frightening dream.

We have now reached the full height of the problem. Yet let us glance at the foothills, above which the pinnacle we have reached is hardly visible to the observer in the plains, before we take a look into the abyss facing us. In what has already been stated, we asked the question whether or not Kant was conscious of the deep significance of the problem formulated in the *Critique of Practical Reason* (p. 121) where he touches upon the higher levels of the problem of freedom for reasons already noted. We gave the answer above by pointing out that the main problem appears only as a special case of the first formulation of the problem in the schematism of critical idealistic thinking, where the identity of the acting and judging subject forms the hidden presupposition throughout the discussion. It presents itself as the application of the moral judgment to the deeds of "born evildoers." Kant came to the conclusion "that the natural nexus of their deeds does not render necessary the evil nature of their wills, but, rather, that it is the result of freely accepted evil and unchangeable principles which make it all the more punishable."

The advance in the level of problems in *Religion Within the Limits of Reason Alone* (p. 19-20) consists in that this view is not activated one-sidedly to account for the evilness of nature, but is also extended to the assumption of the goodness of nature. Not until this double formulation was the problem fully recognized; and all other points in which the development of *Religion Within the Limits of Reason Alone* goes beyond the *Critique of Practical Reason* (p. 121) are only a natural consequence of the two-sided problem that we now have. The act of freedom on p. 121 of the

Critique of Practical Reason from which the nature of disposition is derived, signifies only a greater emphasis on the responsibility of practical behavior, which was established elsewhere already. Contrary to this, pp. 19 and 20 of *Religion Within the Limits of Reason Alone* demonstrate the two-sided problem—that it is really this unfathomable act of freedom which furnishes the basis of the responsibility for our actions. On p. 121 of the *Critique of Practical Reason* the once-assumed-evil maxims are represented as unchangeable and necessarily sensitive to progress, that is, progress toward evil. This view will, likewise, have to be dispensed with as provisional when the two-sided problem confronts us, unless we are to carry absurdity into the problem itself.

Now comes the third and most important step forward. In the episodic form of the problems in the *Critique of Practical Reason* (p. 121) it might appear acceptable that there is a mean between the bad and the good nature of the disposition. In this case, the evil nature of the will would have to be understood as an exception to the average nature of the will inclined toward evil. When the two-sided problem confronts us, this view falls by the wayside: There is no mean between the good and evil nature of the disposition. With this assertion (whose scope one fathoms correctly only when one is mindful that the assumption of an evil and a good maxim as a free act must always again be reduced to a maxim) Kant has arrived at a point at which the genius must of necessity take up the fight with the historically legitimated views. From this standpoint he then hurls his death-dealing missiles against everything within reach: the dogmatic theory of original sin, moral empiricism, as well as the ethical-psychological illusions from Seneca to Rousseau. One opponent above all had to be brought low: the person who robbed moral reflection of its dead seriousness and replaced it with his sickly over-stimulation in which the two extremes, moral indifference and moral exaggeration, could occur equally at will.

Good and evil form absolute contrasts. The actions which rise from the good or evil nature of the disposition must rest upon a free act in order to fall under moral responsibility. Therefore, the moral nature of the disposition itself must be reduced to an act of the subject. The act would not be free if it were based on the existence or nonexistence of sensibility. In rejecting this assumption, as in all other matters, the conclusions from the demands of freedom and the determination of good and evil as opposites, coincide. In this case, this leads to the necessary assumption that the good and evil nature of the disposition rests on the assumption of a maxim.

With this conclusion we have arrived at the limits of our insight. The difficulties now opening up consist in the following. 1) We are continually tempted to apply time perceptions to the act thought last when we trace back the assumption of the maxims, misled by the analogy which urges itself upon us with the causal series in the phenomenal world. 2) In spite of the above insight or, rather, perhaps just because of the fact that owing to it the assumption of an influence of the sensibility on the coming about of the moral disposition is being rejected, the evilness as it occurs, just like the goodness as it appears, becomes completely incomprehensible. 3) In that we go back to the factor of the origination of the rational being for the explanation of the above state of affairs—a reflection which we were completely relieved of in Kant's explanation of the field of investigation in critical idealism—we arrive at the conclusion that the moral condition of the disposition must be thought of as innate and yet may not be represented as such.

These are the main difficulties in the representation of the first origination of the nature of the moral disposition in general. If one keeps in mind Kant's conception of evil (unacceptance of the moral law as the only determining ground for one's maxims), he must add the verifiable fact that in so far as human experience goes, man is, in general, evil in his ethical disposition. But it is exactly with the consciousness of the moral law that, simultaneously, the type of evil disposition is given (which can be noted empirically in man's actions) if one remembers that man, according to Kant, cannot be good and evil at one and the same time. It is implied in the consciousness of responsibility that both motivations coexist in man, who is empirically evil. The following remains as the only possible solution: Evil consists in the form of subordination of the motivations!

Evil is radical in so far as it spoils the ground of all maxims. The consequences of this character of the natural evil inclination are the following: 1) The original *Anlage* toward the good within us consists in the fact that the sensuous drives are, in view of the origin of evil, not only not indifferent but that they may be designated as a natural inclination toward the good in so far as they are the presuppositions of a societal association in which the moral law is to unfold itself. Hence, regaining the original *Anlage* toward the good cannot consist in the acquisition of a lost motivation to do good, but only in purifying it, being the uppermost ground of all of our maxims. 2) The same difficulties as for the general two-sided mode of consideration discussed above appear when we wish to form a mental picture of the act imagined as possible of an assumption of a morally good disposition by reversing the relationship in the usual subordination of maxims. Only the difficulties turn out to be practically soluble here in so far as this timeless act presents itself to man as a development. (This was not possible when we reversed the relationships of the maxim from which follows the radically evil, since the process had to be transported into the condition of our existence as rational beings where it had not yet become conscious.) The timeless intelligible comprehension of this act, which was an insoluble necessity for the occurrence of the radically evil in order to hold on to the responsibility for our actions, loses its cogency when we try to present to ourselves the re-entry of the good principle. Why? Because while he is continually experiencing progress and reflecting on his moral accountability, the rational being does not need to experience within himself that unitary intuition divorced from time and space, but, rather, can leave it to that being for whom "this infinity of progress represents a unity," and to whom this change presents itself as revolution (p. 50).

It becomes perfectly clear in the discussion just concluded that we are in a different field of investigation from that of the *Critique of Pure Reason* and the *Critique of Practical Reason*. In the case of the *Critiques*, the possi-

bility of a moral evaluation of every action was gained by
virtue of the fact that each presented itself as an intelligible act, divorced from its space-time determination, to
which space-time causality could not be applied. This
unity of sensuous world and intelligible world took place
under the more or less conscious presupposition of an
identity of the acting and judging subject. In the present
case, however, where we are dealing with the problem of
Religion Within the Limits of Reason Alone, we can no
longer avail ourselves of the possibility of such a solution.
We may roughly formulate as follows the question as to
the problem of freedom and moral responsibility in its
profoundest form, and we do so with a view to the possibility of man to better himself as laid down in the discussion
on p. 50. How can we hold on to the moral responsibility
for human actions if the transition from the radically evil
to the radically good is presented merely as a character
development by stages while, in essence, it consists in a
timeless act, and is thus incapable of being carried out in
our imagination as rational beings? In these circumstances
there is no longer any solution on the basis of the unity of
man as an intelligible and a phenomenal being; that is, the
solution has become impossible by virtue of the type of
reflection in critical idealism. In order to maintain the
requirement, the solution of the difference must be sought
in the imagined evaluation of a being who represents himself as a postulate, which, according to the *Critique of
Pure Reason* and the *Critique of Practical Reason,* is
possible only on the ground of representing to oneself the
possibility of freedom in an insight which critical idealism
imparts! Here, on p. 50—where the problem of freedom

in its most profound form lies in the shape of a quest after the possibility of changing one's disposition— it is demonstrated, in the juxtaposition of divine and human types of reflection, that the basic question is no longer soluble in the realm of critical idealism as a principle of investigation, because critical idealism is committed to seeking the solution in the juxtaposition of man as an intelligible and a phenomenal being! The difficulty which can no longer be solved here consists in the transference of the idea of development (made necessary by the higher problem of freedom) to the intelligible realm. . . .

The fact that we are involved in the methods of investigation of critical idealism—as is so evidently clear from pp. 128 and 129—is of decisive importance for what follows. Concerning its practical aspect, pure reason has the same need as in its theoretical aspect: to seek in all that is given that which is unconditioned, to comprehend everything in a unity. This unconditioned totality of the object of pure practical reason is comprehended under the name of "the highest good." To arrive at the highest apex of human understanding is a matter of establishing the unity of the total content of our empirical will with the moral law and its demands. However, in pursuance of the investigations of p. 133 ("Concerning the Dialectics of Pure Reason in the Determination of the Concept of the Highest Good") the fact appears that—if we believe we have solved the entire problem of freedom with the methods of investigation of critical idealism—we are completely under the spell of this method of investigation. Beginning at this point, the entire discussion concerning the highest good appears, henceforth, under the presuppositions of the method of investigation of critical idealism.

Up to now, this method of investigation only served to prove that for me as a rational being, and considering all my actions, intelligible freedom and necessary condition are to be thought of as compatible by virtue of the absolute demands of the moral law. From now on, the bringing about of the unity between the moral law and the world in general is carried on under the same special reflection. Thus, the general concept of the highest good is placed in relationship to the individual person, something that was not contained in the original nature of this concept. Here, in the last analysis, lies the cause of all the inconsistencies, mistakes, and inaccuracies which have been levelled against Kant's philosophy of religion, especially in this respect. Therefore, it is odd that all these alleged mistakes in regard to critical idealism are no mistakes at all since they rest merely on the strictly maintained presuppositions of its method of investigation. What, at first sight, one may attempt to explain as an incomprehensible change in the trend of Kant's thought thus appears inevitable. The unity of moral law and world in the highest good which, taken in a general sense, would lead to the demand for a world in which all changes take place according to the causality of the moral law, is necessarily interpreted as related to the individual rational being as a unity of virtue and happiness. That this in turn rests entirely on the isolation of the subject and the identity of the acting and evaluating person and results necessarily from it is clear from the whole presentation on p. 133. Classically formulated, we find the presupposition for this reflection in the following statement: "To stand in need of happiness, to be worthy of it, but, nevertheless, not to partake of it, cannot be reconciled at all with the perfect will of a rational being who is at the same time all-powerful, even though we are just experimenting with such a thought" (p. 133).

"Virtue and happiness together constitute the possession of the highest good in a person." On this basis, Kant now builds further. The connection of these two concepts is necessarily synthetic. The mode of combination may be expressed in this statement: "It is *a priori* (ethically) necessary to produce the greatest good through freedom of the will." "If, therefore, the greatest good is impossible according to practical rules, then also the moral law which demands that it be promoted must be illusory and, to a large extent, false because it is based on empty imaginary purposes." Ordinarily the reader discovers in this sentence of Kant's an exaggerated and illogical assertion. However, it would be more appropriate to look for the illogicality in the judgment of those who are completely in agreement with the presuppositions of the method applied and yet find it objectionable if Kant draws the correct inference. Incorporating happiness into the concept of the greatest good and offering this alternative are the natural consequences of the presuppositions of the method of investigation applied. Nevertheless, everybody feels that in the course of the investigations and between the indubitable assertion of the fact of the moral law and the formulation of the antinomy on p. 137 (which winds up with the objectionable assertion which makes the admitted fact shaky) there must have crept in a logical error which is responsible for the entire formulation of the antinomy.

Concerning the moral person, in so far as it may be determined in his nature by the pre-existence of his self, Kant has stated quite correctly in the first section of *Religion Within the Limits of Reason Alone* that we cannot in any possible statements concerning it go beyond what is given in the phenomenal world, that is, birth, however inexplicable the fact of the lapse into the "radically evil" and particularly our consciousness of responsibility remain in the face of it. If we do not include in the assumption of a continued existence the continuation of the moral person at all, then the above-cited Kantian assertion is based on a change in subject which is covered up by the double meaning of the word, person. Hence, we are also forced to give to the term, person, a coinage strange to the field of investigation of critical idealism. At the same time, the infrastructure which the *Critique of Pure Reason* builds up with respect to asserting the continuation of our self, is not able at all to support the structure reared on it.

These difficulties, which necessarily arise in the imperceptible movement toward a field of investigation foreign to the essence of critical idealism, consist in the fact that in the postulate of immortality the higher, unsolved problem of freedom dominates the development of thought in the manner described above. Now, the question is whether these same difficulties also narrow down the second postulate. From the outset, this seems quite natural since this second postulate, likewise, is reared on the formulation of the concept of the greatest good which is possible only in the apparent solution of the problem of freedom in general. Scrutinized in greater detail, this second postulate of the existence of "God" was already necessary for the assumption of the first one. If holiness consists in the complete appropriateness of the disposition to the moral law--and this condition is thinkable in the intelligence of a sensuous being only as an infinite development—then there is holiness concerning the moral disposition only when there is an intelligence in which we may presuppose such a development as a unitary, timeless act. The necessity of a postulate thus formulated, whose elements may be found in the solution of the antinomy as well as in the *Critique of Practical Reason* (pp. 148 and 149), cannot be dismissed if we are seriously concerned with the Kantian juxtaposition of good and evil in which every condition of the disposition must be thought of as being reducible to an intelligible act.

Kant's train of thought takes a different turn. There must exist a guarantee of the proportionality of virtue and happiness, since otherwise the requirement of furthering the greatest good would falter and the moral law would become illusory. It is on this requirement that the postulate is built. And we have to state again that establishing the postulate in this form is possible only if one leaves the field of investigation of critical idealism. This relocation has only become possible through the apparently solved problem of freedom. Only in this way could a free rational being be equated with the empirical rational being and the proportionality of virtue and happiness in the empirical world be suggested by formulating the concept of the highest good for the rational being. On this is later based the demand for "a cause in the totality of nature different from nature which contains the reason for this connection . . . between happiness and morality" (p. 150). In this connection two different natural causalities having objective validity are cited which, being so contradictory, cannot be justified at all on the basis of critical idealism. It is characteristic that Kant (on pp. 173 and 174) feels compelled to make excuses for this method in that he acknowledges the unjustifiability on the basis of the results of critical idealism: "I have stated above that in the world happiness (which is exactly proportional to moral worth) is not to be expected according to the course of nature alone, and may be deemed impossible, and that, therefore, the possibility of the highest good in this respect can only be admitted under the presupposition of a moral author of the world. I cautiously did not mention the limitation of this judgment to the subjective conditions of our reason in order not to make use of it until the manner of its verification could be determined more closely. In fact, the impossibility mentioned is merely subjective." The object of Kant's excuse is to show that he has concluded from this objectified subjective impossibility to a demand from which not the objective speculative positing of a God, but only the subjective and practical assumption of his existence, would flow. This explanation, however, does not go to the core of the method, since the question concerns not whether the thus posited postulated being is subjective or objective, but whether or not—if the fact of the moral law is not to become illusory— the requirement of proportionality of virtue and happiness in the sensuous world must lead, of necessity, to the additional postulate of a being who comprehends the two causalities into a higher unity, himself being the primary cause of the world. (In all this one should, of course, keep in mind that the juxtaposition of two causalities is founded merely in our subjective view.) The answer on the basis of critical idealism is, of course, only a No, since the mechanism of nature and intelligible causality are represented as different merely in our reason, so that the former is the sensuous appearance of the latter. In order to bring about this unity, the rational being does not ever need to assert an infinite being who differs from a natural cause. To assume one actually contradicts critical idealism.

For the moment it is sufficient to note in the interesting remark on pp. 173 and 174 the following: Kant in this one case admits that the infrastructure of establishing a postulate extends beyond the boundary posts of critical idealism, a fact of which we became aware when a recoinage could be noted in the terms with reference to the first postulate. Furthermore, the demand to further the highest good in this world is basic to establishing the second postulate. The contradictions with which we are concerned in dealing with the possibility of the highest good refer to the juxtaposition of a "realm of nature" and a "realm of morals" (p. 174). The latter distinction does not completely coincide with the juxtaposition of an intelligible and a phenomenal world which is common in critical idealism. The dull identification of the two, which becomes necessary as soon as the postulate of the existence of God takes rise (presumably on the basis of critical idealism), is presupposed when the postulate was established on pp. 149 and 150 ff. and then carried out. The necessary consequence of a juxtaposition of a natural mechanism and an intelligible causality justified merely subjectively in the realm of the investigation of critical idealism, was suddenly regarded as objectively real. This identification of the realm of morals with the intelligible world in itself signifies, in regard to the establishment of the second postulate, what the identification of the personality as an enduring unity in the fluctuations of phenomena was meant to convey in regard to the basis of the second postulate.

Thus, it has been demonstrated for the basic method regarding establishing the second postulate that central to it is the same operation as in the first postulate, that is, identification of a moral magnitude with an intelligible one. This identification cannot be made in critical idealism, however natural it may be in the ordinary view. In the case of the concept of the moral person, we have demonstrated this by showing how the determination of an orderly and steadily progressive development—that is, change—clings to this concept by virtue of its empirical determination. The same now also holds true for the moral world, the realm of ethics. It is already contained in the demand that although the realm of morals cannot be realized until infinity is reached, empirical rational beings should work on it. The realm of morals is the magnification of the moral person. The uppermost moral rational being, God, is the immortal soul magnified as a continuation to perfection of the moral person. In establishing the second postulate there is a large-scale repetition of what we have already experienced in the establishment of the first postulate. Just as in the first postulate the second one was already implied, so the first one is again carried over in a different form in the second one, as if it had not been solved yet.

Now it must be demonstrated that the establishment of the second postulate may be investigated critically according to the same points of view as the first one. First of all, it must appear surprising that the starting point of the second postulate is not at all based on the solution of the first one, despite the fact that it is preceded by the establishment of the first one. It is even identical with it, but is not based on the first one at all. Rather, in the course of the investigation, it again posits the first one covertly, and assumes it. This fact does not come to the fore at all in some of the presentations of Kant's philosophy of religion. The blame lies on the introduction of the investigation of the second postulate where, it is true, reference is made to the solution of the first one as if the second one did require the solution of the first one as a condition (p. 149). However, if there really were a connection between the two, the introduction would necessarily stand on the following reflection —that the highest good consists in the proportionality of virtue and happiness. If, however, happiness is the highest comparison thinkable of every absolutely perfect satisfaction possible, then only the highest moral perfection, that is, holiness, can correspond to it in the realm of morality.

Now, we have shown that holiness can be thought of as being realizable only in infinity, a fact on which the demand for the immortality of soul is based. Hence, in what follows, the postulate of the proportionality of happiness and morality should be justifiable only in this formulation: The fact of the moral law in us which lays down a synthetic combination of virtue and happiness in the concept of the highest good demands that to the holiness of the immortal soul, which has been presented by the above postulate as possible (not as necessary, it is to be noted), the happiness of this immortal soul should necessarily correspond. If the second postulate is not based on the first one by such reasoning, then it is not based on it at all, does not presuppose it in any sense whatsoever, and may turn out to be merely a parallel presentation of the development of the first postulate if, in the end result, the first postulate is presupposed. This assertion is quite to the point if we can show that, presupposing the above reflection, the second postulate is completely impossible. Also, on the basis of the requirement that holiness of the soul must correspond to happiness, no postulate whatever can be based which assumes a being who in himself unites the two mutually contrasting causalities asserted here, since both magnitudes included in the postulate are given in the intelligible world. Indeed, on the postulate of immortality, a second postulate —that of the existence of a highest moral being—can be established just as little as the assumption of a God of the nature described makes certain and real the necessary assumption of the possibility of the immortal soul's holiness. On p. 148, it is shown that the assumption of this highest being is necessary if we are to predicate the holiness of anything at all, since it is in his intelligence alone that infinite moral development presents itself as a condition— as holiness.

This impossibility we can trace back to its first foundations. The establishment of the first postulate has become necessary by virtue of the fact that by laying down the impossibility of holiness in place of the fictional free rational being (concerning which the concept of the highest good was developed in consequence of the problem of freedom, which was solved only apparently) suddenly the empirical rational being appears whom, on the basis of critical idealism, it is possible to prove free. In order to maintain the assertions made regarding the fictionally free rational being, this free rational being is projected into infinity as an immortal soul, possibly already possessing holiness, and conjoined into a unity with the empirical moral rational being by assuming an infinite moral development. Here lies the significance of the postulate of immortality as developed. Now we have, as a matter of fact, incorporated the old fictional free rational being as a subject into all of our assertions, whereby the possibility—or better, the necessity—of establishing postulates is rendered nugatory, and we have moved, once again, back into the position which preceded ascertaining the actual impossibility of holiness for the rational being in the sensuous world. The error uncovered there is again nullified. What has been denied the fictional subject by this assertion, whereby it became the empirical rational being, has been assured it again in another way by the assumption of an infinite possibility of development in its progress towards holiness. And now we have, once more, the subject to which the determination of the concept of the highest good has reference, that is, a free rational being in so far as there is no obstacle to the present or future adequate commensurability of its will with the moral law. The identity of this rational being is thus guaranteed in both cases in that the divine reason seizes upon the infinite progress toward holiness as holiness as an existing act.

Should what follows be incapable of being joined, in the reflection formulated above, with the solution given by assuming the postulate of immortality, then, in actuality, the empirically unfree rational being is posited again as the subject of assertions which were made concerning the free fictional rational being. The postulate developed upon this inconcealable contradiction is merely the repetition of the solution already given but left out of account. Thus, we are, on p. 149, on the same spot as on p. 146. Previously, the example was geared to the concept of virtue as something commensurate with the disposition toward a moral law, while now the example is geared to the concept of happiness. One might just as well have begun with the latter example—in which case one would have also solved the former by implication. For the two concepts of morality and happiness stand in a relation of proportionality to each other, whereby the changes in magnitude must correspond with each other. The example is so construed that at one time a finite concept above is made to correspond with an infinite one below; the next time, the proportion is simply reversed. The solution consists in that through rendering infinite the finite side (the real essence of the postulate), equality is achieved on both sides.

Twice thus far we have made use of the general observations on pp. 158 to 177 and found both times that Kant definitely returns to the position of critical idealism which he occasionally left in establishing the second postulate. But now it turns out that all discussions in this context have the same tendency, that is, to demonstrate the true agreement of the results which the *Critique of Practical Reason* and the *Critique of Pure Reason* have achieved independently of each other. We already noted a similar suggestion after the problem of freedom had apparently been settled: "I may be permitted to call attention to only one more thing at this occasion; that is, that every step one makes with pure reason, even in the practical field, where one does not pay any notice at all to subtle speculation, nevertheless seeks contact, meticulously and involuntarily, with all the factors of the *Critique of Theoretical Reason,* as if each one had been thought through with premeditated caution, just to procure the necessary confirmation" (p. 128).

The postulates were, then, established without concern for the "ideas" of speculative reason in that immortality and the existence of God were arrived at solely by the demands of practical reason, as has been shown in the earlier section, "Concerning the Primacy of Pure Practical Reason in its Connection with the Speculative Reason." When the postulate of immortality was established, the reference that it corresponds to an idea of speculative reason was left out. With reference to the second postulate, it is pointed out nonchalantly on p. 151 that what is postulated here corresponds to a hypothesis of theoretical reason. The structure has now been erected; and in order to insert the capstone firmly, it is merely a matter of showing that through this independent procedure of practical reason only the ideas of theoretical reason have been legitimized. With this intention, the things to be remembered concerning the concept of God are enumerated (p. 166), and transcending the determination of critical idealism, when laying the groundwork for the second postulate, is referred to as unessential (p. 173).

Let us survey once more by way of review the road we have travelled in the investigations thus far before we pass on to a comparison of the results of practical reason and the way in which they are realized with the results of that section of the *Critique of Pure Reason* dealing with the philosophy of religion with which we have already concerned ourselves.

At first, we saw how freedom relative to the moral judgment of our actions was presented, on the basis of the antinomy of the moral law, as imperative and experienced in the fact of conscience in that a sharp distinction was made between it and every empirical motive force for action. The structure was built with the material of critical idealism. The practical idea of freedom was realized according to the scheme of a philosophy of religion in the transcendental dialectic. In consequence of the thus necessitated borrowing of the method of investigation in that scheme, the problem of freedom was looked upon as apparently fully solved; with respect to the free rational being, a demand was made for the highest good presented as a synthetic unity of virtue and happiness. This is the formulation of the demands for a moral world in general, which is imperative, considering the isolated person. Asserting the impossibility of holiness on the one hand, and of happiness on the other, the empirically unfree rational being returns to investigate further. The demand for freedom in the face of the moral law in which the demand for a moral world in general is equally posited (which is immediately clear if we start with the community of all moral rational beings) reappears in the demand for a highest good which, in turn, is again only the demand of the individual for a moral world and leads to the postulates of immortality and the existence of God. Since the solution of the problem of freedom is not possible on the higher levels of stating the problem in the field of investigation of critical idealism, the realm of critical idealism is transcended in all statements at whose base we somehow find this problem. We have proven this for the section on the radically evil. Likewise, we found that the postulates regarding the formulation and statements did not stay within the bounds of critical idealism. They are "postulates" but not ideas. Only one idea is realized, the idea of freedom. In order to reach the triad and the systematic connection by which they could legitimatize themselves as ideas (cf. *Critique of Pure Reason*, p. 385), the three magnitudes realized thus far quit the series and the connection in which they had stood up to now and in which they had been realized. They immediately adopt the sequence and systematic connection which the three ideas in the process of entering the practical field exhibited on p. 385 of the *Critique of Pure Reason*. This procedure, however, is possible because the two postulates are not ideas. At their base lies the higher problem of freedom, which is beyond critical idealism. We may, therefore, reduce the insight won in the tedious investigation thus far to a double expression based on one fact: 1) The problem of freedom as it presents itself in its profoundest formulation on the factual basis of the moral law is insoluble with the means at the command of critical idealism, or 2) the postulates of the existence of a highest moral rational being and the infinite continuation of person (immortality) realized as necessary within us by the practical use of reason based on the fact of the moral law within us, do not lie in the realm of critical idealism and, therefore, do not coincide with the ideas of a highest being and the timelessness of our intelligible existence, which critical idealism has demonstrated as problematic and religiously oriented.

Thus, we can note the curious fact that it is only on the basis of critical idealism that the ideas of God, freedom, and immortality have been established as possible without science being able to claim otherwise in the interest of truth, but that these ideas immediately undergo a transformation as soon as this possibility has been raised into a practically recognized reality by virtue of the experience of the moral law. The transformation is of such a nature that the scientific demonstration of its possibility can no longer be accomplished with the means at the command of critical idealism. The hope of realizing these problematic ideas through the fact of the moral law must, therefore, be given up according to the investigation of the sections of the *Critique of Pure Reason* and the *Critique of Practical Reason* in which the philosophy of religion is dealt with. The assertion on p. 591 of the *Critique of Pure Reason* has not materialized: "In what follows it will become evident, however, that respecting its practical use, reason has the right to assume something it is not authorized by any manner or means to presuppose without sufficient proof in the field of mere speculation."

This means nothing else but that the scheme of a philosophy of religion in the transcendental dialectic which was meant to prepare the way for the philosophy of religion of critical idealism was not thoroughly worked out. Up to now we have considered two attempts in detail which, in temporal sequence, were meant to carry out this scheme, and we found that the first of the two, the sketch of a philosophy of religion, does not yet know the scheme of the philosophy of religion in the transcendental dialectic, while the second one, the *Critique of Practical Reason*, knows it, to be sure, but is not able to execute it logically. Both times the question of in how far the completion of the scheme of the transcendental dialectic has succeeded concerns fixing the position which the idea of freedom during the realization of the ideas occupies vis-à-vis the two other ideas. Let us compare the two attempts briefly.

We have shown that on pp. 608 and 609 of the *Critique of Pure Reason* the practical idea of freedom is understood as if it were not a problem of reason in its practical interest, but merely a question of two problems: Is there a God; and is there a future life? By means of our investigation of the concepts of freedom which come into play in Kant's thinking in general, we have shown that no progress at all was made with the practical freedom thus understood, and that the existence of God and immortality of soul may not be deduced from the presupposed possibility of a moral world (p. 612). Both demands are made on the assumption, recognized as necessary, of the proportionality of virtue and happiness, which is to the same degree implied in the theoretical as in the practical use of reason. "Therefore I say that just as moral principles according to reason in its practical use are necessary, it is just as necessary, according to reason in its theoretical use, to assume that everyone has cause for expecting happiness to the same extent to which he makes himself worthy of it by his behavior; and that, therefore, the system of morality is inseparably connected with that of happiness, but only in the idea of pure reason" (p. 613). Now follows the realization of the two remaining ideas and, to be sure, in the reverse order from that in practical reason: first the idea of God; then the idea of immortality (p. 614). If we take proper note of the motivation, we find that both are based merely on the principle of happiness and the immortality of soul does not result from the demands for infinite moral perfection. Kant is so far removed from this thought that he prefers to presuppose a meritorious moral behavior in this world upon which the future world will follow. "Since of necessity we must, by virtue of reason, think ourselves as belonging to a moral and intelligible world—although the senses give us nothing but a world of appearances—we shall have to assume the moral and intelligible world as the result of our behavior in the sensuous world, but lying in the future, because the sensuous world does not offer us any immediate approach. Thus, God and a future life are two presuppositions not to be separated from the obligation which pure reason, according to its own principles, exacts" (p. 614).

We now also have the confirmation of the assertion made and demonstrated earlier that the realization of the postulates in practical reason may take place in a different sequence and without the distribution according to which the postulate of the existence of God builds upon the postulate of happiness and immortality on that of holiness as the second constituent of the highest good. For, with the one the other is always given, because both reflect (though in different ways) the requirements of the rational being to be placed in a world where the moral law is the principle of events. This difference in the arrangement in the sketch of a philosophy of religion and the *Critique of Practical Reason* lies in the fact that in the former the realized magnitudes are not yet ideas, and in the latter they are no longer ideas. The escalation which drives the realized magnitudes beyond the concept of ideas in the *Critique of Practical Reason* took place by a deepening of the ethical content.

Freedom is also realized as an idea in the *Critique of Practical Reason* as compared with the sketch of a philosophy of religion. What has been brushed aside in the *Critique of Pure Reason* almost as if it were just a preliminary remark (pp. 608 and 609: "Now, then, we should first take note of the fact that for the time being . . .") is again treated in the critical light of the analysis of pure practical reason (pp. 108 to 129 of the *Critique of Practical Reason*) in a discussion where every line once more reveals the mighty struggle of the spirit with the problem. What a difference between the manner in which the problem concerning transcendental freedom is shoved aside as of no concern on p. 608, where it is a question of the practical use of reason, and the confession with which Kant announces his victory in the *Critique of Practical Reason*. He says, on p. 124 of the *Critique of Practical Reason:* "Of such great importance is the separation of time as well as of space from the existence of things-in-themselves as I have accomplished it in the critique of pure speculative reason. However, the solution of the difficulty here expounded, some might say, is weighed down very heavily and is hardly susceptible to a clear exposition. Nevertheless, is every other attempt at solution which has been made and may yet be undertaken easier or more comprehensible . . .?" The resignation manifested in these words has something profoundly stirring about it if one has, by studying the text, experienced vitally with Kant the entire treatment of the problem of freedom in the *Critique of Practical Reason.*

Let us summarize briefly the result offered us by the investigation of the *Critique of Practical Reason* for an insight into Kant's philosophy of religion.

To be sure, the *Critique of Practical Reason* contains Kant's presentation, which is to represent the philosophy of religion of critical idealism. However, this is not the outline of a consistent thought structure of his philosophy of religion, because it carries out the scheme of a philosophy of religion in transcendental dialectics—which rests upon the unity of pure reason in theoretical and practical use—only half of the way, and then reproduces the original plan of the *Critique of Practical Reason* which, in essence, and by virtue of the dynamism residing in the moral law, as it is grasped more fully right along, transcends the bounds of critical idealism. The scheme of a philosophy of religion in transcendental dialectics was never realized in full by Kant. It would have led him into a philosophy of religion of "pure reason in practical use," while the *Critique of Practical Reason* has already offered us the philosophy of religion of "practical reason."

Thus, at the conclusion of our scrutiny of the *Critique of Practical Reason,* we find Kant's philosophy of religion in the process of moving steadily and necessarily toward a field which no longer lies within the bounds of critical idealism. This movement is most pronounced in the emergence of the higher problem of freedom in the *Critique of Practical Reason.* And, thus, we proceed to that piece of writing which we have already utilized in the treatment of our problem of freedom.

Religion Within the Limits of Reason Alone

◨ The first part of the essay *Concerning Radical Evil in Human Nature* is an exposition of the higher problem of freedom. In the first essay of *Religion Within the Limits of Reason Alone,* the problem of freedom is also basic. A certain dependence on the biblical and dogmatic use of language which obscures the clarity of exposition in this first piece is noticeable. If we survey the work as a whole, a new difficulty in the way of clarity in the development of thought raises its head—lying in the conception of this work and resting mainly on the independent nature of the first essay as compared with the others. Both difficulties together have as consequence that one does not immediately see clearly how the inner development of thought in *Religion Within the Limits* proceeds in complete analogy to that of the *Critique of Practical Reason,* but only that it presents itself as a repetition of the latter on the basis of the more profoundly grasped problem of freedom, whereby similarities and deviations appear almost at once. The

· 293 ·

questions as to the relationship of the *Critique of Practical Reason* and *Religion Within the Limits* is almost insoluble, should one presuppose the former in evaluating the latter.

We shall start with a comprehensive review of the first essay. Earlier we tried to show that the problem of freedom in its higher version lies at the basis. In view of the moral evaluation of human actions, how can we think of a possibility of one natural state of our disposition passing over to another one in so far as this is absolutely required for the maintenance of our freedom to act? The impossibility of a solution is further increased by Kant's version of an absolute contradiction between good and evil in so far as the occurrence of the good or evil nature of the disposition —in respect to necessity and point of time—lies as an intelligible act beyond human understanding, and we can think of a change in the moral sense only as a constant progress. The task of the first section consists in the presentation of the entire profundity of the problem as is already indicated in the title, "Concerning the Indwelling of the Evil Principle Beside the Good One."

In the interest of moral stamina, Kant offers a summary solution to the problem by asserting that the intelligence of God comprehends moral development—thought of as infinite—into a unitary act according to which "change" may be considered "as revolution" in the moral judgment of God. At this point both difficulties work together, that is, the one founded in the conception of the work itself, as well as the one brought about by reliance on the religious, biblical, and dogmatic views. The result is that the further pursuit of this thought is not permitted to come clearly to the light of day. To say it plainly, Kant overlooks the lack of justification for introducing the concept of God at this point. The problem of the possibility of the fall and resurrection exists for the moral self-evaluation of man, not for the imagined evaluation of God, whose existence must first be proven to rest upon the practical demand of the moral law. Thus, we are dealing here with an accompanying realization of the idea of God as we had already occasion to note when Kant established the postulate of immortality in the *Critique of Practical Reason.* In general, it may be said that the last-mentioned passage has great affinity with the one at hand and rests upon the same procedure.

It may still be fresh in our memory how establishing the existence of God in the *Critique of Practical Reason* went hand in hand with the practical assumption of immortality and how, in the postulate of the existence of God as guarantor of the intelligible moral world, immortality was established right along with it, in so far as it is thought of as participation in that world. The same is the case with *Religion Within the Limits of Reason Alone,* when the first difficulty is dissolved. It is brought about in that we think of the total moral evaluation of our existence as taking place in the absolute intelligence of the highest moral being. In this way, the existence of this being is practically demonstrated as real. At the same time, however, our supersensuous existence is established right along with this as the imagined continuation of our earthly existence in so far as we are meant to receive the reward for our conduct in the judgment of the highest moral being. This section of *Religion Within the Limits of Reason Alone* also arrives at the practical assumption of the continuation of our existence; but this result is radically different from the practical assumption of immortality in the *Critique of Practical Reason*. The two trains of thought have absolutely nothing in common and move in different directions at every point. In the *Critique of Practical Reason* immortality is postulated in the interest of the infinite moral development. In *Religion Within the Limits of Reason Alone,* this development is thought of as finished with life on earth, and positing a future life which takes no interest whatever in moral development offers difficulties, particularly because of the fact that it prolongs the moral contradictions into eternity and thus renders an intelligible moral world impossible—the very thing for which the *Critique of Practical Reason* established immortality as a postulate! Now we become aware that the identification of the intelligible substratum of the rational being and the moral personality is incompatible with maintaining the moral evaluation of our existence on earth and that it can be brought in harmony with it only if and when we can justify assuming the most thoroughgoing dualism. The latter assumption, however, contradicts the requirement of the realization of the highest good thought of as a moral, intelligible world. Thus also the moral law becomes illusory and the whole investigation returns to nothingness.

In analyzing the first section in *Religion Within the Limits of Reason Alone* one becomes aware of all these difficulties without being able to fathom their scope fully; the dogmatic use of language covers up the complete otherness which lies in the expressions "immortality" and "a future life" concerning their relationship to the infinite moral development required by the moral law.

That advancing and developing the thought of the continuation of our existence exhibits a deep cleavage between the sketch of a philosophy of religion and the trend of thought of the *Critique of Practical Reason,* has already been shown. Now we have found that regarding this problem *Religion Within the Limits of Reason Alone* is closer to the *Critique of Pure Reason* and the *Critique of Practical Reason* in that both speak of a future life and do not motivate this idea with the necessary assumption of an infinite moral development of our personality. This assumption constitutes the basis for establishing the postulate of immortality in the *Critique of Practical Reason* which is apparently realized in the identification of the moral person with the intelligible substratum of the rational being on the basis of critical idealism. The comprehensive moral evaluation of our existence on earth is of no interest in this reflection, especially on account of the continuity of the moral development which brings our earthly existence together with intelligible existence in the concept of the postulate of immortality. Intelligible existence is unhesitatingly equated with existence in the moral world by the identification of the latter with the intelligible world. Contrary to this in the sketch of a philosophy of religion and in *Religion Within the Limits of Reason Alone* there reposes, on the threshold between this world and the next, a moral judgment which strikes the balance of our behavior in the sensuous world. The sketch of a philosophy of religion expresses it in this manner on p. 614: " . . . we have to look at the moral world as a consequence of our behavior in the sensuous world." On the same page, however, the identification of the moral world with the intelligible one wants to be kept. But in doing so, the interpretation of the future world as a consequence of our moral behavior in the world of sense has become illusory because the presupposed moral judgment of our behavior on earth has to maintain the possibility of a double ending—in which case future existence cannot be equated with life in the moral world. Thus, the sketch of a philosophy of religion occupies a position midway between the *Critique of Practical Reason* and *Religion Within the Limits of Reason Alone*. With the latter it shares the concept of a "future life" and the relationship between the continuation of our existence and the moral evaluation of our behavior on earth. With the former it shares the identification of the moral world with the intelligible one, a difficulty which makes itself noticeable in the use of the indefinite articles when the concept of the intelligible world is introduced. Thus, the sketch of a philosophy of religion encompasses a contradiction regarding the continuation of our existence relative to the moral evaluation of our earthly life, a contradiction which the deeper probing of the problem in the *Critique of Practical Reason* and *Religion Within the Limits of Reason Alone* brings right out into the open. The two reflections are joined together in the sketch of a philosophy of religion because the practical assumption of a highest good, of a moral world ruler, and of the highest derived good precede the moral world, the positing of a future life. At the same time, it has been established that the concept of God as a moral lawgiver and judge was introduced into the investigation prior to the assumption of a future existence, and, thus, the personality is being developed which can evaluate its existence in a future moral world as the consequence of its behavior in this sensuous world. It is characteristic that in the reflection which derives a future existence from a moral pronouncement of God as judge of the moral behavior in this world and which arrives at the concept of God as moral creator of the world and lawgiver, there must precede the introduction of a demand for the infinite continuation of our existence. In the *Critique of Practical Reason*, where the moral judgment concerning our terrestrial existence has no connection whatever with the postulate of immortality, the postulate of immortality is consistently disposed of prior to the postulate of the existence of God as a moral creator of the world and lawgiver. *Religion Within the Limits of Reason Alone* is in a similar position; a future existence is implied in assuming a moral judgment of our existence by God's intelligence. The relocation of moral judgment into God's infinite intelligence is the only possibility of solving the difficulty, which consists in the fact "that the distance between the good we ought to do and the bad with which we start is infinite and, in so far as the act is concerned (that is, the commensurability of a way of life with the holiness of the law), is not attainable at any time."

Now, with the fact of the moral law, first of all my own personality is given as the subject of moral evaluation. If the moral evaluation is to be transferred into God's infinite intelligence because of the difficulties which result from defining good and evil as absolutely contradictory concepts, then it is absolutely necessary that in a preliminary discussion the concept of God as a moral lawgiver and moral judge be demonstrated as a practically necessary assumption. This, however, is not the case in the section of *Religion Within the Limits of Reason Alone* under consideration. The concept of God as moral creator of the world, lawgiver and judge is, to be sure, presupposed in so far as the entire presentation is made to depend upon Christian dogmatic thoughts and phrases. The real act of establishing this concept by moral deliberation does not occur until p. 101 ff., as we have shown at the beginning of this section. The connection between the concept of God and the moral law also met with in this section of *Religion Within the Limits of Reason Alone* is not to be supported by Kant's earlier writings, since the deliberation is entirely different in the *Critique of Practical Reason,* and the moral concept of God is arrived at only after the postulate of immortality. Thus, the foundation is lacking for solving the difficulties on p. 68 ff. By leaning on the dogmatic statements of Christianity, an apparent foundation is invented and the main moral difficulty of the Kantian philosophy of religion, that is, of the connection of the moral law with the concept of God, is apparently overcome. The basic intention of Kant's "philosophic doctrine of religion," to derive all statements made on the basis of the moral law and the practical requirements resulting therefrom, has been given up as a matter of fact.

These difficulties, which have been solved only by an unintentional deception, all go back to the one thought of the inappropriateness of the duration of our existence as a postulate for infinite moral development. They caught our attention by virtue of the fact that in the place of man in general, individual man as a subject entered Kant's thinking. At the moment when general considerations come to the fore again and man is introduced as the subject of investigation, especially on account of his standing in a societal relation with mankind, the difficulties disappear and the infinity of moral development is in consonance with the unimaginable duration of mankind in general. The investigation at the beginning of the third section of the philosophical doctrine of religion is on level ground. The phrasing of this title, "Concerning the Victory of the Good Principle over Evil," is meant to express the progress of thinking in this third section vis-à-vis the second section ("The Struggle of the Good Principle with Evil"). The question is now merely whether thought has progressed organically. If we keep in mind that in the second section it is a matter of man considered as an individual, and that man in general (in so far as he comprehends within himself the societal bond with mankind) is the subject under consideration and dominating the presentation in the third; and if, furthermore, one is aware of how little the third section refers back to the second one, one will rather incline toward the assumption that in both sections basically the same problem is treated under different presuppositions about the subject. The resolution of this problem depends on the investigation of the reflections in this third section.

Concerning our comparison, we have seen that the sketch of a philosophy of religion is much closer to the discussions of *Religion Within the Limits of Reason Alone* than the *Critique of Practical Reason*, because the former implies the thought of developing and expanding a moral community in its concept of the highest good, while it shares with the latter the formulation of the concept of happiness.

Thus, the sketch of a philosophy of religion occupies, in regard to all points adduced above whose consequences extend to every imaginable point of comparison, a transitional place between the *Critique of Practical Reason* and *Religion Within the Limits of Reason Alone*. This is particularly plain in the formulation of the concept of the kingdom of God in its relation to the development of the moral community of mankind and the concept of God derived from it. The sketch is aligned with the thought of the *Critique of Practical Reason* because in both, the practical moral investigation point, by formulating the concept of happiness beyond the boundaries of the world in which man is understood as a moral person and his action in general is placed in opposition to what is happening in the world. In that the endpoint of the moral development is relocated in the beyond, the value of the moral appraisal of the this-worldly moral development is weakened. This is shown in that neither the *Critique of Practical Reason* nor the *Critique of Pure Reason* occupies the standpoint at the end of their discussions from which the necessity, or, perhaps only possibility (cf. the *Critique of Practical Reason*), may be derived of taking up the ethical evaluation of the moral and societal institutions of mankind in regard to the final moral purpose which is envisaged as the highest good. *Religion Within the Limits of Reason Alone*, however, is forced, in spite of the difficulties facing it, to bring the ideal magnitudes into relationship with their empirical historical presentation and to bring the religion of reason into union with the pronouncements of historical religion. Although the latter is done at the expense of the perspicuity and independence of the reflections, incorporating this intention into the scheme of the presentation is quite characteristic. It is in line with the possibility of appreciating the political, civil community as a precondition for the ethical community. Now we have seen how, in the *Critique of Practical Reason,* when we were going beyond the present world (taking our stand on the fact of the moral law and looking toward the endpoint of ethical development), we were led to the absolute impossibility of appreciating human conditions ethically as soon as we tried to reverse the reasoning. In *Religion Within the Limits of Reason Alone* we meet the case that the emphasis in the presentation lies particularly on the possibility of bringing historical phenomena into relationship with the ideal magnitudes of moral deliberations. The question now is whether this presentation may, with attaining the final moral purpose in view, go consistently beyond the limits of the given world, as concerns the moral person in his individuality or in his wholeness.

This is not the case for the concept of the kingdom of God as a moral end which was reached under the general mode of reflection, as is already evident from the subtitle of the third section: "Concerning the Founding of a Kingdom of God on Earth." However, the second section, which deals with the individual moral person, goes beyond these limits in that it posits a future existence in which, as we are about to enter it, a divine judgment points to happiness or damnation. We have already shown above that the thus-understood supersensuous existence presents itself as a "future life," not as "immortality of soul," because it has no connection with the ethical development of personality regarding infinite perfectibility. This supersensuous existence has no moral interest. The above reflection still requires proof that the assertion of such a "future existence" cannot be established at all on the fact of the moral law, taking into consideration the presuppositionlessness demanded by the moral investigation.

The transfer of the final moral judgment into the intelligence of God—in so far as a future existence is implied in it—was executed in the second section only under the presupposition that the practical reality of the concept of God may be assumed as given and the connection of the same with the moral law as already accomplished. However, this was not actually the case, and the recognition that the moral concept of God is not actually reached until well along in the third section remained under cover by virtue of the confusion of the presentation with the religious-dogmatic pronouncements of historical Christianity. Thus, the motivation of the future existence introduced hypothetically into the second section crumbles of its own weight by recognizing the deceptive appearance of its basic presuppositions.

We now proceed to summarize briefly the ideas by which a place may be assigned to *Religion Within the Limits of Reason Alone* in the entire development of Kant's philosophy of religion. If one leaves the concealing cover out of account for the moment, we find that *Religion Within the Limits of Reason Alone* seizes upon three ideas as problems, and deals with them. In spite of the identical expression, we are not operating on the ground of critical idealism. For the ideas which are being discussed in *Religion Within the Limits of Reason Alone* have reference to the community of ethical beings and stand in connection with the clearly recognized main problem of freedom which is discussed in the first section. On this are then established the ideas of a perfected ethical personality, of a perfected moral community and the highest moral personality, that is, the moral lawgiver. Now, the first and second ideas form one whole because they can be brought to perfection only in a mutual relationship. The moral personality arises and becomes reality only in the ethical community. The question as to the possibility of the perfection of the ethical personality, however, coincides with the problem of freedom on the higher level of the problem. Thus, we have only two ideas in *Religion Within the Limits of Reason Alone*—the higher idea of freedom and the idea of God. The idea of immortality has dropped out because its ethical interest comes to the fore in the higher formulation of the problem of freedom. But also the idea of God in *Religion Within the Limits of Reason Alone* is only a subsidiary concept called in to make the "ethically common being" in whom the ethical personality is to perfect itself, comprehensible. In reality, *Religion Within the Limits of Reason Alone* knows only one idea, the idea of freedom in its higher formulation. The whole of Kant's philosophy of religion, complete in this form, oriented toward one question, is: How is the ethical personality of man as a moral creature regarding his essence and perfectibility possible in this world? In that *Religion Within the Limits of Reason Alone* is being guided by this questioning into stressing the ethical community, a modern trend wafts through these thoughts in spite of the dogmatic and churchy phraseology, a trend which is invigorating because of the great profundity of the moral consciousness which here struggles into form. The vitality of ethical thought has pushed thinking out of the narrow track in which critical idealism had coerced the Kantian philosophy of religion. Simultaneously, with the freedom of mobility, it garners in the full wealth of thought which it exhibited already in its undeveloped form before it was put in a consistent relationship to critical idealism. *Religion Within the Limits of Reason Alone* refers back to the sketch of a philosophy of religion, while it shows almost no contact with the *Critique of Practical Reason*. The *Critique of Practical Reason* represents a stage in the development of Kant's philosophy of religion. It is, as it were, a narrow pass through which Kant's mental army had to go on its march from the area of precritical rudimentary development to the area of complete maturity of thought. Thus, *Religion Within the Limits of Reason Alone* represents the highest perfection of Kant's philosophy of religion. Its thoughts are modern. In this treatise Kant stands far above his time in his thinking, if not in the language he used. This is shown also in that he is able to fuse the contradictory trends of the religious thinking of his time, rationalism and pietism, into a higher unity, as if they already belonged to the past, and he does so by fighting them in their one-sidedness from his higher position. If we have comprehended this innermost core of the thinking in *Religion Within the Limits of Reason Alone* in its entire depth, we must doubly bemoan the fact that Kant, forced by unfavorable circumstances, cloaked his up-to-date thoughts in the stiff dogmatic form of the church language of his day, perhaps more than was called for by his pedagogic wisdom; and thus, the depth of his thought became veiled almost to the present day, making it possible to look upon his profoundest work in the philosophy of religion as a retreat from the *Critique of Practical Reason* and, thus, to leave it out of account in the treatment of his philosophy of religion.

The *Critique of Judgment*

It is hardly necessary after what has been said, and without concern over the chronology of Kant's writing, to justify our having treated *Religion Within the Limits of Reason Alone* prior to the *Critique of Judgment*. The detailed investigation of the solution to the problem of freedom led us to pursue further the development of a thought in *Religion Within the Limits of Reason Alone* left incomplete in the *Critique of Practical Reason*. Thus, also, it became necessary to compare the further development in thinking in both works which an interpolated treatment of other works would have made more difficult. The points of comparison of the *Critique of Judgment* concerning its thought on the philosophy of religion lie, to a large part, more toward the sketch of a philosophy of religion. The *Critique of Judgment* brings to a conclusion the thoughts of the series of ideas that stood foremost in the sketch of a philosophy of religion in that it furnishes a capstone to the introduction of the concept of "the final end of creation."

Thus, there also occur odd agreements with the thoughts in the sketch of a philosophy of religion in the treatment of the individual problems, while the *Critique of Practical Reason* moves closer to being included in the comparison not until the end of the *Critique of Judgment*, because of the unjustified introduction of the immortality concept and, at the same time, shifting the entire thinking away from its original aim.

We shall start with an investigation of the problem of freedom. The *Critique of Judgment* treats the problem as solved. It no longer occupies itself with it but goes back to earlier formulations in those passages where it touches upon the problem. In this way the dependence on the sketch of a philosophy of religion becomes more pronounced than in the *Critique of Practical Reason*. The main passage which is in question here may be found on p. 370 of the *Critique of Judgment:* "The idea of freedom is a fact whose reality, as a special kind of causality (whose concept, theoretically considered, would be an exaggeration), may be demonstrated in the practical laws of pure reason and, in accordance with these, in real actions, hence in experience. It is the only one among all ideas of pure reason whose object is a fact and which must also be reckoned among the *scibilia*."

Here is the idea which we can pursue into the details of terminology, on the basis of which in the *Critique of Pure Reason* (pp. 608 and 609) practical freedom was disposed of before the practical attainment of the two religiously oriented ideas. Again, the *Critique of Judgment* picks up once more the scheme of a philosophy of religion in transcendental dialectics and incorporates an exposition of it.

In this side-by-side arrangement of ideas which before had determined the entire presentation of a philosophy of religion, and in the offhand manner in which they are inserted into the *Critique of Judgment* in a subordinate place, is demonstrated that the *Critique of Judgment* occupies a far more developed position and carries fragments of a past exposition with it just as a river carries debris with it. The idea which touches upon the scheme of a philosophy of religion in transcendental dialectics stands in connection with the explanation in the *Critique of Pure Reason* (p. 591) before the play of transcendental hypotheses begins: "It will be shown in what follows that regarding its practical use, reason has the right to assume something which it would in no wise be authorized to presuppose without sufficient proofs in the field of mere speculation."

The basic idea is that what will later legitimize itself practically as "idea" in the moral conception of existence has already turned out to be a hypothesis on attempting to grasp scientifically the totality of the world and as such was in equilibrium, as is seen in the fencing match on pp. 591 to 595 of the *Critique of Pure Reason*. Adding a practical moral interest becomes decisive. It procures the right of domicile in the practical field to the ideas that were born in the speculative field, but were not domiciled there. "An advantage appears on the side of one who maintains something as a practically necessary presupposition (*melior est conditio possidentis*)." The *Critique of Practical Reason* had abandoned this thought entirely; along with the practical need for postulates it maintained their practical assumption without going for support to the preparatory work of unity-seeking theoretical reason. This is especially clear when the concept of God is arrived at whereby no attention is paid to the teleological sketches of theoretical reason in the *Critique of Practical Reason.* The individual magnitudes are arranged in series and the reader is supposed to conceptualize for himself how what follows is based on what precedes it. The schematism of the projected reflection and the rather odd poverty of "ideas" as compared with those of the *Critique · of Pure Reason* thus become understandable. The *Critique of Judgment* again guides us into the old tracks. Practical reason procures reality for the ideas which begin to appear over the horizon in the field of theoretical reflection. This thought is developed concerning the concept of God.

Let us look back over the road travelled thus far. We started with the basic problem lying at the root of the projected work: why progress in thinking, which lies at the base of the entire planning of the work, comes so little to the fore in the presentation of esthetic judgment. It is due to the fact that the main question which constitutes the peculiarity of synthetic judgments and the *a priori* principles of the ability to judge, as compared with all other means of knowledge, is not put at the beginning of the investigation. All difficulties which we have traced relative to this assertion were reduced to this circumstance. They consisted mainly in the irregularly occurring and vague coinage of new concepts whereby we were compelled to determine more closely the basic subject of the statements after we had started with the investigation of the use of the concept of the supersensuous in relation to the intelligible, unconditioned, and infinite, as well as its position and connection with the world of experience. While we were presenting the matter, we implied that the main question—that is, in how far the esthetic comprehension of the world is a connecting link between appraising it by means of understanding and reasoning morally—was neither taken note of nor solved in the plan of the *Critique of Esthetic Judgment*. It is a critique of taste aimed at arriving at and presenting the concepts of the beautiful and sublime without reference to the generality of esthetic judgment of the entire world of appearance; and, therefore, it is also incapable, in principle, of showing the connection with the other faculties of knowledge regarding which, when investigated, no barriers were drawn as to the field in question. And yet, achieving this connection together with insight into its necessary nature lies in the consistency of Kant's thinking, taking the whole field of esthetic judgment into consideration. This is already evident in the fact that Kant—although without native artistic ability and without ever having come in closer contact with the performing arts—was driven, almost against his own will and merely through the logic of his own thinking, into the comprehensive investigation of the *Critique of Esthetic Judgment*. So mighty, however, was the logic of his thinking that Kant (although still caught up in the narrowing down of the esthetic investigation as if it had reference only to the beautiful and sublime) breaks down the barriers which still cling to the plan of the *Critique of Esthetic Judgment* in the conclusions he reached. Moreover, he pointed out a new path for esthetic investigations whose course, however, is visible only for a short distance. But the leg no longer has the ability to start on a new journey.

In these reflections, the task of the second part of our present investigation is delineated. It is a matter of highlighting and tying together the passages where Kant's investigation points beyond the self-imposed limits (the presentation of the beautiful and the sublime) and establishes reference to the essence of the esthetic grasp of the world in general, whereby the nature of the synthesis accomplished by the esthetic judgment and the peculiarity of the basic *a priori* principles appear. At the same time is won the knowledge of the necessity and solubility of the difficulties just alluded to. In finding the reasons for the last of the difficulties which concern the fixation of the subject implied in the esthetic judgment, we grasp the nature of the fact and the innermost essence of the link which the esthetic judgment forges between our grasp of the world according to the understanding and according to moral reason as well.

If . . . an opposition of nature and art really misses the point, a differentiation of the two from another consideration (if Kant seems to have achieved the identification of the products of nature and of art in esthetic appraisal) has been rendered possible by virtue of the fact that in an esthetic evaluation nature and art are not to be differentiated in so far as nature ceases in the traditional concept to be nature if evaluated according to formal and logical concepts of expediency and is evaluated in analogy to the products of a reasonable being. In this case a differentiation between natural events and human actions becomes impossible in that it is a matter of indifference for the evaluating subject whether the expediency grasped in the esthetic appraisal of an object logically preceded the object as a conceptual pattern or not. The nature of the esthetic judgment is in no wise affected by such knowledge; it still remains only subjective with a claim to objective validity. Thus, it is really impossible for Kant to divide nature and art, be it by juxtaposition or by parallelism. In the former case, it is impossible to point to a principle which legitimizes itself on the basis of critical idealism by which a realm of art could separate out from the general field of phenomena. In the latter case it is impossible to point to a principle by which nature could be distinguished from art in an esthetic appraisal. At one time art is already included in the concept of nature in so far as it forms a constituent of the world of appearance; the next time nature is thought of in the concept of art as an object of esthetic judgment. This is patent in the final classification of the general introduction (p. 38) : Nature is cited as an object of the understanding which relates to the *a priori* principle of regularity. Here nature comprises the world of appearances which actually is first created by the intuitive understanding. Thus, every type of art is also included in nature. The power of judgment, with its *a priori* principle of expediency, has reference to art according to the same classification. This classification is only justified when we understand by art the totality of all appearances to which *a priori* principles of expediency may be applied for the purpose of evaluating them. Since this applies, however, to the entire world of appearances, if one brings esthetic evaluation to bear equally upon pleasure and displeasure, the entire world of appearances is, again, included in art so that in both sides of the classification each time the same is included under a different name. Therefore, on the basis of

Kant's investigation, nature and art are completely coincident. They both designate the world of appearances as a whole, be it as a creation of our understanding, be it as an object of our judgment. The tripartite division respecting the faculty of knowledge thus arrived at is possible only by virtue of the fact that the same concept has been included twice under different names, but with the same content, for two faculties of knowledge.

By the same token, it may be shown that the field of art embraces at the same time the field of freedom, because the concept of freedom is a presupposition for the delineation of the field of art in so far as the latter, being a spontaneous happening, does not take into consideration the mechanism of nature when the possibility of appraising expediency is involved. Thus, art is already an appraisal of what is happening as taking place spontaneously. This same impossibility of making a separation in principle appears when one tests the classification in line with the *a priori* principles in that every principle of expediency, no matter what, must, if thought through all the way, lead of necessity to the idea of a final purpose to which it is oriented. This is a thought which Kant himself later incorporated as a principle in his presentation in that he has the teleological judgment attain to perfection only in moral theology. In this manner, the very same object is again included in this tripartite division under the field of freedom, as in the two first-mentioned ones. It is the world of appearances which is presented to view here in analogy to moral activity in so far as the principle of its happening was generally understood from the point of view of art.

What about the *a priori* validity of the concept of expediency in regard to an "objective" purposive evaluation? ...

Let us take up the principal passage on p. 32 where Kant follows through with the bifurcation of judgment: "We can imagine expediency in an object given in experience for some objective reason, as agreement of the form of an object with the conceptual possibility of the thing. The concept precedes the object and contains the reason for its form."

If we consider this teleological power of judgment which judges "logically according to concepts" in all seriousness, the question will be suggested strongly to us, from where did the power of judgment get these concepts according to which it judges the real world? Whereon does its validity rest since it lays claim to general validity? If Kant had followed through with the critique of teleological judgment corresponding to this classification, he would have necessarily had to give up his conception of the *a priori* in general, in that he would have been able to base the "concepts of things which precede them and imply their form" either only on generalized experience or on an *a priori* form in Plato's sense. In doing so he would have furnished a critique of the expediency of things instead of the *Critique of Teleological Judgment*, just as he introduced a critique of taste in place of the *Critique of Esthetic Judgment*.

Now, the employment of the expression "concept" as basic to the judgment of expediency shows that Kant here operates with the terminology of ancient thought instead of with the *Critique of Pure Reason*. The ancient concept of art in sole reference to the beautiful also forces the teleological judgment of the world in the present classification (so that some relationship with the ancient concept can be established) into the ancient garb of expediency which is supported by the concept of expediency preceding the evaluation of objects. With this, Kant's formulation of the *a priori* is eliminated automatically.

Now, this unhappy description of teleological judgment on p. 32 came about only respecting the connection with the critique of taste. Just as the spell is broken, so also the Kantian interpretation of expediency throws off its ancient garb. It becomes again what it was on p. 16 ff. and seeks its foundation not upon "concepts" but on "principles." The designation of expediency as a principle becomes dominant now, and the term concept is used with the same meaning as the term principle. Specific examples may be found on p. 18. Expediency is that principle which has reference to the connection of objects themselves; hence it is not based on the expedient "concepts of these objects in so far as they precede the appraisal of them." In this rudimentary form expediency as a principle of judgment coincides with unity as a principle of grasping events in general. To that extent, expediency itself is an *a priori* principle of judgment. It is to these general ideas, not the classification on p. 32, that the *Critique of Teleological Judgment* refers, as it is developed on p. 238 ff. The views which were to make possible the classification on p. 32 disappeared without a trace. They were introduced in order to relate superficially esthetic and teleological judgment by means of the concept of expedience, which was impossible from the start in the ancient understanding of art. The investigation, henceforth, moves along the course originally plotted on p. 16 ff. This wonderful structure is thus reared which, starting with the principle of uniformity in respect to an expedient evaluation of the world, leads to the question as to the final purpose and permits teleology to fulfill itself only in an ethico-theology.

ᶦ The entire *Critique of Teleological Judgment* takes its rise on Kant's original idea on p. 16 ff., and leaving out of account its formulation on p. 32 becomes intelligent right from the start as having been founded on necessity from the following observation. The reader may remember how we proved earlier that the context in which Kant's original ideas on p. 16 ff. moved has a one-sided reference to "nature" without our being able to discover a principle to distinguish art from nature. However, on p. 32 ff., the statements are made solely with a view to art, in that it is impossible to distinguish nature from art, provided one rejects the popular distinction. Thus, we have won the original concept of purpose concerning nature as nature (p. 16 ff.) and the difficulties in the concept of purpose do not arise before we meet the statement (on p. 32 ff.) that art really includes nature in itself. At the moment when nature as nature again dominates the reflection (p. 236 of the *Critique of Teleological Judgment*), the original concept of purpose likewise comes into its own and all difficulties disappear.

Thus, the *Critique of Judgment* is arranged on the broad basis of nature as nature as is shown first in the concept of expediency. Only the endeavor to fit a critique of taste into this frame as a critique of esthetic judgment resulted in the concepts in question becoming inadvertently differently oriented. This came to the fore clearly in the classification on p. 32, and may be demonstrated mainly with respect to the concept of expediency.

We have just demonstrated the consequences of this subterfuge for the validity of the "*a priori* principle" of the judgment in question and have shown how the critique of taste loses its claim to *a priori* principles by virtue of the transformation of the concept of purpose, while the *Critique of Teleological Judgment,* going back to the original formulation of that concept, is able to deduce especially from this very fact the right to carry along *a priori* principles in the judgment. With this we are forced to make a second conclusion. It has reference to the main question with respect to which the investigations thus far derive any value at all. "Does the *Critique of Judgment* perform the task which it undertakes to perform, that is, to demonstrate the connection between understanding and reason by virtue of the power of judgment?"

The question has, in principle, already been decided: The *Critique of Judgment* does not undertake a solution because it cannot by itself establish the connection between esthetic and teleological judgment, but unites both only superficially in the concept of expediency. Naturally, if one looks more closely into the formulation of the concept of expediency, the poorly concealed discrepancy reveals itself especially in the classification which Kant offers. Thus, the *Critique of Judgment* joins understanding and reason in that it carries the distinction into the power of judging itself.

This conclusion may be reached even in a purely formal way if we recall the statements made thus far concerning the significance of the feeling of pleasure and displeasure.

On the one hand, in the main passages—where it is a matter of the connection made in judgment between understanding and reason—the feeling of pleasure and displeasure respecting them is, in general, brought in relation to the power of judgment. From the start, the preparatory step taken to accomplish the connection on p. 16 is characteristic of the role which here falls to the feeling of pleasure. It is stated on p. 16: "The feeling of pleasure is lodged between the faculty to know and the faculty to desire, just as the power of judgment is lodged between understanding and reason." This recognition is, then, utilized to demonstrate as possible that the power of judgment contains a principle *a priori* and that, furthermore, through the connection of the feeling of pleasure and displeasure with the faculty of desiring, a transition may be made from the field of concepts dealing with nature to the field of the concept of freedom, which, then, makes possible the transition from understanding to reason (p. 16). Here, the core of the thinking lies in that the power of judgment as such is brought in connection with the feeling of pleasure and displeasure, because only thus can the connection with the faculty of desiring be accomplished.

Right in line with these reflections, we read next, on p. 25 ff.: "Concerning the Connection of the Feeling of Pleasure with the Concept of Expediency in Nature." What is now being discussed in regard to "nature" the main classification on p. 38 seeks to convey in regard to "art." Here also the feeling of pleasure and displeasure is brought into relation with judgment in general. In between, on p. 32, lies the classification into formal and logical expediency in which case only the former may, under reversal of the logical relationship, be brought into relation with the feeling of pleasure, while the latter, on the contrary, has to do not "with a feeling of pleasure in things, but with the understanding when we judge them." This logical judgment is attributed, on p. 33, to understanding and reason. Thus, either the concept of pleasure and displeasure conceals the imperfectly accomplished contact between esthetic and teleological judgment (cf. pp. 17 and 38), or the expression "expediency" apparently holds together esthetic and teleological judgment if one has to drop the general relationship of the feeling of pleasure in the interest of a possible classification.

Since, however, the separation continues factually as the work progresses, it is not a question of the connection between understanding and reason through the power of judgment; rather, esthetic and teleological judgment each of itself and independently of the other endeavors to establish this connection with reason without having the ability to maintain such a connection among themselves.

Should one now reflect that, according to our earlier demonstrations, an investigation of the sublime spills over the narrow framework of the critique of taste, which, therefore, independently of the latter, must establish for itself the connection in question, then the *Critique of Judgment* occupies itself with the solution of the task, generally called into being by the *Critique*, in three separate areas: How is the connection between understanding and reason to be proven scientifically (as having been accomplished by the power of judgment) by research into 1) the beautiful, 2) the sublime, and 3) teleology in general?

In the general survey of the difficulties which are founded in the plan of the *Critique of Judgment,* we have already touched upon the concept of the supersensuous. This concept plays a predominant role in the investigation concerning the sublime. This becomes apparent in the fact that of those places where the concept of the supersensuous occurs in the *Critique of Judgment,* more than half are devoted to the investigation of the sublime. The characteristic thing in the concept of the supersensuous which is related to that of the sublime is the difficulty we experience in making it coincide with the concept of the intelligible. This is attested to also by the extremely rare appearance of the concept of the intelligible. On pp. 108 and 109 we gain an insight into the difficulties. In this narrow space, the terms which we are endeavoring to equate clash with each other. Starting with a comprehension of the sublime, one arrives at the concept of the supersensuous only by detouring over the concept of the infinite. That object is sublime, and that alone, when nature as a whole is suited as a measure: "The real, unchanging, basic measure of nature is the totality of nature herself which, as phenomenon, is comprehended infinity" (p. 109).

How does one get from this concept of the absolute whole of the world of appearances (for it is only with this that we are dealing when it is being considered a measure for estimating mathematical magnitude) to the concept of the supersensuous? Kant's auxiliary idea is as follows: "Since this basic measure is a self-contradictory concept (on account of the impossibility of the absolute totality of a progress without end), it is that magnitude of an object of nature on which the imagination expends its entire faculty of comprehension fruitlessly, which must lead the concept of nature to a supersensuous substratum (which at one and the same time underlies nature and our faculty) which is great beyond all measure of sense" (p. 109). This reflection does not lead further than to the concept of a "supersensuous substratum" whose derivation proclaims itself in the contradictory statement "that it is great beyond all measure of sense." A "substratum" to which an estimate of magnitude is applied positively or negatively is, however, no longer a substratum. Thus, the flaws in the reflection show themselves in that passage where Kant undertakes to justify scientifically the equation of "nature as totality" with its "intelligible substratum" in a discussion which he already used in the *Critique of Pure Reason.*

A coalescence of the infinite with the supersensuous, apparently also a coalescence of the infinite with the intelligible (if it is a question of investigating the sublime), may be based on the impossibility of a *progressus in infinitum,* but not the identification of the supersensuous with the intelligible. Thus, in investigations of the sublime, the "supersensuous"—and not the "intelligible"—dominates one's thinking, and the attempted coalition of both which takes place on a large scale unnoticed in the *Critique of Pure Reason* when the antinomies are under discussion, . . . turns out to be infeasible in the section at hand when one consults the numerical relationship of the terms "supersensuous" and "intelligible" in researching the sublime. . . . The sublime is conjoined with reason as the faculty of progressively unifying experience up to the unattainable absolute. The supersensuous in question is both times the "totality of possible appearances," experienced at one time by virtue of the impossibility of a perfectly unified comprehension of the totality of appearances, the next time by virtue of the impossibility of applying the relative measures of magnitude and power to certain appearances. Therefore, we may say that the sublime rests on the comprehension of an appearance by reason. Consequently, it is really no longer a matter of a union of judgment and reason regarding the sublime, but both faculties of knowledge pass over into each other without distinction in this problem, as is indicated by the same subject in both cases, that is, man as moral being, and the agreement in formulation of the concept "supersensuous" in so far as it maintains contact with the concept of the infinite.

Our investigation has arrived at a decisive point: The subject of the esthetic valuation is the person. The entire thought and idea content of the person comes to the fore in a progressive crescendo when we comprehend esthetically the world of appearance, beginning with the simplest esthetic formal unity and ending in the most complicated, and apparently incomprehensible, progressive esthetic comprehension. Let this be imagined as a sort of process of empathy, or let the attempt be made to describe the process by utilizing the terms "mood" or "imagination"; the fact is well established that nature as appearance becomes art in that the person discovers within himself an idea which, related to appearance, seizes upon the principle of an esthetic unity. The process of the esthetic apprehension of a landscape, the explanation of which Kant has to forego, may, accordingly, be described in main outlines. The whole series of appearances is held together in a unity by a thought. Thus, from being an appearance, the landscape in spring becomes an object of art, as does the dreary sandy desert. These processes presuppose a personality which has developed thoughts and ideas to a significant degree of refinement. Therefore, it is explainable that in the development of mankind, as in that of the individual, not until a certain point in the development has been reached, to cite an example, does the landscape become art. Descriptions of landscape and landscape painting are relatively of recent date. It was not until the Renaissance that an esthetic apprehension of the landscape really came into being, while the ancient literature offers relatively few examples of it and leaves the esthetic evaluation of the landscape still in a certain dependence on the feelings of pleasure and displeasure relative to the pleasant and unpleasant.

It, likewise, corresponds to what has been said when each thought entering anew in the history of mankind's development manifests its influence through an enrichment of the esthetic field. Thus, the proliferation of historic insight, which places past epochs of civilizations vividly before our eyes, signifies an advancement of the esthetic comprehension of objects which otherwise would hardly be sensed as art because a multitude of historical ideas are brought to bear upon them. Thus, a heap of rubble on a mountain becomes art because around it hovers the romantic spell of the Middle Ages. At the moment when we might be convinced that it is contemporary, it would be impossible to accomplish an esthetic unity with respect to it; it would remain appearance, a picture of loathsome disorder. A couple of broken columns and a bit of blue sky and the landscape becomes art if the appraiser's memory and insight into the ancient Hellenic splendor awaken. If this is not the case, the infertile imagination cannot complete the insight, and the object remains appearance. Kant's example of the imitated song of a nightingale (p. 168) and, likewise, the example of artificial flowers transplanted into nature (p. 164) are, thus, disposed of. Why does all esthetic interest fade after the deception has been discovered? Because the person is no longer capable of comprehending the unity in the objects and their environment by bringing their ideas to bear upon them. It is no longer the melancholic, mild, moonlit summer's night which allows us to construct the song of the little bird as a harmonious unity, but it is a succession of notes which, as noise, we sense as unpleasant because we cannot accomplish a sense of oneness between it and peaceful nature.

That Kant's example is, taken by itself, correct, but the explanation of it made from the context into which it has been pressed, totally wrong, becomes clear if we undertake a modification of the example. If, for instance, one substitutes the warbling of the nightingale by a beautiful human song modulated in soft rhythms, the esthetic effect of nature is not diminished despite Kant who would not acknowledge it as nature. Rather, the esthetic effect of nature will become intensified because the appreciator can now construct once more a unity among the succession of notes, their origin and nature. However, the esthetic unity can also be constructed for the imitated bird song, as shown by Beethoven's Pastoral Symphony. The imitation of the song in this composition is not felt as a noise, but as art because it is incorporated into an esthetic unity even though only for the one who is able to accomplish the unity intended by the composer. Thus, it is demonstrated especially in the most complicated examples that nature does become art in that the person brings to bear his entire wealth of ideas and thoughts to the appearance and seizes them in an esthetic unity. The richer this content, the larger the area of art for the person who is the judge.

Thus it is the evaluating person "who enlarges our concept of nature from a mere mechanism to the concept of it as art" (*Critique of Judgment,* p. 98). On the same high level is a statement on p. 182: "The faculty of imagination (as a faculty of productive knowledge) is, it must be said, very powerful in that it creates, as it were, another nature from the material which is presented it by the real one. We enter a discussion with her in which our experiences appear to us as commonplace; we reshape them, perchance, always, to be sure, according to the laws of analogy, yet also according to principles which are on a higher level of reason (and which come just as naturally to us as those according to which the understanding comprehends empirical nature), in which case we become aware of being free from the law of association (which is part of the empirical use of that faculty) to the end that the material may be loaned us by nature according to the law of association, but transformed by us into something else, that is, something that surpasses nature."

The principle of classification and progression in the arts, rooted in a grasp of the essence of art in its true scope, contains not only an indication of a combination of the esthetic judgment with practical reason, but, if thought through consistently, furnishes the proof for it so independently that the investigation concerning the combination in question could be terminated merely by pursuing the problem of the classification and stepwise sequence of the arts.

The second problem, which we also want to investigate in its relation to Kant's philosophy of religion, concerns the section which Kant devotes to the understanding of genius. This is, perhaps, the most unsatisfactory part of the entire *Critique of Judgment*. Here, the narrowing down process initiated by Kant's concept of art draws the ultimate conclusions. The investigation of genius extends only to art in so far as it concerns human activity. This unjustifiably constricted circle is further contracted. Genius is being investigated in its relation to the "fine arts," and of these only the graphic arts are taken into account. In this way, however, every connection between the investigation of the esthetic genius and the investigation of the nature of genius has, in general, been made impossible. Should the investigation of the esthetic genius be confined to its proper boundaries, it must take into consideration genius in its relation to its entire field of operation, the world of appearances in general. However, a principle of differentiation between the world of appearances and the field of human activity cannot, then, be discovered. The nature of genius consists, namely, in the singular crescendo of the faculty for understanding the world of appearance as art, if we define genius in connection with the main esthetic problem. Before genius becomes a cause of appearances which it manufactures in order to be judged as art, it must have understood these appearances in nature as art. The painter, before he presents a process in which the art of a genius may be sensed, must have previously understood this process as appearance by virtue of his genial talent. Thus, the artistic production is not a characteristic mark, but only a result, of genius.

Now, the occurrence of genius, in whatever art, denotes a progress in that art. Furthermore, every progress in art consists in the fulfillment of its principle of unity. Genius is, thus, characterized as a unique ability to accomplish an esthetic unity in a field of appearances at a point where it had not been accomplished up to that time, or to accomplish it in such a manner as would not be possible with the customary means of unification. In that it introduces a more perfect principle of unity into art, the genius seizes upon something as art that up to that time was mere appearance, or enhances art in such a way that the others, who are incapable of accomplishing this unity with the customary means, believe art has been reduced to appearance. Thus, it lies in the nature of genius to be misunderstood and in the nature of the progress of art (that is, the art of the genius) to be looked upon, in the average sensibility of contemporary art appreciation, as appearance. Thus, when Bach breathed into counterpoint, which in itself is an empty pattern, the idea of a unified development, by virtue of which all his works possess such a surprising perfection and unity, his music was felt, particularly by capable contemporary musicians, to be noise, and it was first Beethoven who possessed the genius to discover art in Bach. Likewise, every progress in the graphic arts, if it can be traced back to the genius of individuals, is felt by most contemporaries as a "senseless imitation or distortion of nature."

This definition of genius as the unique faculty of seizing the esthetic unity in objects leads us to recognize their connection with genius also in other fields as soon as one returns to the subject problem. The subject is the person. In so far as it has the talent to accomplish an esthetic unity, one calls it artistic genius. If it is the religious or ethical nature of the person which seizes the world of appearances and its events in a corresponding unique unity, one calls it moral or religious genius. Therefore, the nature of every religious genius is shown in that he constructs a unity by working over the wreckage of a religion destroyed either deliberately or unconsciously as the exigencies of his religious personality dictate it without concern as to whether, for the average person, the broken pieces do fit together into a structure or not. The genius seizes what is only in the light of its own converging into a unified image —and the rest becomes blurred in the shade. Thus, for Jesus of Nazareth, only that exists in the Old Testament which proves to be in harmony with his religious talent. It is from here that light is shed: "On these two hang all the law and the prophets." In this manner Augustine unites the contradictions of a Neoplatonic world view and Catholicized Christianity into one whole; he establishes the higher unity of both without feeling the contradictions. Thus Luther, being the religious genius that he was, fits together the most contradictory portions of medieval dogma because he brings a unified principle to bear on it; he voiced contradictions, but he never felt them. In every religious genius progress toward the principle of unity is documented just as in the esthetic genius. Because progress cannot be achieved on the basis of the customary or the habitual, it is especially the religiously interested masses who sense the new structure not as religion but as appearance—that is, as a conglomerate of religious pronouncements—and the religious genius becomes a deluded heretic.

In analogy to the religious genius, the moral genius likewise presents itself as the accomplishment of a higher unity in evaluating phenomena on the basis of the dominant moral determination of the person. Socrates accomplished this unity in appraising the world of appearances morally without feeling the need for extending this unity to the whole field of events and seizing as unitary all happenings in the world in a moral evaluation. Kant, too, is a moral genius like Socrates—and one of overwhelming magnitude. He is a moral genius in that he comprehends and undertakes scientific research merely for the purpose of demonstrating the reality of the moral law. At the moment when, in the development of the epistemological problem posed by Descartes, the consequences were drawn from his moral indifference—which a Spinoza could still pass over lightly—Kant, in his critical investigations, so transforms the setting and solution of the problem that it tends toward a moral interpretation of the world. The unity which he, as a moral genius, accomplished consisted in that he brought the division made by critical idealism into an intelligible and phenomenal world into a unified combination by virtue of the fact of the moral law without his noticing the divergent tendencies of these two elements and without being obliged to draw the consequence that the moral law, when incorporated into the distinction of the intelligible and what is of the nature of appearance, renders a moral appraisal of happenings impossible.

Thus, the common element of geniuses in all fields is that genius accomplishes a new unity according to the determination of its subject as a person. The ascent from the esthetic to the moral and religious genius takes place to the extent to which a person becomes a moral person and, in turn, a religious person.

With this we conclude the difficult investigation concerning Kant's *Critique of Esthetic Judgment* in its relation to his philosophy of religion. The result is, for all points in question, the same: Kant, even though without artistic ability and training, feels the union which the esthetic judgment brings about with other faculties of knowledge. Often he describes them in a very striking manner, but is able to give reasons for it at no turn of the problem because he destroys the connection between judgment in general and esthetic judgment by introducing the popular concepts of art and expediency, and furnishes, instead of the esthetic judgment, critiques of taste and of the sublime, critiques which cannot solve the problem.

With this formulation of the result the investigation can rest satisfied. It has approached the *Critique of Esthetic Judgment* for the purpose of illuminating its place in the development of Kant's philosophy of religion. However, in the analysis of the thinking which we recognized as necessary and have followed through, still another result has urged itself on us which is related to the *Critique of Esthetic Judgment*. The place of the *Critique of Esthetic Judgment* has been taken by a critique of taste, while the general introduction of the *Critique of Judgment* has delineated the area of a *Critique of Esthetic Judgment*. Here, too, the suspicion is in order that as the sketch of a philosophy of religion was inserted into a later reflection after a slight revision, thus also the critique of taste, which belongs to an earlier epoch of Kant's thinking, may have been taken up with slight revisions into the *Critique of Judgment* in place of the *Critique of Esthetic Judgment*. The original frame of thought to which this critique of taste belongs documents itself for the first time in clear outlines in the classification of judgment into an esthetic and a teleological one (p. 33). There, a view of teleological judgment is expounded according to which it is supposed to have reference to "the agreement of the form with the possibility of the thing itself, according to a concept of it which is antecedent and contains the ground of this form." The *Critique of Teleological Judgment* offered later takes no cognizance of this determination but occupies a far less developed standpoint.

Thus, at the end of this long investigation, we are face to face with an antagonism between Kant's understanding and definition of religion, on the one hand, and the concept of religion which the philosophy of religion of critical idealism has produced spontaneously, on the other.

Let us, then, close by summarizing the result of the investigation of the *Critique of Judgment* with reference to Kant's philosophy of religion.

Kant seeks to work up a connection between the understanding and the practical moral reason through esthetic and teleological judgment, presupposing their mutual independence. In spite of valuable starts, the attempt undertaken in the field of esthetic judgment miscarried because he adopted an uncritical esthetic concept of art and expediency. In the field of teleological judgment, the attempt is carried through with strict logic up to the point where the ethico-theology builds upon teleology. From hence forth the influence of the concept of the highest good, uncritical regarding the formulation of ethico-theology, asserts itself. Furthermore, Kant's attempt to erect, in the field of teleological judgment, a philosophical-religious structure is not carried out consistently to the very end because for the last part of the structure, the material which was already utilized in the sketch of a philosophy of religion and in the *Critique of Practical Reason* is again being utilized. The adoption of otherwise oriented thoughts is made possible by virtue of the fact that in some respects the moral theology transcends the rigid forms of the *Critique of Practical Reason* and, driven by moral interests, reaches back into the richer thought content of the sketch of a philosophy of religion. Once taken up, some of these thoughts can no longer be brought into relationship with moral theology, and they pass once more through the development leading to the thought structure of the *Critique of Practical Reason*. That train of thought in the sketch of a philosophy of religion which is geared to general reflections is further developed in the ethico-theology in the direction of *Religion Within the Limits of Reason Alone*. Through the concept of moral mankind as the final end of the world, we see how preparations are being made in the ethico-theology for the moral valuation of earthly conditions as good, the receding into the background of the ethical interest in the continuation of our existence, the act of relating the concept of God to the "ethical common being" and the moral concept of happiness. These magnitudes, then, lay the condition for the advancement of thought in *Religion Within the Limits of Reason Alone* in their pure formulation. Without a preceding ethico-theology, *Religion Within the Limits of Reason Alone* would be incomprehensible in the developmental process of the Kantian philosophy of religion. The ethico-theology again picks up the thoughts which the formation of the philosophy of religion of critical idealism had eliminated, in the *Critique of Practical Reason,* from the Kantian philosophy of religion. The ethico-theology gives them a more logical formulation and brings to them a deeper grasp of the moral law by which these thoughts attain an enrichment of their moral worth. However, the ethico-theology points forward to *Religion Within the Limits of Reason Alone* and backward to the sketch of a philosophy of religion. Through slight contact with the *Critique of Practical Reason,* it shows that Kant's philosophy of religion is engaged in a stage of development which presents itself as a movement away from the philosophy of religion of critical idealism. In the *Critique of Judgment,* the terms supersensuous and intelligible still struggle for equal place. In *Religion Within the Limits of Reason Alone.* the struggle has been decided in favor of the term supersensuous.

General Summary and Conclusion

◻ We have made our investigation in the manner projected in the general introduction in the four writings which are of special interest for Kant's philosophy of religion. Every type of reflection has been investigated by itself and only after it was thoroughly understood compared with the reflections in other writings and brought into relationship to them. Hence, in the presentation of Kant's philosophy of religion we have already prepared the solution for the problem which was broached in the introduction. It has reference to the question whether and in how far a philosophy of religion rising above the basis of critical idealism is possible.

No matter at which point the investigation starts, the result is the same: A philosophy of religion tailored and oriented to the presuppositions of critical idealism is a product which is self-disintegrating. The opposing forces are in equilibrium so long as they have not reached their full intensity; in this manner the sketch of a philosophy of religion can unite reason in its theoretical and practical use. The *Critique of Practical Reason,* however, can no longer reach the attempted union of practical and theoretical reason; the perfected philosophy of religion of critical idealism dissolves itself.

The later reflections only carry with them the debris of the burst structure of the *Critique of Practical Reason.* They are clearly distinguishable from the new thoughts expressed and resist every new attempt at joining them together. Thus, in the ethico-theology we meet a concept of the highest good which was under the influence of the *Critique of Practical Reason* and, subsequently, a concept of immortality divulging the same influence. These two foreign thoughts prevented the perfection of the ethico-theology according to the plan projected for it in the combination with general teleology. In the presentation of *Religion Within the Limits of Reason Alone* the influence of the thinking of the *Critique of Practical Reason* recedes into the background completely. The concept of immortality hardly ever occurs. The hypothetical positing of a "future life" shows that the continuation of our existence is not required by interest in an ethical perfection. The concept of a moral world and, at the same time, the idea of the highest good, have gained a relation to the moral society which does not suggest any attempt to realize these magnitudes in the intelligible field.

Thus, the *Critique of Practical Reason* forms the apex of that type of thinking in Kant's philosophy of religion which seeks its connection with the determinations and presuppositions of critical idealism. The trend toward this point is presented in the thinking of the sketch of a philosophy of religion. The trend downward from the apex is expressed in the successive retreat of the thoughts of the *Critique of Practical Reason* when presenting the ethico-theology in *Religion Within the Limits of Reason Alone*.

Thus, there exists an insoluble contradiction, traceable to its ultimate reasons, between the presuppositions of critical idealism and the fact of the moral law which renders impossible any philosophy of religion resting upon a union of these two factors in that the logical assertion of the one factor neutralizes the effect of the other. In the relationship of these two factors with respect to each other lie the two tendencies which we were able to pursue through the entire Kantian philosophy of religion.

In the final summing up we have assembled for comparative study the results of those trends of thinking in Kant's writings in which we could note the prevalence of the critical idealist factor over the moral one: It is Kant's philosophy of religion as the philosophy of religion of critical idealism. It reached its most complete formulation in the *Critique of Practical Reason* in the philosophy of religion conjoined with the thus formulated epistemological presuppositions. The contradiction asserting itself between both elements is covered up only tediously, and the fact is veiled that as soon as the intelligible and the moral world are brought in coalition, morality and the formulation of the moral law in Kant's sense cease to exist. This trend in the modern philosophy of religion is logically continued by the one who was able to develop Kant's epistemology to its ultimate implications because he did not possess Kant's moral depth: Schopenhauer. He drew the consequences which Kant was not able to draw because his gaze all the while strayed toward the fact of the moral law. Kant was not able to realize the ideas in the formulation as secured against all attacks in the transcendental hypotheses. His moral interest compels him to go beyond this formulation which, in view of critical idealism, is the most complete, whereby the ideas of the continuation of our existence and freedom no longer exhibit the correct coinage of critical idealism. It is no accident if Schopenhauer returns again and again to the transcendental hypotheses in questions involving continued existence and freedom, and starts with the *Critique* only at that point where Kant allows the fact of the moral law to enter his investigation. He completes the de-ethicalization which principally lies already in the consistency of the presentation of Kant's *Critique of Practical Reason;* he does away with the moral law in Kant's formulation, carries to completion the identification of the knowing subject with the moral person, defines the relationship between the intelligible and phenomenal world by rejecting every attempt at bringing it home in analogy to the relationship of reason and consequence, and makes no attempt to distinguish between human action and the area of general appearances. Implied in this is that, for the purpose of realizing the intelligible, it is necessary to start with a principle which, unlike the moral law in Kant, is given as related only to a definite area of appearances but is applicable to the determinations of relations between every appearance and the intelligible sphere whereby, however, the starting point may be taken solely from the knowing subject. Thus is completed the de-ethicalization of the philosophy of religion of critical idealism in Schopenhauer's theory of the will; and the moral indifference of the Occidental epistemological problem, which seemingly had been overcome by Kant, comes to the fore again at the moment when a follower of Kant who does not comprehend the ethical depth of the founder of critical idealism begins to sift the results of the *Critique of Pure Reason* and develop them logically.

This, in brief strokes, is the entire thinking of Kant's philosophy of religion. The presuppositions of critical idealism withdraw entirely into the background. Moral mankind, not the rational being, is the subject of investigation. To the extent that these presuppositions give way, the purely ethical formulation of the statements becomes more and more noticeable. The world is considered in them only as far as the moral law extends and world events and world order refer to moral mankind. The concept of God is realized with a view to the ethical community, and the subject as moral individual is considered only in his mutual relationship with this community. Immortality does not enter into this thinking. The entire thought structure culminates in the concept of God as a moral person.

Thus, each one of the two types of thinking which may be pursued in Kant's philosophy of religion forms a system of philosophy of religion by itself if taken in the context of its consequences. At the same time either the critical idealistic presuppositions neutralize their ethical determination, or the latter cancels the former. It is implied in the logical consequences of these facts that every one of these trends of thought in the course of the history of the philosophy of religion received a logical treatment, in which case the dependence on Kant, who gave it that treatment, must have been more or less present to the thinkers who pursued them.

We have arrived at the end of our investigation. The main result can be briefly formulated thus. The Kantian philosophy of religion is fulfilled in a great development which is conditioned by the relationship between two parallel ways of thinking. The philosophy of religion of critical idealism contained in the *Critique of Practical Reason* is but a stage in this development. That it no longer is able to carry out the scheme of a philosophy of religion in the transcendental dialectic proves that, impelled by the developmental principle of the Kantian philosophy of religion, it itself is in the process of transcending the limits of the area of critical idealism. The driving factor in this development is the conception of the moral law which becomes more and more profound. It is Kant's self-perfecting ethical personality which is at the root of this development. Only in this development does the wealth of thought of Kant's philosophy of religion proclaim itself. However, his thought will also be able to exercise its influence upon today's philosophy of religion when the insight attains widespread acceptance that Kant's philosophy of religion may not be expounded and evaluated solely upon the schematism of the *Critique of Practical Reason*.

Acknowledgments and Sources

REVERENCE FOR LIFE

Acknowledgment is gratefully made to the following for permission to quote from the works cited below:

I   *Memoirs of Childhood and Youth*, by Albert Schweitzer, translated by C. T. Campion, published 1924 by George Allen & Unwin, Ltd., London.

II   *Goethe: Five Studies*, by Albert Schweitzer, translated by Charles R. Joy, copyright 1948 by the Beacon Press, Boston.

III   "Busy Days in Lambaréné," The Christian Century, Vol. 51, No. 11, copyright 1934 by Christian Century Foundation, Chicago.

IV   "Religion and Modern Civilization," The Christian Century, Vol. 51, Nos. 47 and 48, copyright 1934 by Christian Century Foundation, Chicago.

V   "The Ethics of Reverence for Life," Christendom, Vol. 1,

No. 2, copyright 1936 by Willett, Clark & Company, Chicago; by permission of World Council of Churches, Inc., New York.

VI "The Relations of the White and Colored Races," Contemporary Review, Vol. 133, No. 745 (January, 1928), London.

VII "Albert Schweitzer Speaks Out," reprinted from the 1964 World Book Year Book; copyright, Field Enterprises Educational Corporation, Chicago.

VIII *African Notebook,* by Albert Schweitzer, translated by Mrs. C. E. B. Russell, copyright 1939 by Holt, Rinehart and Winston, Inc.; reprinted by permission of Holt, Rinehart and Winston, Inc., New York.

IX *Out of My Life and Thought,* by Albert Schweitzer, translated by C. T. Campion, copyright 1933, 1949, by Holt, Rinehart and Winston, Inc., reprinted by permission of Holt, Rinehart and Winston, Inc., New York.

THE LIGHT WITHIN US

D *The Decay and Restoration of Civilization.* London: Black, 1929.

E *On the Edge of the Primeval Forest.* New York: The Macmillan Company, 1956.

K *Aus meiner Kindheit und Jugendzeit.* Munich: Verlag C. H. Beck.

M *Memoirs of Childhood and Youth.* New York: The Macmillan Company, 1955.

O *Out of My Life and Thought.* New York: Henry Holt and Company, 1933.

S *Selbstdarstellung.* Hamburg: Verlag Richard Meiner.

V *Verfall und Wiederaufbau unserer Kultur*. Munich: C. H. Beck.

PILGRIMAGE TO HUMANITY

Acknowledgment is gratefully made to the following publishers for permission to reprint and translate from the works of Albert Schweitzer: George Allen & Unwin Ltd., London; Beacon Press, Boston; C. H. Beck Verlag, München; A. & C. Black Ltd., London; Breitkopf & Härtel Verlag, Wiesbaden; Dodd, Mead & Company, New York; Harper & Brothers, New York; Freies Deutsches Hochstift Frankfurter Goethe Museum, Frankfurt; Holt, Rinehart and Winston, New York; Kommissions-verlag der Strassburger Druckerei und Verlagsanstalt; the Macmillan Company, New York; Richard Meiner Verlag, Hamburg; J. B. C. Mohr Verlag, Tübingen; Verlag Philipp Reclam, Stuttgart; and Mr. G. Woytt, Strasbourg.

The English-language publishers who gave permission for new translations of works to which they held translation rights are named under the proper titles in the list of references.

1—Par	15—Afr. G
2—Kph. I	16— "
3—LD	17— "
4— "	18— "
5— "	19—WU
6—Par	20—LD
7—KE	21—LD
8—Par	22— "
9—LD	23—Lb
10—Ex	24—LD
11—Str. A	25— "
12—KE	26—KJ
13— "	27—LD
14—LD	28— "

ACKNOWLEDGMENTS AND SOURCES

29—LD

30— "

31— "

32— "

33— "

34— "

35— "

36— "

37— "

38— "

39— "

40— "

41— "

42— "

43— "

44— "

45— "

46— "

47— "

48— "

49— "

50— "

51— "

52— "

53— "

54— "

55— "

56— "

57— "

58— "

59— "

60— "

61— "

62— "

63—WU

64—LD

65— "

66— "

67— "

68— "

69— "

70— "

71— "

72— "

73—Tgb

74— "

75— "

76— "

77— "

78— "

79— "

80— "

81— "

82—LD

83—CW

84— "

85— "

86—LD

87—KE

88— "

89—Ind

90—LD

91— "

92—Jb

93—Goe

94— "

95— "

96—B

97—"

98—"

99—"

100—"

101—LD

102—B

103—"

104—"

105—"

106—"

107—"

108—"

109—"	127—KE
110—"	128—LD
111—"	129— "
112—"	130— "
113—"	131— "
114—H-Kn	132— "
115—SRVbl	133— "
116—SThU	134— "
117— "	135— "
118—LD	136—Kph. I
119—LJ	137— "
120—MP	138— "
121—LJ	139— "
122—Mess	140— "
123—LJ	141—Oslo
124— "	142—LD
125—LD	143—KE
126— "	144— "

Afr. G *Afrikanische Geschichten.* 1938. By permission of Richard Meiner Verlag, Hamburg, A. & C. Black, Ltd., London, and Macmillan Co., New York.

B *Joh. Seb. Bach.* 1947. By permission of Breitkopf and Härtel Verlag, Wiesbaden, A. & C. Black, Ltd., London, and Macmillan Co., New York.

CW *Das Christentum und die Weltreligionen.* 1924. By permission of C. H. Beck Verlag, München, George Allen & Unwin, Ltd., London, and Macmillan Co., New York.

Ex Excerpts from various communications.

Goe *Goethe: Vier Reden.* 1950. 3rd ed. By permission of C. H. Beck Verlag, München, and Beacon Press, Boston.

H-Kn Elly Heuss-Knapp, *Ausblick vom Münsterturm.* 1934.

Ind *Die Weltanschauung der indischen Denker.* By permission of C. H. Beck Verlag, München, and Beacon Press, Boston.

Jb *Jahrbuch des Freien Deutschen Hochstifts.* Frankfurt-am-Main, 1928.

KE *Kultur und Ethik (Kulturphilosophie II).* 4th ed. By permission of C. H. Beck Verlag, München, A. & C. Black, Ltd., London, and Macmillan Co., New York.

KJ *Aus meiner Kindheit und Jugendzeit.* By permission of C. H. Beck Verlag, München, George Allen & Unwin, Ltd., London, and Macmillan Co., New York.

Kph. I *Verfall und Wiederaufbau der Kultur (Kulturphilosophie I).* 1925. 2nd ed. By permission of C. H. Beck Verlag, München, A. & C. Black, Ltd., London, and Macmillan Co., New York.

Lb *Mitteilungen aus Lambaréné I/II.* 1925. By permission of C. H. Beck Verlag, München.

LD *Aus meinem Leben und Denken.* 1932. By permission of Richard Meiner Verlag, Hamburg, and Holt, Rinehart and Winston, New York.

LJ *Geschichte der Leben-Jesu-Forschung.* 1933. 5th ed. By permission of J. B. C. Mohr Verlag, Tübingen, A. & C. Black, Ltd., London, and Macmillan Co., New York.

Mess *Das Messianitäts- und Leidensgeheimnis.* 1901. By permission of J. B. C. Mohr Verlag, Tübingen, and Dodd, Mead & Co., New York; and Macmillan Co., New York.

MP *Die Mystik des Apostels Paulus.* 1930. By permission of J. B. C. Mohr Verlag, Tübingen, A. & C. Black Ltd., London, and Macmillan Co., New York.

Oslo *Das Problem des Friedens in der heutigen Welt.* 1954. By permission of C. H. Beck, München, A. & C. Black, Ltd., London, and Harper and Bros., New York.

Par *Pariser Rede von 1952* in Fischer-Bücherei "Genie der Menschlichkeit." 1955.

SRVbl *Schweizerisches Reform. Volksblatt.* 1947.

SThU *Schweizerische Theologische Umschau,* 1953.

Str. A *24 Aufsätze zur Jahrhundertwende,* "Die Philosophie und die allgemeine Bildung im neunzehnten Jahrhundert." 1900.

Kommissionsverlag der Strassburger Druckerei und Verlagsanstalt.

Tgb *Zeitschrift Universitas*. Beitrag Schweitzers: "Tagebuch im Kriege." 1946.

WU *Zwischen Wasser und Urwald*. By permission of C. H. Beck Verlag, München.